ANIMALS AND SOCIETY

Animals and Society uses a variety of historical sources and a coherent social theory to tell the story of the invention of animal rights. It moves from incidents like the medieval execution of pigs to a discussion of the politics and strategies of modern animal rights organisations. The book also presents radical interpretations of nineteenth-century animal welfare laws, and the accounts of the Noble Savage. The insights generated by social science are always at the core of the discussion and the author draws on the work of Michel Foucault, Norbert Elias, Claude Lévi-Strauss and Mary Douglas.

This wide-ranging and accessible book provides a fascinating account of the relations between humans and animals. It raises far-reaching questions about the philosophy, history and politics of animal rights.

The book will be of interest to students of sociology, history, philosophy and politics.

Keith Tester teaches in the School of Social and Historical Studies, Portsmouth Polytechnic.

ANIMALS AND SOCIETY

The humanity of animal rights

KEITH TESTER

London and New York

First published in 1991
by Routledge
11 New Fetter Lane, London EC4P 4EE

Simultaneously published in the USA and Canada
by Routledge
a division of Routledge, Chapman and Hall Inc.
29 West 35th Street, New York, NY 10001

Reprinted 1992

© 1991 Keith Tester

Typeset by NWL Editorial Services, Langport, Somerset

Printed and bound in Great Britain by
Mackays of Chatham PLC, Chatham, Kent

British Library Cataloguing in Publication Data
Tester, Keith
Animals and society: the humanity of animal rights
1. Animals. Treatment by man. Ethical aspects
I. Title
179.3

Library of Congress Cataloging in Publication Data
Tester, Keith, 1960–
Animals and society: the humanity of animal rights/Keith Tester.
p. cm.
Includes bibliographical references (p.) and index.
1. Animal rights – History. I. title.
HV4705.T47   1991   90–8763
179'.3 – dc20   CIP

ISBN 0–415–04731–5
0–415–04732–3 (pbk)

CONTENTS

Acknowledgements   vi

1 THE CLAIMS OF A DOG   1

2 THE OTHER ANIMAL   17

3 CIVILISED ATTITUDES   48

4 A PIG'S LIFE   72

5 A DIFFERENT KIND OF BEAST   94

6 A SIMILAR NATURE   121

7 A COMPREHENSIVE PRINCIPLE   147

8 ANIMAL MAGIC   170

9 IF A LION COULD TALK   194

Bibliography   209

Name index   216

Subject index   218

ACKNOWLEDGEMENTS

I have inevitably benefited from the advice and support of a number of colleagues and friends whilst I have been working on this project, which began life as a doctoral thesis at the University of Leeds. I am especially grateful to Zygmunt Bauman and Ian Burkitt for their perceptive comments and encouragement. Greater although very different help was constantly given by Linda Rutherford. The book is dedicated to her.

I feel obliged to stress that none of the people who have lent their assistance is at all to blame for the analysis developed here. Neither should it be imagined that any of them would necessarily wish to be associated with what I have said. The responsibility is mine alone.

I am very grateful to Jon Wynne-Tyson, Centaur Press, and the Society for Animal Rights, Inc. for kind permission to quote extensively from Henry S. Salt, *Animals' Rights Considered in Relation to Social Progress*.

Chapter One

THE CLAIMS OF A DOG

Our environment has many unpleasant features. One is dog excrement. Piles and pats of it abound, waiting to slip up the inattentive pedestrian. But what do we do if we see a squatting dog? We either express haughty contempt, turn away, or blame the owner. Would any of us kick or punch the dog? Probably not; instead we are more likely to shout at the person holding the lead. On the one hand we seem to believe that the dog is not entirely responsible for its actions, on the other we feel that it should not be deliberately hurt simply because it is doing what it must. We are not certain what we should do about the dog that fouls our front garden, indeed we are not sure we can rightly do anything. Our treatment of the animal is difficult. Animals present society with ambiguities; with companionship, food, clothing, fun, but also with demands for compassion, abstinence and kindness. They disgust and please us; we can do with them what we will yet pull back with horror from open cruelty. The dog makes claims upon us, although we are not entirely sure what those claims are. But they still profoundly influence our treatment of the animal.

This book is about those claims and how they affect the way individuals relate to, and understand, animals. At its broadest, this book is concerned with the relationship between animals and society, but mostly it is about the special claims which are made for animals' rights. This explanation of animal rights will discover many surprising incidents in the attitudes and beliefs of humans. I will emphasise the situation in Britain – perhaps *England* is better – and only refer to events in other countries if they support any case or illustrate it particularly vividly. This is not because Britain is more respectful of animal rights than anywhere else (just

1

because we see ourselves as a nation of 'animal lovers', we should be wary of falling into any national chauvinism), but simply because Britain is the environment I know best. I hope that the story told in this book has some relevance elsewhere. In a sentence, I will explore the social processes and relationships which lie behind the many assertions which are made in Britain for the moral relevance of animals, and show how those relationships influence people's lives.

Concern for animals has a long history. To give just one example, when he wrote the great radical Romantic poem *Queen Mab* in about 1812, Shelley bewailed the treatment of animals by which 'the bull must be degraded into the ox, and the ram into the wether' (Shelley 1905: 818). Yet he was only interested in the sufferings of animals because they reflected 'manhood blighted with unripe disease' (Shelley 1905: 770). He was not concerned with the relevance of animals so much as with the decay of humanity. The idea of animal rights is rather different precisely because it does say something tangible about animals and advocates that individuals should think about how they treat them. Animal rights does not seem to be as selfish as Shelley's self-serving pity for a castrated ram. The wish to say something morally irreducible, something real, about animals and then establish that statement as a guide for human behaviour is a relatively recent phenomenon. In Britain the concern with animals' rights has been an especially widespread and lively social issue since the middle of the 1970s (although, as we will see, the roots of the idea are to be found in the eighteenth century). The surge of interest can be attributed to the debates stimulated by the book *Animal Liberation*, written by the Australian philosopher Peter Singer and first published in Britain in 1976.

This chapter will give an introductory survey of the three clearest, most influential, and sustained statements of the claims of animals: that by Singer and later contributions by Tom Regan and Stephen Clark. It might seem curious that the whole complex issue of the relationship between animals and society is so quickly reduced to just three philosophy books: surely they cannot say everything that is important? No, they cannot, but between them Singer, Regan, and Clark do cover virtually all the ground which must be mapped in order to understand modern moral attitudes towards animals.

The argument of *Animal Liberation* is powerfully simple. Singer writes from within the utilitarian tradition of moral philosophy. Broadly speaking, utilitarianism holds to the central theme that pleasure is good and pain is bad. As John Stuart Mill put it, utilitarianism asserts that 'pleasure and freedom from pain, are the only things desirable as ends' (Mill 1910: 6). It goes beyond individualistic hedonism. Certainly, Mill tells us, the individual should follow the path of pleasure and avoid pain (such a life is morally good), but the individual lives in a social world and, consequently, should act to promote global pleasure, or at least defend the preference to avoid pain. Utilitarianism asks the individual to aggregate the consequences of his or her actions for the promotion of pleasure and avoidance of pain, and demands that she or he should morally only follow that course which causes more pleasure than it does pain. This is a morality which can be imagined as a pair of scales, and the moral act is the one which tips the individual and social balance in favour of pleasure. An act is not moral *as such*; rather, morality is a product of the consequences which the act has on the balance of pleasure and pain. Utilitarianism is inherently social. Singer holds to a slightly modified version of Mill's position; for Singer the moral act is that which takes account of the preference of all sentient creatures not to experience increases in pain or suffering.

Now, utilitarianism can have important things to say about the social treatment of animals because, if animals are able to experience pleasure and pain, it is logical to assume that they prefer not to undergo any increase of suffering, and they should therefore be included in the calculations which must be made to deduce the moral consequences of any act. For utilitarians, the experience of pleasure and pain cannot be ignored simply on the grounds that the experiencing subject is an animal. Utilitarians like Singer assert that the preference for pleasure rather than increased pain demands equal consideration whether the experiencing subject is the Queen of England or a laboratory rabbit. Peter Singer calls this the *principle of equality* and, obviously, it is a *prescription* for equal ethical consideration, and not a *description* of equality. The principle refers to the equal consideration of interests and preferences (Singer 1976: 5). All beings that can suffer pain have an equal interest in avoiding it. Singer has no doubt that this is the essence of morality:

3

If a being suffers there can be no moral justification for refusing to take that suffering into consideration. No matter what the nature of the being, the principle of equality requires that its suffering be counted equally with the like suffering – in so far as rough comparisons can be made – of any other being. If a being is not capable of suffering, or of experiencing enjoyment or happiness, there is nothing to be taken into account. So the limit of sentience (using the term as a convenient if not strictly accurate shorthand for the capacity to suffer and/or experience enjoyment) is the only defensible boundary of concern for the interests of others. To mark this boundary by some other characteristic like intelligence or rationality would be to mark it in an arbitrary manner. Why not choose some other characteristic, like skin color?

(Singer 1976: 9)

The only morally relevant characteristic is the ability to suffer and the preference not to, and so according to Singer the moral terrain is a plateau of morally equal preferences in which features such as skin colour, sex or species are as morally important as the differences between green and brown eyes. Indeed, to subordinate the question of sentience to some secondary feature is utterly reprehensible, and just as overriding sentience on the basis of skin colour is morally condemned as racism, or on the basis of sex as sexism, any qualification of the principle of the equal consideration of interests on the grounds of species should, Singer asserts, be rejected as *speciesism*. The word was first used by Richard Ryder in a critique of the use of live animals in medical experiments (Ryder 1975) and Peter Singer defines the *speciesist* as a person who 'allows the interests of his own species to override the greater interests of members of other species' (Singer 1976: 9). *Animal Liberation* asserts that the truth of animals is their ability to suffer on a morally equal basis to ourselves, and they have a preference in the avoidance of suffering as we likewise do. To argue the contrary is to give voice to speciesism. Singer intended his book to be read and adopted as a persuasive repudiation of the acts of speciesism: the point is not so much that animals have a right to be treated well, rather it is that if we are to be good utilitarians, we should not act in any way that violates their preference not to suffer.

4

This is important. Singer does not believe that animals have rights. No, he is more concerned with the morality (or otherwise) of the acts of society and individuals. This is why the book is called *Animal Liberation*; Singer argues for moral, utilitarian acts, not a respect for intrinsic rights. He wants the acts which will liberate animals from speciesism. Indeed, in subsequent essays, Singer has often taken pains to distance himself from any talk of rights: 'when I talk of rights, I do it . . . as a concession to popular rhetoric (*Animal Liberation* was not written primarily for philosophers)' (Singer 1980a: 327). Singer is more concerned with acts, a position which has caused him to fall between two stools. Popularly he has been taken up as a prime advocate of animal rights (it must be said that *Animal Liberation* is not as explicit as it might have been on why it rejects talk of rights: Singer was quite prepared to play the rights card when it leant the case greater strength). Meanwhile, rights theorists have expressed grave doubts over the applicability of utilitarian calculations to the relationship between society and animals. This is especially true of Tom Regan.

Regan tears out the heart of Singer's thesis. Singer asks that account be taken of the consequences of an act for the preference of sentient beings not to suffer, before that act is performed. It should only be carried out if, on aggregate, it does not increase the sum of pain amongst morally relevant creatures. For Regan, such an approach not only betrays a 'significant conservative bias' because it considerably reinforces existing social attitudes by making them the yardstick against which all else is measured (Regan 1984: 138), but, more importantly, the utilitarian emphasis on aggregates can provide no foundation for the claims of an individual over the group.

Singer does not talk about rights; he gives the individual no priority outside of the global equality of the preference or interest not to suffer. Tom Regan believes that this position is quite unsatisfactory. He is right to say that according to the utilitarian approach to morality:

> we must choose that option which is most likely to bring
> about the best balance of totalled satisfactions over totalled
> frustrations. Whatever act could lead to this outcome is the
> one we ought morally to perform – it is where our moral duty
> lies. And that act quite clearly might not be the same one that

would bring about the best results for me personally, or for
my family or friends, or for a lab animal. The best
aggregated consequences for everyone concerned are not
necessarily the best for each individual.

(Regan 1985: 20)

Think of Raskolnikov in *Crime and Punishment*. Notwithstanding
his egoistic justifications for murdering the old moneylender,
Raskolnikov reasoned that by taking her money he could pay his
debts and help his family; certainly the benefits of the murder
would far outweigh the suffering of one unloving, decrepit old
woman. In strict utilitarian terms, the murder was an exceedingly
virtuous act. But, as Regan would object, this cannot mean that it
is morally acceptable for us to rob and murder lonely pensioners.
There is no doubt that Peter Singer would be totally horrified by
mass murder of the elderly but his moral philosophy cannot totally
overcome the tyrannical potential of the rule of the aggregate. For
utilitarians, in certain circumstances, anything might be
permissible.

Regan defends the individual by stressing that all subjects of a
life, and a being is a subject of a life when it has goals, preferences,
emotions and an identity over time, have an intrinsic value in and
of themselves (Regan 1984: 264). In Singer's theory sentient
creatures only enter the frame of reference at the moment they
are about to be acted upon, but Regan believes that the subjects of
a life (a category which he argues must extend beyond humans)
are always morally relevant whether they live in a cage, on a
factory farm, or on a desert island. Regan accepts Peter Singer's
slogan that 'All Animals Are Equal', but where Singer sees a
prescriptive equality of preferences, Regan identifies an equally
possessed inherent value, and individual subjects have a right to
expect the respect of that value. He tells us that the inherent value
of subjects should be treated as a categorical concept since 'One
either has it, or one does not. There are no in-betweens. Moreover,
all those who have it, have it equally' (Regan 1984: 240–41). As
Regan says in a passage which he also wants applied to animals:

Human beings have inherent value because, logically
independently of the interest of others, each individual is the
subject of a life that is better or worse for that individual.
Because of the type of value human beings have, it is wrong

(a sign of disrespect and a violation of rights) to treat humans as if they had value merely as means (e.g. to use humans merely to advance the pleasure of the group). In particular, to harm human beings for the sake of profit or pleasure or curiosity of the group is to violate their right not to be harmed.

(Regan 1983: 39)

Regan's approach is comparable to Peter Singer's in that they both focus on harm to animals. Yet they follow different paths to this destination. Singer looks at the speciesist immorality of the consequences of certain acts, Regan at the disrespect of intrinsic rights.

Humans disrespect the intrinsic value of animals, and the rightful claims extending from it, because of conceit and chauvinism. Conceit because we attribute to ourselves a unique and privileged place in the universe, chauvinism because we refuse to recognise that the qualities which we suppose give us universal importance 'are also possessed by individuals other than one's self or the members of one's group' (Regan 1984: 151).

The disputes amongst the protagonists of the view that animals make morally relevant claims upon humans are thrown into sharp relief by the sincere and respectful debates between Tom Regan and Peter Singer. (Their disagreements have not prevented them working together. See, for example, the collection they edited in 1976.) Where Singer rejects all a priori assumptions except the preferences of sentient subjects, and attempts to deduce a practical ethics from it, Tom Regan's work suggests a more Kantian flavour when he recognises the authority of a reworked definition of the categorical imperative; for Regan other subjects of a life should be treated as ends in themselves and not as means to something that violates their integrity. (Kant, of course, accepted the moral relevance of only rational subjects.) Indeed, if Regan's concern had not been to develop a philosophically consistent and weighty case for animal rights, his convincing demolition of Singer's plea for animal liberation could have made the grip of speciesism even tighter. As it is, Regan is exceptionally careful not to throw out the baby with the bathwater, and in fact his critique of utilitarian arguments has served to consolidate the claims which are made for animals. This has been possible because, like Singer, he believes that society should begin to treat animals radically differently and, especially, stop eating them. They believe, although inevitably for different reasons, that we should all become vegetarian.

Like all else in *Animal Liberation*, Singer's affirmation of vegetarianism is splendidly simple and developed with considerable intensity. Vegetarianism is a practical, personal testimony to the rejection of speciesism. Our interest in lamb cutlets is less important than the interest of the lamb in leading a life without pain, in so far as the present methods of meat production override the preferences of nonhuman creatures. Vegetarians (like Singer and Tom Regan) are people who 'once they have broken away from flesh-eating habits . . . can no longer approve of slaughtering animals in order to satisfy the trivial desires of their palates' (Singer 1976: 175). To do anything else, to continue to eat meat, is profoundly speciesist and therefore immoral. Moreover, in the utilitarian scheme meat-eating is wrong since, if all sentient creatures are of equal moral relevance because their preferences count equally, clearly one human eats many animals in the course of a life, and the amount of suffering thus caused to animals far outweighs his or her culinary delights. George Bernard Shaw once said that he would be followed to his grave by the herds of cattle and shoals of fish that did not have to die because he, too, was a vegetarian (cited in Singer 1976: 177). But the rejection of speciesism goes beyond questions of cuisine; *Animal Liberation* asserts that speciesism also provides the rationale for using living animals in scientific experiments (vivisection) and so, too, the products of that immoral practice should be denied by any individual who accepts the requirement to act in accordance with an uncompromising utilitarian demand for equal consideration.

It is interesting to see how the argument of *Animal Liberation* is developed. Peter Singer does not rely on an extended consideration of a logically compelling philosophical case (we have already seen that the book was not primarily aimed at the academy). Instead he makes a highly emotive appeal that is powerful because it inspires disgust and outrage, and then offers an idea as to what the horrified reader can do to assuage guilt. The book begins by outlining the prescription of how animals should be treated before moving on to spend two chapters describing what actually happens to animals in factory farms and laboratories. Only then, when the emotional card has been played to the full, is the case for vegetarianism spelt out, along with tips on the potential implications of the renunciation of meat. Peter Singer has written a handbook for action as much as, perhaps more than, a philosophical treatise.

Tom Regan takes an opposing stance. *The Case for Animal Rights* is not an emotional book. On the contrary, it is carefully and deliberately philosophical and attempts to be influential solely on the grounds of its logical impact. Regan stimulates action through contemplation, and it is no surprise to learn that he finds Singer's utilitarian vegetarianism unpersuasive. We have already seen that Singer demands vegetarianism on the grounds that, firstly, meat-eating is speciesist and, secondly, disutilitarian. Tom Regan shows that the second strand of Singer's case is highly problematic.

Singer concentrates on the immediate immorality of one person eating hundreds, thousands, of animals. Clearly this diet flies in the face of the principle of equality; in these terms, Singer is right to say that by utilitarian criteria you and I should, strictly speaking, leave off eating meat because the way it is gained in industrialised societies forgets about the preferences of the animals. However, Regan points out that Singer's calculation of meat and eater is far too limited; after all, the meat on our plate has to be produced. The meat industry is quite massive. In the middle 1980s, the United Kingdom's food industry, ranging from farmworkers to meat pie makers and workers in fast food restaurants (which universally sell meat), employed around 2.8 million people, or 13 per cent of the national workforce (Sheppard 1980). Regan's point is that Singer cannot ignore the preferences and interests of those nearly 3 million people whose livelihood is closely tied to continued meat-eating. Singer's argument collapses: 'Since there are many more humans who prefer a continuation of this industry than who oppose it, it is quite unclear how the preferences of the latter can outweigh those of the former' (Regan 1984: 222). Singer would reply to this argument by pointing out that there must be a threshold at which the aggregate preferences of non-speciesist vegetarians outweighs the prefer-ences of everyone associated with the food industry. By the utilitarian argument there must be a point at which the sheer number of vegetarians will make the meat industry uneconomic. The speciesists would then be morally obliged to turn vegetarian. For Regan, this defence of utilitarianism is little more than nonsense, since:

on this view, all that nonvegetarians need to do, in order to insure that they personally escape the obligation to be vegetarian, as this is determined by the vegetarian's impact on factory farming, is to continue doing precisely what it is that they are presently doing – namely, eating meat! For there is, on this view, no obligation to abstain from eating meat if too few people do abstain, so that those who do eat meat do nothing wrong. And if, perchance, the ranks of vegetarians were to swell to such an extent that their collective impact on factory farming could, other things being equal, close this or that intensive rearing operation, the nonvegetarians, given Singer's position, could still take steps to escape the obligatoriness of vegetarianism, as this is assessed by the impact of vegetarians on factory farming. All that nonvegetarians would need do is *eat more meat*, thereby negating the collective effect of the vegetarians and so, on Singer's view, thereby negating the meat eater's obligation to be vegetarian.

(Regan 1984: 225–6)

Tom Regan argues that vegetarianism is a moral duty founded on a requirement to respect the intrinsic value of all subjects of a life, to treat them as an end in themselves. Eating animals, or experimenting upon them, or using them in sport, is to reduce them to means and, therefore, to deny the value they possess irrespective of whatever we may want them for. As Regan argues: 'The individual is right not to purchase the products of an industry that violates the rights of others, independently of how many others act similarly' (Regan 1984: 350–51; emphasised in the original).

Tom Regan and Peter Singer ultimately imply rather similar things. Their philosophies for animal liberation, which explicitly denies that animals have rights, or for animal rights, which rejects the usefulness of any aggregates, could not be more different, yet they have the same impact on the practices of the individual. The moral person, the moral society, should be vegetarian, anti-vivisectionist, and should not use animals for sport. Morality entails leaving animals alone. A similar set of conclusions is reached by Stephen Clark, although his account is different again. Clark's perspective is contained in his book *The Moral Status of*

Animals. He agrees with the moral requirement for vegetarianism. He too is outraged by vivisection and hunting, sentiments which arise from his belief that humans should, must, respect the integrity and goodness of the commonwealth of the biosphere. Clark mocks utilitarian accounts because they are 'notoriously ill-suited to a defence of *rights* which are precisely the individual's defence against factitious calculations of the greater good' (Clark 1977: 22). Clark believes that all creatures have natural wants and ways of behaving which they have an interest to pursue and act out. To prevent their achievement, either by deliberately causing them to suffer pain, or by keeping them in too small cages, is a restriction of their right to fulfil their 'genetically programmed potentialities' or achieve self-realisation. Potentiality makes moral claims (Clark 1977: 55,58). Clark believes that all creatures have an equal right to fulfil their potential, because all are vital to the commonwealth: 'My suggestion is that society is much . . . like a household, including different age-groups, ranks and species and that a similar analogical process reveals the wider household which is the community of living creatures' (Clark 1977: 35).

According to Clark, humans are unable to see the Household, which was presumably built by God and encompasses the universe, because we live in societies which ritualise all life. And we can ritualise because we are the only species that can verbalise to any level of complexity. He believes that social culture is a 'world-at-fantasy' which corrupts the 'text' of nature; in the rituals of culture, 'Nature is a grand mirror for humanity' (Clark 1977: 119). We ritualise the world, make it a complete fantasy, because we are ashamed of the fact that we are merely one equal part of something which far transcends us: 'we wish to create a world where we are masters, and where . . . reminders of our real defencelessness as wild nature are kept firmly in their place' (Clark 1977: 133). The great symbols of that mastery, which Clark sees as invariant indications of corruption, are meat-eating and science. Indeed blame for the denial of the true human sensibilities of affection and love for all creatures is directly attributable to the cultural idealisation of objective science.

Stephen Clark is certain that our rejection of the commonwealth of nature will eventually herald the apocalypse. If we do not acknowledge the moral importance of animals, the earth will crack and explode:

If we recognize the claims of other creatures in this
community, we may still perish – we have no security on that
– but if we do not respect them, we shall perish the sooner. So
long as we *civilized men* imagine ourselves to be apart from
the land, and from our fellow creatures, we shall attempt to
exploit them for our private gain, and the attempt will kill us.

(Clark 1977: 164)

We must respect the importance of the interest of all creatures to
fulfil their potential, and we should, rightly can, do nothing to
impinge upon that.

The practical implications of Clark's argument are very wide
ranging. He agrees with Singer and Regan that it is immoral to
cause animals to suffer or treat them merely as a means, but he
moves beyond the emphasis on animals to suggest that the
commonwealth also includes plants and bacteria, ozone and water.
This unity of life demands respect: 'The First Cause, if it chose
anything, chose that the members of the world it made should be
mutually dependent' (Clark 1977: 177). Humans can eradicate
bacteria, but only if such an act does not harm the important place
of Bacteria; we can mow grass but only because that will enhance
the growth of Grass, and it should always be remembered that, 'in
speaking of "the fox" we falsely forget that there are foxes, with
individual interests and points of view, and that even if there be
the Fox we have no dealings with Him' (Clark 1977: 170). Stephen
Clark wants us to act in a way that respects the importance and
integrity, the individuality and unity, of the biosphere: to lead a life
that sees through the cultural rituals that mask the commonwealth
and pander to human arrogance. In other words, the moral status
of animals is precisely the same as the moral status of ourselves.
We all have equal importance and it is immoral to pretend or act
differently. We should all live a life that glories in the commonwealth, but Christians in particular should turn away from the
rituals of meat because 'It is open to the Christian . . . to say that
all such sacrifices, all such flesh-sharings were ended with the one
perfect and sufficient sacrifice' (Clark 1977: 178).

It would be absurd to try to deny the great differences between
Singer, Regan, and Clark, who between them encompass the main
points in the field of animal rights. It would also be wrong to
underestimate the degree of practical agreement that their ideas

finally produce. Consequently, it is reasonable to use 'animal rights' as an umbrella term for the wider debates; all the disagreements are within the common field of trying to work out the morally good relationship between society and animals. Notwithstanding the disagreements, it is fair to read this book as a study of animal rights: Why? Firstly, and as Peter Singer acknowledged, the phrase 'animal rights' is a powerful rhetorical gesture that has been accepted as a largely self-explanatory term in social debates and, secondly, the positions of Singer, Regan, and Clark broadly have the same practical implications. Empirically, they have similar consequences and cover the sides of the same debates. To some extent they are refighting the squabble between Tweedledee and Tweedledum.

The various definitions share the assertion that, for one moral reason or another, social behaviour and attitudes towards animals should be changed and constrained. Animal rights brings together four areas which independently question the suffering visited upon animals: vegetarianism: the opposition to hunting; the campaign against the use of vivisection in science and medicine; and the concern with animals' welfare. With their central themes of equality, value, or commonwealth, Singer, Regan, and Clark explicitly link these four empirically discrete worries. Each is a separate area of concern about the different ways society treats animals, and any one may, but need not, be linked with any one or any combination of the remaining three. The point to note is that animal rights is a moral principle which brings the four concerns together in something more than an accidental way, and makes them consistent and mutually supporting. It unifies otherwise separate worries; it is a complete and all encompassing attitude towards animals.

Now, Singer, Regan, and Clark manage to provide clear and internally consistent arguments as to why the four areas should be pulled together and made into a moral principle which demands action. Animal rights is a moral umbrella under which one cannot oppose hunting without at the same time accepting vegetarianism, animal welfare, and antivivisection. Stephen Clark tells us that 'All those who believe that animals are not utterly beyond moral consideration, that they should be spared all avoidable pain are duty-bound to abstain from meat, and to campaign against vivisection' (Clark 1977: 169–70). Everyone who accepts a notion of animal rights would only criticise Clark because he does not explicitly (but does implicitly) include animal welfare – that is, the belief typified by the Royal Society for the Prevention of Cruelty to Animals that cruel behaviour is wrong, but uncruel behaviour is acceptable – and antihunting.

The umbrella term can be understood in realist terms. It is arguing that somewhere behind the veils of speciesism, chauvinism, or ritual, hides a true reality of animals that must be uncovered. Once that reality is brought into the light, for the first time in many centuries, humans will recognise its truth and change their actions. But here something curious, and very interesting, begins to happen. Animal rights wants a recognition of the truth of animals, but *animals* is such a broad category that it is almost meaningless. It talks of animal rights, and then forgets that animals are very different. Mary Midgley points out that writers like Singer (and Regan, and Clark) talk

> in a very wholesale, *a priori*, French-revolutionary sort of way about all animals being equal, and denouncing 'speciesism' as being an irrational form of discrimination, comparable to racism. This way of thinking is hard to apply convincingly to locusts, hookworms and spirochaetes, and was invented without much attention to them.
>
> (Midgley 1983: 26)

Now, the fascinating point is that although Midgley has high-lighted a shortcoming in some of the main categories which are used to express the importance of animals, animal rights is not intended to cover all animals. Peter Singer and Tom Regan are quite open that they are not arguing for the respect of the rights or preferences of all animals, and even Stephen Clark's discussion is not as universal as all the grand talk of the biosphere and commonwealth might lead us to expect.

Animal rights is restricted to the animals who are most like us. Of course, seemingly valid philosophical explanations for the restriction are provided, but the fact that barriers are erected after mammals and only ambiguously encompass reptiles, fish, and molluscs is sociologically important. As we know, Singer believes that a creature is morally important to the extent that it can suffer; the point of *Animal Liberation* is that this prescriptive situation does not, but should, also describe the relationship between society and animals. In a subsequent book, *The Expanding Circle*, Singer spelt

14

out his belief that morality is rooted in altruism: 'Ethics starts with social animals prompted by their genes to help, and to refrain from injuring, selected other animals' (Singer 1981: 91). That selection is made on the basis of those 'other animals' that the individual recognises as being similar to him or herself. Singer agrees with W.E.H. Lecky that the circle of moral concern successively expands from the egoistic individual to the family group, community, nation, humanity, and ultimately, animals. Indeed: 'The idea of equal consideration for animals strikes many as bizarre, but perhaps no more bizarre than the idea of equal consideration for blacks seemed three hundred years ago' (Singer 1981: 121). Now if, as Singer suggests, the moral claims of animals are a product of the extension of altruism ultimately beyond the species barrier, it is likely that such altruism – which is essentially a recognition of the Other as the Same – can only go so far. In *Animal Liberation*, Singer has no doubt that mammals are sentient and therefore morally equal to humans, but his certainty begins to fade with fish and, eventually, 'somewhere between a shrimp and an oyster seems as good a place to draw the line as any, and better than most' (Singer 1976: 188). In *The Expanding Circle*, the line is drawn somewhere after the far more vague group of 'most animals' (Singer 1981: 120).

A broadly similar limitation of the constituency of animal rights can be found in Tom Regan's work. Regan bases his case for animal rights on reasonable assumptions; we can reasonably assume that other animals are the subjects of a life and that awareness should inform, and be reflected in, our moral systems. He suggests that because we know about the relationship between humans' conscious subjectivity and biology, 'it is reasonable to conclude that mammalian animals are likewise conscious' (Regan 1984: 29). Regan is only unequivocally prepared to include in the group of beings possessed of intrinsic value those which are most like us, and it is little coincidence that they are also the animals we know best. Similarly, Stephen Clark rests much of his plea on the assumption that

> the need for language as a medium for effective compact-making has been much exaggerated: common sympathies and purposes, mutual attractions and puzzlements are quite enough to provide a mutual sense of fair dealing at least with

our most immediate, mammalian, kin, and according to
some, admittedly bizarre, accounts even with members of
entirely different biological phyla.

(Clark 1977: 34)

So, Mary Midgley's comment would be quite right if animal rights
was meant to be applied to all animals, but it is not. This book will
show that this apparent paradox is not without profound
sociological and moral significance.

Indeed, it would be interesting, and not too deliberately
polemical, to explore the hypothesis that animal rights is not
concerned with animals at all; that, on the contrary, the idea says
rather more about society and humans. Animal rights might really
be about social actions and only incidentally focus on animals. This
is clearest in Singer, who wants to make us think about the
utilitarian consequences of our acts; animals – and remember the
category only definitely includes mammals – are creatures to
which something happens. Morally, the only important consideration about animals is their ability to experience pleasure or
pain. Although Regan talks of the intrinsic value of individuals
independently of any use they might be put to by others, the lens
through which moral issues are focused is precisely the possibility
that animals are reduced to means by humans. Again it is the
acting human who creates difficulties. Finally, Stephen Clark emphasises the commonwealth, but the crucial point in his analysis is that
it is only humans and society which deny that community in the
first place. Animal rights only wants to talk of the animals with
which people are most familiar, and it only talks of animals to the
extent that we do something to them. It is not a morality founded
upon the reality of animals, it is a morality about what it is to be
an individual human who lives a social life. The crucial facet of
animal rights is precisely that it states claims which we are asked
to do something about; animal rights is a social problem.

This book explains why there is a worry about the rights of
animals. I have surveyed the arguments which have most recently
stressed a respect for animals' rights and preferences, but we now
need to explore why the ideas take the form they do. In particular,
why does animal rights only properly include nice cuddly
mammals? Why are rights only accorded to the animals which are
most easy to anthropomorphise?

Chapter Two

THE OTHER ANIMAL

George Orwell believed that the person who abstains from meat is 'out of touch with common humanity', and 'willing to cut himself off from human society in hopes of adding five years on to the life of his carcase' (Orwell 1959: 174). Is there a vegetarian who has not been asked, 'What do you have to eat, then?' Or someone expressing sympathy for animals who has escaped mockery for caring more about animals than the suffering of other humans? But the questions might be well founded. Perhaps it is true; perhaps some individuals do only give animals rights because they are in some way unable to meet social expectations.

Karl Menninger certainly thought so. According to him, both excessive kindness to animals, which could obviously take the form of moral prescriptions, and wanton cruelty could be explained by the knowledge that might be uncovered in psychoanalysis. Menninger built his argument on the Freudian thesis that we all have conscious and unconscious incestuous erotic attachments. The point is, of course, that they cannot be expressed; society harshly forbids and punishes any hint of incest. Now, these feelings do not just 'go away' because they cannot be freely expressed; on the contrary they are sublimated and displaced on to other objects. Animals are other objects par excellence:

> Many persons . . . who are very fond of certain pets, become dimly or even clearly aware of the erotic element involved, and here I mean the physically exciting sexual element. But few, I am sure (and in my experience none), become aware except through psychoanalysis of the fact that the animal represents a sister, mother, father, or other relative.

Similarly, cruelty to animals may be characterized by the
perpetrator as uncontrollable rage, justified sport, necessary
evil, or even sadistic perversion, but this much insight never
extends to a recognition that the real objects of this
mistreatment are human figures toward whom such
behaviour could not be exhibited.

(Menninger 1951: 44)

I caress a cat because I cannot caress my mother or sister, whilst I
spurn dogs because I am jealous of my father's claims on my
mother. Attitudes towards animals are sublimated expressions of
inclinations that cannot be expressed towards the human love
object who stimulated them. Animals become totems. Menninger
explained his own childhood affection for dogs and horses in this
way.

The psychoanalytic approach could provide one explanation as
to why animal rights – which would be interpreted as a
rationalisation of sublimation – is only fully accorded to mammals.
In Western European societies, most concern is expressed about
mammals because they are the animals which individuals know
best whilst they are attempting to come to terms with their desires.
We applaud animal rights precisely because we are able to
anthropomorphise mammals, and we anthropomorphise because
we cannot freely love. Horses, in particular, have long been a
totem animal simply on account of their familiarity; they are the
second best, and most common, objects of our love. Menninger
cautiously suggests that the interest of contemporary young
children with cars can be explained in the same way. Children who
presently live in towns or cities do not see many horses, but they
see many cars and consequently machines become the focus of
displaced incestuous affections (Menninger 1951: 43).

Although this line of thinking has been used in an attempt to
stigmatise fox-hunters (Duffy 1984), and despite Menninger's
certainty that the animal-directed habits of a number of
individuals are clinically revealed to be the sublimation of socially
condemned desires, it is not convincing as a sociological explanation. No doubt some individuals who are concerned with the pain
and suffering of animals may be dubbed psychotic or pathological,
but a similar proportion of sociologists probably can be as well,
and it would be quite implausible to suggest that all sociology can

therefore be explained as sublimation and displacement. Menninger would have us extrapolate too much from the individual to the social; at least Freud's contributions to sociology and philosophy were openly speculative. The idea and practice of animal rights is far too complex to be subjected to any psychological reductionism.

Moreover, it is likely that the moralists of animal rights, such as Peter Singer, Tom Regan, and Stephen Clark, would reject Menninger's method on the grounds that it is over-humanised. For Menninger, animals are little more than blank objects on which we can inscribe our own definitions and concerns. Now, notwithstanding the paradoxical *lacunae* in the various versions of animal rights, Singer and the others demand that humans are seen as simply one kind of animal; they press the claim that the crucial aspect of being human is not intra-social relations but rather the linkage between the human and the animal. Indeed, perhaps their hints can be taken up and perhaps animal rights is best interpreted as a human response to animality. Certainly the utilitarianism of Singer, Regan's rights and Clark's commonwealth move along such a path, but, going beyond them, it is possible to ask whether the roots of animal rights might be buried deep in biology.

Ethologists, who study and compare the behaviour patterns of animals to produce an all-inclusive knowledge ranging from the activities of humans to sticklebacks or insects, would indeed explain animal rights by reference to biology and its evolutionary features. Perhaps the best-known ethologist is Konrad Lorenz, 'a gristly silver-spade-bearded man with arctic blue eyes and a face burned pink in the sun' (Chatwin 1987: 121).

Lorenz is a convinced Darwinian. He fundamentally assumes that all living species are involved in a long-term, never-ending quest for survival, and succeed to the extent that they accept the compulsion of external reality and adapt to it. Evolution is the process of adaptation for survival. Lorenz contends that all the 'peculiarly human' characteristics, including knowledge, culture, thought, and perception, are directly attributable to the quest for species survival (Lorenz 1977: 6–7). Moreover, since all species are linked in evolution – we have all evolved by adapting to our external situation just as 'the horse's hooves are adapted to the prairie, or fish's fins to the water' (Lorenz 1977: 37) – it is logically reasonable to assume that 'an enormous animal inheritance remains in man to this day' (Lorenz 1952: 152), From a Lorenzian perspective, the origins of the human concern to treat animals morally would be found in the animal instincts which remain in all humans, and the tension between them and social, cultural life. Lorenz sees culture as nothing more than the resisted modification of 'inherited behaviour patterns' (Lorenz 1977: 190).

Humans possess innate patterns of behaviour which are qualified and diverted by society. In *King Solomon's Ring*, Lorenz writes that animals are important precisely because they help us come to terms with tensions generated by the nature-culture dichotomy. Animals are important because they connect us to the external reality hidden by social life. So far the story has a similar narrative to Menninger's work, but there is a fundamental divergence. Menninger concentrates on what humans can make of the animal, Lorenz on what the animal makes of humans. In a typically personal vein – and as Lorenz got older the amount of tedious personal anecdote which allegedly gave his work world-historic importance increased – he writes:

> The pleasure which I derive from my dog is closely akin to the joy accorded to me by the raven, the greylag goose or other wild animals that enliven my walks through the countryside; it seems like a re-establishment of the immediate bond with that unconscious omniscience that we call nature. The price which man had to pay for his culture and civilization was the severing of this bond which had to be torn to give him his specific freedom of will. But our infinite longing for paradise lost is nothing else than a half-conscious yearning for our ruptured ties.
>
> (Lorenz 1952: 126)

In the evolutionary scheme, humans are unique because we have freewill, because we have managed to tear ourselves away from simple objective and instinctual compulsion. But Lorenz bewails the price of freedom; we have only been free to lose paradise. Animals are the only way left for humans to reclaim a place in the great tide of history. If we treat animals properly, and uncover our innate behaviour, which society can never finally distort, we will be able to restore the primeval unity between social culture and natural biology (Lorenz 1977: 217–18). Such is the paradise of ethology.

Lorenz argues that humans will only live well and properly when the demands of evolution, and in particular the connections between humans and animals, are accepted. Animal rights could be defined as one product of this. Lorenz's work can also be used to explain the concentration on mammals. Evidently, humans possess innate instincts to nurture (and Lorenz knows this because he has observed nurturing amongst jewel fish, for example, and forged the evolutionary links to humans) which are naturally triggered by certain features. We care for human babies, not simply because they are our kin, but because they have the triggering features of short, chubby limbs, big eyes, and big heads in relation to body size; because they are generally soft and round. Lorenz says that our response to these characteristics is the result of an evolutionary demand to care for the survival of helpless humans. The 'fact' that our innate desire to protect and nurture human infants 'is also released by less appropriate objects is merely a trivial flaw in a system which is otherwise efficient and highly adaptive'. Indeed, according to Stephen Jay Gould, the success of Walt Disney characters is due in part to the exploitation of infantile features (see Serpell 1986: 61–2). So, by this account, animal rights represents a concern to protect and nurture those creatures which falsely trigger the innate desires which evolution has enhanced in order to help the survival of human infants. We only give rights to those animals which are soft and cuddly like babies, and so we worry about dogs but not slugs, pigs but not prawns. The work of Singer, Regan, and Clark would be reduced to nothing more than an attempt to spell out that which is truly innate and, presumably, only hidden by culture.

But Lorenzian ethology has a darker side. It is not solely concerned with the restoration of a lost omniscience or the pampering of cuddly babies and animals. It more fundamentally emphasises human aggression. Indeed, the main focus of Lorenz's concern for the survival of the human species is how we work out and practise our aggressive instincts. All creatures have aggressive weapons and strategies to protect their immediate kin and territory, but the tragedy of humanity is that we uniquely wantonly kill trespassers and, more importantly, have developed weapons which go beyond our bodies and beyond our stage of evolution. Lorenz assumes that 'All living beings have received their weapons through the same process of evolution that moulded their

21

impulses and inhibitions; for the structural plan of the body and the system of behaviour of a species are part of the same whole' (Lorenz 1952: 198). Except in humans. In the always beneficent workings of evolution, weapons and behaviour are intimately linked; the creature develops a set of innate inhibitions against using the weapon in any way which will endanger the existence of the species. However, humans have succeeded in destroying that delicate bond. We build weapons of mass extermination and slaughter which are utterly beyond our evolutionary ability to control. For Lorenz this is the explanation of the two world wars of the twentieth century and the nuclear holocaust of the future. Humanity has conjured its Mephistopheles.

Lorenz argues that the ability of our aggressive impulses to herald global destruction can only be held in check by the 'strait-jacket of ritualization into which most of our social intercourse is so uncompromisingly pressed'. Evolutionary inhibitions are no match for nuclear warheads. Aggressive impulses must be restrained by tightening, in an increasingly vice-like grip, the social rituals which bring 'most or all of the instinctive urges inherent in our species under sufficient control to impose upon them the normative pattern drawn up by the culture in question' (Lorenz 1977: 217).

The analysis would lead to a two-part understanding of animal rights (which would, of course, complement the nurturing aspect mentioned above). Firstly, according to Lorenz, culture is caught in a spiral which pushes it ever further away from the objective reality and paradise of the entwined evolutionary and social and makes culture a force in its own right. If it were not, if culture did not take on an inhibiting reality of its own, world war would be unstoppable. In this picture, the happiness which Lorenz found on his country walks with a dog, and more broadly a respectful consideration of animals, would be last straws by which we can clutch at true reality. Secondly, Lorenz argues that culture can only control aggressive impulses by tying us into ritualisation and pacification; animal rights would then be seen as an extension of these rituals. Animal rights would be understood as one more strand of an inhibition of aggression without which we would kill each other; animals must be made the focus of worries about cruelty and kindness in order to maintain the normative patterns of the social life which presently assists human evolution.

Lorenz's approach seems appealing. It can offer a coherent, evidently scientific, explanation of why it is that a concern with animal rights has developed in some of the world's most advanced societies, by linking social rituals and the joys of glimpsing an extra-social reality to the demands and difficulties of evolution. Moreover, Lorenzian ethology appears to provide considerable insight into why writers like Singer, Regan, and Clark limit the strict constituency of animal rights, and why those limits are placed in some grey area after mammals. He appears to offer a great deal, but that appearance only deceives.

Initial doubts with Lorenz's work arise when one contemplates his ethological method. Certainly, Lorenz knows a tremendous amount about animals, and he writes well and vividly (especially in *King Solomon's Ring*). He claims that observation has led him to distinguish the core of the animal and instinctual that is the basis of human behaviour. He talks of love, nurturance, affection, and aggression amongst sticklebacks in precisely the manner an anthropologist would talk of the same behaviour amongst, say, Trobriand Islanders. Lorenz is confident that the procedure is viable: 'And if I have just spoken of a young male jackdaw falling in love with a jackdaw female, this does not invest the animal with human properties, but, on the contrary, shows up the still remaining animal instincts in man' (Lorenz 1952: 152–3). This is Lorenz's central methodological principle, but it has no analytic validity whatsoever. For example, the concept of 'falling in love' is not a natural trait. It is a social phenomenon which is peculiar to certain societies at certain times, usually modern West European ones. Lorenz relies on anthropomorphism to ground his evidently scientific work. He forgot that the culture he condemned also created the spectacles through which he observed and understood animals. Lorenz makes simple assertions which he wants accepted without providing any reasoned justification why they should be. When the assertion is removed from Lorenz's work, the remaining analysis is either non-existent or commonplace. This is especially clear in some of his later work. For example, he begins *Behind the Mirror*, which attempts to understand the 'ills' evidently besetting modern social life, by asserting that 'The progressive decay of our civilization is so obviously pathological in nature, and so obviously shows the symptoms of mental sickness' (Lorenz 1977: 18). Presumably, if the signs are so obvious, it would be a fairly easy task to marshal some evidence to support the assertion, but Lorenz is reticent to do so. The common-sense assertion is all and everything. Lorenz was a great observer, and no doubt a splendid biologist, but he was a baleful social theorist and philosopher. Lorenz does not explain the problem of why and how humans use animals as the basis of certain social ideas and practices. On the contrary, he merely compounds the difficulty.

However, the entire ethological enterprise should not be rejected simply on the grounds of Konrad Lorenz's tendency to produce arrogant exegeses on the commonplace. A far more serious addition to the project has been made by Edward O. Wilson. Wilson is not a simple heir to Lorenz's sticklebacks; although they operate within the same broad tradition of enquiry their work is importantly different. Lorenz is a conventional ethologist; he observes a vast number of animal species and attempts to deduce the fundamental capacities they all share. He is able to cross-reference those capacities from one species to another because evolutionary theory tells him that any differences will be of degree and not of kind. Wilson shares the concern to observe the behaviour pattern of species (he is a fan of the social insects), but he works at a greater level of abstraction than orthodox ethology. A researcher like Lorenz does not really go beyond small groups of animals; Wilson does. Wilson's basic unit of analysis is the gene and the adaptations it makes in the evolutionary struggle for survival. Lorenz stops with the innate behaviour of the body, whereas Wilson goes further to explore the biological core of behaviour. Wilson remains an ethologist, but more than that, he supports *sociobiology*. Peter Singer succinctly defines sociobiology as 'the belief that all social behaviour, including that of humans, has a biological basis and is the outcome of an evolutionary process that selects some genes or groups of genes in preference to others' (Singer 1982: 42).Wilson's concern with the evolutionary selection of genes is such that he is reticent to talk of humans as this implies some prior nonbiological community or already existing body. Instead, he refers to the 'hypothalamus and limbic system' (Wilson 1975, 1978). The key issue in Wilson's work is the problem of altruism.

Altruism – unselfish concern for the welfare of others – presents sociobiology and evolutionary theory in general with a very real difficulty. For writers like Edward Wilson, the behaviour patterns of species and individuals are totally susceptible to biological explanation; some creatures are altruistic because they are driven by their genes to sacrifice themselves for the well-being of others. For example, a small bird will give a warning cry when a predator approaches, and so risk its life to safeguard its fellows. The difficulty is that, in Wilson's words, 'fallen heroes do not have children' (Wilson 1978: 152). If altruism is rooted in genes, the individuals with those genes would disappear (the altruists would all be killed), and only those possessing selfish genes would survive. However, altruism continues to exist: how can evolutionary theory explain this?

Wilson's answer explains why he turns to genes rather than merely groups or species. A Lorenzian analysis would doubtless explain that altruism persists because it assists group survival. Wilson rejects this and, instead, suggests that continued altruism is due to the evolutionary motivation of genes to defend and protect the species gene-pool. The meaning of altruism is thus reworked: what seems like the unselfish behaviour of the individual becomes, when properly understood, the product of the selfish gene. Wilson distinguishes 'hard-core altruism' which is unconcerned with social rewards and is restricted to the altruist's immediate family (and therefore the gene's kin); it is 'likely to have evolved through kin selection or natural selection operating on entire, competing family or tribal units'. Meanwhile, 'soft-core altruism' is a more social concern: 'The capacity for soft-core altruism can be expected to have evolved primarily by selection of individuals and to be deeply influenced by the vagaries of cultural evolution' (Wilson 1978: 155–6).

The point to note is that for Wilson altruism is essentially an intra-species affair. The individual is altruistic, not because his or her personal existence is important, but because the species' genes must survive. Since social life depends on high levels of reciprocity, hard-core altruism, which is purely self- or at most family-oriented, must be subordinated to soft-core altruism which enhances the survival of the entire social network upon which species evolution depends. Wilson uses this notion to explain the maintenance of social reciprocity and selfishness. We must be soft-core altruists to allow hard-core altruism:

Individual behaviour, including seemingly altruistic acts

25

bestowed on tribe and nation, are directed, sometimes very circuitously, toward the Darwinian advantage of the solitary human being and his closest relatives. The most elaborate forms of social organization, despite their outward appearance, serve ultimately as the vehicles of individual welfare. Human altruism appears to be substantially hard-core when directed at closest relatives. . . . The remainder of our altruism is essentially soft. The predicted result is a melange of ambivalence, deceit, and guilt that continuously troubles the individual mind.

(Wilson 1978: 158–9)

This might all be well and good, but what does it imply about the relationship between society and animals? Wilson himself says little about inter-species reciprocity, and it is up to us to follow his leads. Animal rights could be effortlessly, and probably validly, interpreted as soft-core altruism, but the simple assertion still begs the question; why do humans worry about their treatment of animals? Wilson suggests that since the Ice Age soft-core altruism has been a problem of the relationship between the in-group and the out-group. The form of soft-core altruism is rigid and universal, it is always and everywhere 'characterized by strong emotion and protean allegiance', but what Wilson calls the 'genius of human sociality' is that the content, the 'precise location of the dividing line' between the in-group and the out-group, 'is shifted back and forth with ease' (Wilson 1978: 163). According to this analysis, then, humans in advanced societies presently express a moral attitude towards animals because they, or at least the mammals, are included in the definition of the in-group which demands a soft-core altruism. But again, the insistent question must be asked: Why animals?

It is at this point that a Wilsonian account, which is at best somewhat speculative, begins to edge into fantasy. Sociobiologists would appear to be able to account for inter-species soft-core altruism only on the grounds that one species (in this case the human), develops an ultimately self-serving interest in the preservation of other species' genes. Animals become the focus of altruism because humans want to maintain the global gene pool. We realise that our continued evolution is prejudiced without it. In other words, the circle of our selfishness successively expands from our immediate kin to our nation, race, species, and eventually to other mammals and, perhaps, all living creatures. To some extent the broad picture is similar to Peter Singer's notion of an expanding circle (certainly the stages of expansion would be identical), but where Singer saw the growth as a cultural response to a recognition of sentience, Wilson is in no doubt that the gene-pool is the prime mover:

> Can the cultural evolution of higher ethical values gain a direction of its own and completely replace genetic evolution? I think not. The genes hold culture on a leash. The leash may be very long, but inevitably values will be constrained in accordance with their effects on the human gene pool.
>
> (Wilson 1978: 167)

Wilson can explain why the idea of animal rights emerged so strongly only in some societies at a specific time by linking its appearance to evolutionary processes (although an insidious ethnocentrism, indeed racism, could creep in), and he can tie the problem of animals to a wider ecological concern whereby we are only concerned with the survival of the global gene-pool in so far as it is fundamental to the survival of our own. Wilson's sociobiology deserves far more serious consideration than Lorenz's ethology, but this is not to say that it should be accepted.

Sociobiology falls into the trap of an almost ludicrous biological determinism. Although Wilson frequently mentions the relevance of the social and cultural, when he is forced to allocate importance, primacy is always given to biology and, more specifically, to the evolutionary survival of genes. We may be socialised humans, but for Wilson we are more importantly gene carriers. Yet according to Mary Midgley, Wilson has performed the important tasks of denying human centrality in the universe, highlighting the differences within the human and, finally, he has established the importance of the genetic perspective over any stories of great men or women (Midgley 1979: 91). Midgley wants to take up what she sees as the incisive points in sociobiology, but make them more amenable to an account which still says something about humans *qua* humans. Midgley cannot accept Wilson's claim that all morality and all behaviour can be ultimately reduced to genes and biology. Midgley's book *Beast and Man* (1979) is also important because it explicitly attempts to approach a rich understanding of

27

the relationships between humans and animals which pays full heed to both.

She is in no doubt: the key thing to recognise is not that humans are just rather like some animals; we *are* animals (Midgley 1979: xiii). She attempts to provide an appreciation of what it is to be human which combines theories of innate instincts (shared by all animals) with a notion of human difference. The central theme running through Midgley's long book is the assertion that 'nature and culture are not opposites at all'. She tells us that the essence of humanity is that we are culture-building animals and 'what we build into our culture has to satisfy our natural pattern of motives' (Midgley 1979: 29). According to Wilson, morality can be explained solely by reference to biology; Midgley agrees that humans possess innate instincts which help our survival, but the crucial divergence from Wilson occurs when Midgley says that instincts do not follow a fixed pattern and are, on the contrary, fairly 'open' and in need of guidance by social definitions of priorities (Midgley 1979: 81–2).

Midgley's position has, and is meant to have, implications for the social treatment of animals. If humans *are* animals, we should recognise our entwined kinship and difference with at least other mammals. Humans should sympathise with animals and treat them as individuals. She argues that all animals should be regarded as morally relevant subjects whether they are humans or of another species (Midgley 1979: 225). If we are to treat animals morally we should tread the thin line which accepts, and glories in, both their sameness and radical otherness. We should accept that we are a natural part of a natural system which our ability to build cultures to some extent hides, but is, in any case, beautifully unknowable. Midgley demands respect of the different subjectivities existing in the world, subjectivities which are quite beyond our comprehension but relevant because we are merely one amongst them. She quotes Iris Murdoch's statement that 'we take a self-forgetful pleasure in the sheer, alien pointless independent existence of animals, birds, stones and trees', and continues:

> The world in which the kestrel moves, the world that it sees, is, and will always be, entirely beyond us. That there are such worlds all around us is an essential feature of our world.

28

> Calling the bird's existence 'pointless' means only that it is
> not a device for any human end. It does not need that
> external point. It is in some sense . . . an end itself.
>
> (Midgley 1979: 359)

Animals constitute a world that is an end itself, regardless of
whatever humans and society might make of it. Midgley wants our
treatment of animals to understand and respect the otherness of
nonhuman animals. In this reading, animal rights would be a
celebration of animals' self-dependent difference; animal rights
would be one way of happily coming to terms with a world that is
and will remain quite beyond our grasp. Midgley's turn to
otherness, which she arrives at from a critical appreciation of
sociobiology, ironically involves a turn away from the materialism
of a Singerian reading of animals as bodies that can suffer. To be
sure, Midgley repudiates cruelty, but because such a treatment of
animals denies their apartness, rather than because it causes pain.

Midgley relies on Kant's theory of the sublime. The comment-
ary on the sublime is not amongst Kant's clearest work, but the
concept refers to a supersensible *boundlessness*; the sublime is that
which transcends sensual perception. It is that which is pleasing
because it goes beyond our sensual ability to know it: 'The sublime
is that in comparison with which everything else is small' (Kant
1988: 377; emphasis removed). This is precisely how Mary
Midgley understands animals; she gratefully accepts the pleasure
that animals' sublime boundlessness can give. (Kant's theory of the
sublime might be linked to ideas of divinity, an implication not
absent from Midgley's work.) However, Midgley has not pursued
the Kantian sublime to its fullest extent. Had she done so, her
comments on the rightful treatment of animals would be made
rather difficult.

Certainly Kant defined the sublime as that which is
supersensible but, simply by the act of writing about it, Kant
demonstrated that 'The sublime is that the mere ability to think
which shows a faculty of the mind surpassing every standard of
sense' (Kant 1988: 377; emphasis removed). It is a faculty of the
mind which judges, classifies something as beyond the sensual.
Aesthetic judgement classifies a thing as sublime by referring

> itself to reason in order that it may subjectively be in
> accordance with the Ideas, no matter what they are; it does so

that it may produce a state of mind conformable to them and compatible with that brought about by the influence of definite . . . [i.e. moral] ideas upon our feeling. Hence we see that true sublimity must be sought only in the mind of the judging subject, not in the natural object the judgment upon which occasioned this state. . . . This feeling of the sublime in nature is respect for our own calling (*Bestimmung*), which by a certain subreption we attribute to an object in nature, converting respect for the idea of humanity in our own person into respect for the object in nature.

(Kant 1988: 377–78)

Midgley ignores this vital part of the Kantian sublime. A thing, say a species of animal, may well be beyond human sensual perception, but Kant asserts that it does not and cannot remain outside the faculties of judgement. The supersensible is made sublime – boundless – in the mind of the rational judging subject. Turning Midgley's terminology against her, animals are only sublime because they are judged (by individuals, by society) to be purposeless. In other words, the recourse to the sublime, which Midgley intends to answer the question of animals by saying that no answer is possible, falls into the same trap as Lorenz's ethology: it becomes part of the problem. It is society, it is 'the idea of humanity in our own person' that says animals should be respected because they cannot be known. But exactly that conclusion does make animals known; they are classified as the unclassifiable.

Moreover, the sublime cannot be the basis of a morality. Kant defined the sublime as the boundless and Mary Midgley believes that humans should glory in the fact that the universe, and more precisely the animal, is quite beyond sensual understanding. However, Burke pointed out that confrontation with the infinite might also induce feelings of horror, fear, and loathing. Certainly, animals might be beyond our senses, but Midgley can provide no explanation why we should react to the sublime with humility; it is equally possible, and perhaps more likely, that humans react to the unknowable by trying to extirpate it. Jean-François Lyotard states that confrontation with the sublime in art gives rise to 'a contradictory feeling, because it is a feeling of both pleasure and displeasure, together' (Lyotard 1989: 22). Midgley refuses to see this ambivalence which can also apply to the experience of animals, and takes up only one side of the sublime whilst quite illicitly denying any other. She does not accept that any assertion that animals are sublime can imply their annihilation as much as their rights. Boundlessness has no moral relevance whatsoever; *Beast and Man* turns around an empty rhetoric.

Mary Midgley tries to unravel the nature of humanity and animality by taking up clues in sociobiology. Her enterprise is an attempt to provide the ontological grounding of a viable, all-encompassing morality. Midgley stresses animals' a priori existence and wants it to have a place in our practical moral behaviour: 'A triangle without three sides ceases to be a triangle. But a flightless bird does not cease to be a bird, nor a flying fish a fish' (Midgley 1979: 206). Yes it might. Those three ironic words are a key to the sociology of animal rights.

A flying fish might be a fish, but it could be classified as a bird or even a magical anomaly. Societies do not just intuitively experience animals; societies seek to know and explain them. We do not simply see or feel animals, we classify them, and it is those classifications, those ideas, which shape our practical actions. Moreover, societies classify animals through a knowledge which attempts to establish unambiguously *what it is to be human*. This broad thesis obviously owes a debt to the social anthropology of Claude Lévi-Strauss, Mary Douglas, and Edmund Leach. Social anthropology offers fascinating accounts of various social attitudes towards animals, accounts which provide a wealth of insight for an explanation of animal rights in modern Britain.

According to writers like Lorenz and Wilson, and notwithstanding their frequent declarations to the contrary, humans are best understood as animals which simply respond to external reality, response itself being dictated by innate drives. Even Mary Midgley's philosophical project ultimately suggests either that morality should be reconciled with biology, or that biology is sublime and must therefore be respected as boundless. All three adopt a position which to some extent reflects the naturalism of Peter Singer, Tom Regan, and Stephen Clark; they see the social dimensions of human relationships, and all cultural endeavour, as an abstraction from the natural. They all attempt sharply to distinguish being from the knowledge of being. Culture is reduced to nothing more than an ideological distortion of True Reality. And so Lorenz attempts to observe the core behaviour patterns of

31

all animals; Wilson sees the gene as the prime mover and basic unit of evolution; and Mary Midgley tries to lay the foundations for a morality which is fully aware of human nature.

It is not good enough simply to assert that humans blindly, naturally, respond to external reality (nature). Whilst it is undoubtedly fair to follow Wilson and see humans as bearers of genes, or Lorenz and Midgley and believe that humans are not just like animals but really are animals, they do not provide the whole story. It is much like saying that J.S. Bach once strung a few musical notes together; the reductionism is similarly absurd. Bach did not write haphazard ditties any more than humans only react to external reality, any more than society and culture are just glosses on some objective nature. The crucial dimension of humanity is precisely the ability to go beyond nature, and the ability to produce a knowledge of being which shapes action more than being itself. Lorenz, Wilson, and Midgley are unable to give this unique capacity its full weight because their methodologies necessarily dismiss it. It may be trite, but it is nevertheless valid to point out that there are certain things in this world which only humans have done and presumably can do, compared to which the natural dimensions of being human are fairly trivial. One of the important dimensions of humans is that we are uniquely social and cultural. We do not only react to nature, we attempt to understand it, and our place in it.

A core of social life is the attempt to establish what it is to be properly human, to establish human uniqueness in contra-distinction to the otherness of the natural environment. Culture makes sense of, and controls, a world which humans did not make but, long ago, found themselves thrown into. Humans everywhere live a social life which is not the product of genes or innate behaviour, but is how we guarantee and make sense of our existence. We do not *see* the world naturally, we *perceive* it socially.

Claude Lévi-Strauss accepts that the natural environment constitutes a reality external to society. But its 'naturalness' is a less important influence on the actions of individuals than how it is appropriated in human perception. Perception classifies the natural environment; the wholeness of external reality is put into categories which are dictated by the faculties of the mind. Indeed: 'The coherence of each system of classification depends strictly on constraints specific to the functioning of the human mind'

(Lévi-Strauss 1987: 103–4). In particular, the human mind depends on the mediation of the senses through language to classify the world into separate parts. Lévi-Strauss is suggesting that humans mentally perceive external reality as other, and classify its boundlessness into rationally intelligible and discrete categories. He defines his project as an attempt to analyse 'the conceptual scheme by the operation of which matter and form, neither with any independent existence, are realised as structures, that is as entities which are both empirical and intelligible' (Lévi-Strauss 1966: 130). He talks of structures, firstly because he believes that the social classification of nature depends on structural capacities in the human mind, and secondly because 'all classification proceeds by pairs of contrasts', that is, by means of a formal taxonomy (Lévi-Strauss 1966: 217). Moreover, because Lévi-Strauss states that perception is mind-dependent, and believes that *Homo sapiens* is an internally consistent biological species, his anthropological project has a universal intent. He examines 'so-called primitive societies' to understand advanced industrial societies better: their 'customs are very much closer to our own than they appear and present us with an enigmatic image which needs deciphering' (Lévi-Strauss 1966: 209).

Lévi-Strauss's structural anthropology demands that analysis concentrates on how societies classify the natural world, how humans understand themselves as humans, and examines the impact of these social interpretations of being on individual practices. Clearly, the naturalistic assumptions of the ethological-sociobiological tradition, and, indeed, the moralists of animal rights, have been totally reworked. Statements about what is true are social artifacts rather than approximations to a real nature which culture hides.

Now, Lévi-Strauss contends that animals create problems for any clear-cut social classification of the world. They are, at one and the same time, comparable to humans and yet totally different; they have bodies which are reminiscent of our own, but they cannot perform many simple tasks. Moreover, animals are frequently involved in social life; many of us share our lives with cats and dogs, or lavish attention on horses. Animals are given a place within the circle of social relationships, but that place is always ambiguous. How, then, can social classification cope with these contradictions whilst retaining an effective formal structure?

Lévi-Strauss shows us with a brilliant analysis of how different animals are named in modern France.

Names are important for Lévi-Strauss because they may be read as something like labels on the various boxes in which the natural world is stored and kept for social use. He points to a paradox: some animals are readily given human names, but the names are denied to others, whilst some names of natural categories are allowed for humans and others are not. He believes that birds are particularly interesting since they are biologically dissimilar to humans but given human names (Robin Redbreast, Jenny Wren). The curious situation Lévi-Strauss identifies is that:

> girls are sometimes called Rose or Violet and conversely
> several animal species are allowed to share christian names
> commonly borne by men or women. But why should it . . .
> particularly be birds who profit from this liberal attitude?
> They are further removed than dogs from men in their
> anatomical structure, their physical structure and their mode
> of life, and human christian names cannot be given to dogs
> without causing uneasiness or even mild offence.
>
> (Lévi-Strauss 1966: 204)

What is his explanation? Birds are given human names, or girls the names of flowers, precisely because they are so different, exactly because birds and flowers are so obviously 'other'. Meanwhile, dogs cannot be given human names, despite the fact that they share our world with us, in order to classify them as quite separate from the realm of social relationships. We give similar names because difference is perceived, we give different names because similarity could be perceived. Names help to firmly establish and confirm the social criteria of difference from the human:

> Birds are given human christian names in accordance with
> the species to which they belong more easily than are other
> zoological classes, because they can be permitted to resemble
> men for the very reason that they are so different. They are
> feathered, winged, oviparous and they are also physically
> separated from human society by the element in which it is
> their privilege to move. As a result of this fact, they form a
> community which is independent of our own but, precisely

because of this independence, appears to be like another society, homologous to that in which we live: birds love freedom; they build themselves homes in which they live a family life and nurture their young; they often engage in social relations with other members of their species; and they communicate with them by acoustic means recalling articulated language.

(Lévi-Strauss 1966: 204)

Birds are totally removed from human social relations, and this distance means that their relationships can be perceived as a *metaphor* of our own (they are a parallel society). Now, because birds are a metaphor for humans – it is possible to speak of them as if they were us – their names can be *metonymical* to human names; they can be an extension of the system of human names.

The situation is totally different with dogs. Lévi-Strauss points out that dogs have no social life of their own and are, indeed, an extension of human society; they are metonymical to us. Consequently, names must be used to represent the otherness of dogs. Their names are drawn from a metaphorical system (Lévi-Strauss 1966: 205). Lévi-Strauss extends this analysis to include the names of cattle and racehorses. He suggests that cattle are technically and economically metonymical to human society, but where dogs are treated as subjects (pets), cattle are objects (meat) and are given descriptive names which reflect either the colour of their coats or temperament. Meanwhile, although racehorses do not represent an independent society like birds (because they are shaped by human endeavour), neither are they subjective or objective parts of human society; racehorse names follow rules of rigid individuation and have no descriptive function. Racehorses 'constitute the desocialised condition of existence of a private society: that which lives off race-courses or frequents them' (Lévi-Strauss 1966: 206).

Lévi-Strauss summarises all these observations in a cryptic statement: 'If, therefore, birds are *metaphorical human beings* and dogs, *metonymical human beings*, cattle may be thought of as *metonymical inhuman beings* and racehorses as *metaphorical inhuman beings*' (Lévi-Strauss 1966: 207). In either case, the names serve to classify animals in contradistinction to the human, and serve to delimit rigidly what it is and is not to be a fully social being. The names of animals are part of a system, a structure, of classification which makes the perception of human difference intelligible.

Lévi-Strauss understands social restrictions on meat-eating in much the same way. Social prohibitions on meat represent attempts to deny human and animal consubstantiality (Lévi-Strauss 1966: 107). Consubstantiality is rooted in the ability of humans to 'assimilate the flesh' of animals, and it is repudiated because, Lévi-Strauss suggests, any overt acceptance of the ability of human bodies to take in the bodies of animals 'would imply recognition on the part of man of their common nature. The meat of *any* animal species must therefore not be assimilated by *any* group of men' (Lévi-Strauss 1966: 108). In other words, humans perceive the fact that we are like animals in that we are similarly corporeal, but that recognition is the basis of a system of dietary classifications which seek to deny it and, once more, entrench the gulf between humans and animals. Social restrictions develop around meat-eating because, by saying that humans and animals are the same, society is able to demonstrate that they are different.

A vivid example of this structure of classification can be found in the Bible. The first five books of the Bible (the Torah of Judaism or the Pentateuch of Christianity) laid down strict regulations on what the Hebrews could and could not eat. These rules establish the edibility of certain meat by determining whether the animal it comes from is classified clean or unclean (Soler 1979). In the biblical system, all animals are classified according to the element in which they live (land, sea, air) and by their natural food source. Before the Fall, when man was unambiguously clean, the God-ordained human diet was exclusively vegetarian; food only became problematic, and potentially unclean, after the eviction from Eden. The biblical classification of food is a response to ambiguities produced by the post-Fall Mosaic toleration of meat-eating. Jean Soler suggests that some meat was made taboo because the animals it came from could not be given a single place in Mosaic classification. An animal was only clean and edible if it unambiguously fitted the categories of knowledge; for example, 'the clean animals of the earth must conform to the plan of the Creation, that is, be vegetarian; they must also conform to their ideal models, that is, be without blemish' (Soler 1979: 134). The Hebrews could eat cows and sheep because they were vegetarian, and the dietary cleanness of the animals was reinforced by their

36

hooves which were defined as the ideal foot form for land animals. However, the pig is unclean, and uneatable, because it has the cloven foot of carnivorous animals. It is unclean because it is blemished and cannot be placed in any single place in the system of classification.

Moreover, carnivorous animals are unclean because they eat flesh and therefore deviate from the ideal diet of Creation; the meat which humans eat is only clean if it is drained of blood. Soler suggests that in the scheme of Creation God created life, and meat-eating was denied because it involved stealing life from God, but the Mosaic system works around this problem. Before the Fall, life was signified by flesh, after it, life is signified by blood. Consequently, meat is clean when it contains no blood and when the animal it came from did not drink the blood of any prey. If Hebrews consume blood either directly or indirectly they are usurping God's rule over life and destroying the basis of all classification: it is impossible for humans to be as God or for animals to deviate from their ordained ideal. The Mosaic system is a taxonomy in which God, humans, and animals all have a proper place in an oppositional system. Humans could not consume the blood that belonged to God, pigs were unclean because they were herbivores with the feet of carnivores: 'The Hebrews conceived of the order of the world as the order underlying the creation of the world. Uncleanness, then, is simply disorder, wherever it may occur' (Soler 1979: 136).

An almost identical analysis, although drawn out much further and related to the schemes and rituals of tribal societies, has been provided by Mary Douglas. In *Purity and Danger* (1966) Douglas accepts the Lévi-Straussian position that 'It is part of our human condition to long for hard lines and clear concepts' (Douglas 1966: 162). The book concentrates on how society responds when the natural objects of perception do not fit these 'hard lines and clear concepts'. Hence the book's title: things are pure, clean, when they can be easily and rigidly classified, dangerous and unclean when they cannot. Society responds to unclean objects by making them the focus of ritual cleansing or taboo. By this scheme, an animal is pure when it is classified, dangerous and dirty when it is anomalous in respect of the systems of classification. Culture provides the rituals of classification and standardises and normalises them. It is culture and classification which make us social and human. 'Social rituals create a reality which would be nothing without them' (Douglas 1966: 62). Douglas also holds to the oppositional understanding of classification developed by Lévi-Strauss and used by Soler, and argues that if the clean is that which is classified and not anomalous, 'uncleanness is matter out of place', and 'we must approach it through order. Uncleanness or dirt is that which must not be included if a pattern is to be maintained' (Douglas 1966: 40).

The implication of this situation for the social treatment of animals should not cause any surprise. Societies will only condone the consumption of animals which are 'pure'. If an animal is dangerous or anomalous, societies either create distanciation through taboo or acceptance through ritual. Where Lévi-Strauss looked at naming patterns and related them to how society sees animals as either metaphorical or metonymical beings – that is, where Lévi-Strauss examines the formation of certainty – Mary Douglas explores the implications if those distinctions are blurred.

Although Douglas was not at all influenced by Soler (indeed they worked quite independently, see Soler 1979: 138), their discussions of the social creation of cleanness and uncleanness are strikingly similar. Usually, when a creature is taxonomically anomalous it is rejected as dirty, as unacceptable food or as something to be abhorred. The Mosaic condemnation of pigs worked in this way, indeed Soler hesitantly suggests that the divine status of Jesus is rejected by Judaism precisely because Jesus' position as half-god, half-human is an abomination to Mosaic classification (Soler 1979: 136). This is one answer to anomaly, the other is exemplified by the Lele attitude towards the pangolin; they ritualise it.

Douglas's discussion of the Lele's pangolin cult is very rich and should be read at first-hand for its many dimensions to be laid out; only one strand is relevant here. Douglas calls the pangolin a 'benign monster'.

> Its being contradicts all the most obvious animal categories. It is scaly like a fish, but it climbs trees. It is more like an egg-laying lizard than a mammal, yet it suckles its young. And most significant of all, unlike other small mammals the young are born singly. Instead of running away or attacking, it curls in a modest ball and waits for the hunter to pass. . . .

38

Instead of being abhorred and utterly anomalous, the
pangolin is eaten in solemn ceremony by initiates.

(Douglas 1966: 168–9)

There can be no doubt that the pangolin is a problem for any
structure of classification. The important aspect of the Lele cult is
that exactly because the pangolin transcends all categories it is
treated as a ritual, magical animal. The Lele are always acting
upon their perceptual and cultural interpretation of external
reality and systematically punish and denounce any infringement
of the socially constructed order as pollution. The pangolin is
important on precisely those grounds:

> The Lele pangolin cult is only one example of which many
> more could be cited, of cults which invite their initiates to
> turn round and confront the categories on which their whole
> surrounding culture has been built up and to recognise them
> for the fictive, man-made, arbitrary creations that they are. . .
> As they prepare to eat they visibly enact the central
> discriminations of their cosmos no less than the ancient
> Israelites enacted a liturgy of holiness.

(Douglas 1966: 169–70)

By eating the pangolin, the Lele are practising their taxonomic
system and reinforcing their definition of their own place in it.
They may reveal the concepts which order perception to be the
product of culture, but 'The rituals enact the form of social
relations and in giving these relations visible expression they
enable people to know their own society' (Douglas 1966: 128). The
pangolin is an anomaly which helps the Lele establish their
certainty; it is an object of disorder which consolidates the
categories of order. More broadly yet: Animals are natural objects
which help determine what it is to be a human social subject.

The interpretation of the relationship between society and
animals which Lévi-Strauss and Douglas inspire would be
profound, but their work does contain some difficulties. Perhaps
the most obvious problem with Lévi-Strauss's analysis is his refusal
to accept that it might be wrong or disproved. He has written of a
letter he received from a British correspondent who pointed out
that in Britain dogs are frequently given human names. This
would seem to fly in the face of Lévi-Strauss's scheme, but he will

39

have none of it. One of the main props of his structuralist enterprise is the idea that 'facts can never be viewed in isolation but must be seen in relation to other facts of the same category' (Lévi-Strauss 1987: 155). The social ordering of the world must be understood as a complete structure, and it is only possible to understand any one part by reference to its position in the global scheme. Consequently, the British correspondent merely proves Lévi-Strauss's point: 'the fact that the French and the British use different types of names for their dogs lends further support to my argument' (Lévi-Strauss 1987: 155). It lends support because the different naming habits simply demonstrate that the French and the British give dogs different structural meanings. It is difficult to know where this leaves a structuralism which has a universalising intent, other than at the level of the most abstract and reified methodological prescriptions.

The analyses of Lévi-Strauss and Douglas also tend to overdraw simple oppositions. For them, classifications are based on metaphor/metonymy, purity/danger, known/unknown, and so forth. But according to Edmund Leach in an important paper which attempts to make Lévi-Strauss's work on the naming of animals rather more subtle, it is necessary to introduce gradations within classification (Leach 1964). The animal is not only that which is distinct from the human; Edmund Leach insists on a recognition of degrees of otherness.

Leach makes an assumption similar to Lévi-Strauss and Douglas; humans do not just respond to external reality. On the contrary, we seek to understand and classify it. However, where Lévi-Strauss seems to concentrate on mind-dependent perception, Leach leans more to Mary Douglas's emphasis on the social and the cultural. 'Such classification is a matter of language and culture, not of nature. It is a classification that is of great practical importance, and it is felt to be so' (Leach 1964: 31).

Leach implies that dogs are the site of special taboos in Britain (we do not eat and should not beat them) because they are ambiguous in the cultural division of the world. At this point, Leach's discussion can be read as an extension of Lévi-Strauss's definition of dogs as metonymical to human society, although he does take a linguistic turn: 'Man and dog are "companions"; the dog is "the friend of man". On the other hand man and food are antithetical categories. Man is not food, so dog cannot be food either' (Leach 1964: 32). Dogs are taboo because they have an ambivalent status in respect of human society. As Lévi-Strauss pointed out, they are an extension of the social world which is not, however, human. Leach relates this categorisation of dogs as companions which are not food to verbal abuse; to call a human a dog is effective as an insult and a taboo phrase because it plays on ambiguity and puts the human outside the properly social. The taboo is that which is interstitial.

Leach believes that social attitudes towards different animals reflect human familiarity with them. Those which are closest to humans are the most taboo and insulting, those furthest away most readily eaten. (Although all these relationships must hold together in a coherent structural system, wild animals are outside of rigid classification and therefore ambivalent food and of varying use as insults.) Clearly the discussion attempts to add subtlety to Lévi-Strauss's rigidity:

> we arrange the familiar animals in a series according to their
> social distance from the human SELF . . . then we can see that
> the occurrence of taboo (ritual value), as indicated by different
> types and intensities of killing and eating restriction, verbal
> abuse, metaphysical associations, ritual performance, the
> intrusion of euphemism, etc., is not just randomly distributed.
> . . . Taboo serves to separate the SELF from the world, and
> then the world itself is divided into zones of social distance
> corresponding here to the words farm, field, and remote.
> (Leach 1964: 52. Tambiah (1973) offers more on the division of
> the world into zones of social distance.)

The animals with the greatest value are those closest to us, and, importantly, *those from which we must most clearly separate ourselves*. Leach suggests that we worry about cruelty to birds and mammals because they are warm-blooded and have sexual intercourse in a way humans can understand; we worry about them on account of their similarity to us. We can only be cruel to those animals which are closest to us, and which therefore present the greatest difficulties for the ordered classification of the world. Leach points out that 'the concept of *cruelty* is applicable to birds and beasts but not to fish' (Leach 1964: 42). A similar story was told earlier by the moralists of animal rights, and by Peter Singer's doubts in particular; now that story is becoming intelligible.

It might seem that the discussion has moved a long way from any intention to provide a sociological account of why animals are frequently given rights in modern Britain, but it has not. The anthropological literature goes to the heart of the relationship between animals and society. Moral philosophers, and indeed society broadly, classify animals as the same as humans precisely to prove that humans are different. The paradox at the heart of animal rights is that humans do, as Tom Regan asserted, identify animals as part of the same metaphorical and metonymical world as society, but that identification is only possible, can only take place, through the culturally created taxonomic structures that make similarity or difference intelligible and which also assert that social life is uniquely possessed of culture. It must be remembered that the world is socially classified in order to establish what humans are; animals are taboo, a pollution, or possessors of rights, only in relation to the taxonomies which establish the basis of human society. Despite Mary Midgley's protestations, animals *are* a blank paper; they are only important because they can tell us something about ourselves; they are only subjected to certain types of behaviour to the extent that such treatment is classified as the demonstration of the uniqueness of humanity. They are nothing other than what we make them. Society invests animals with moral significance and presses codes of normative behaviour. Society uses animals to understand itself. This must be the basis of any sociological explanation of animal rights. Unfortunately, however, the explanation is not that simple (or else, what is the rest of this book about?).

Animal rights may be understood as a taboo which helps to maintain the differential ordering of living objects. It establishes precisely how and why humans are different from the animals they know best and most nearly resemble; it makes humanity different by making humanity moral. Moreover, whilst animal rights establishes the importance of animals' congruity to human society, it does so by making them metaphors for each other. All other living creatures are collapsed into the objective category 'animal' which muddies over more than it clarifies. Animal rights serves to classify nonhuman animals as a morally indistinguishable 'other'. It makes the subjective human adopt normative behaviour towards objective animals.

The anthropological literature makes the vital point that

culture attempts to order the world logically in a way which makes every part of external reality intelligible and assigns it a place in a taxonomy. As Douglas and Leach point out, the places where those logical orders overlap, or where an object can be allocated to more than one category, become sites of danger or taboo. The interstices are places where the 'fictive reality' (Douglas's phrase) maintaining social life is threatened with dissolution. One of the most fundamental interstices is the metaphorical and metonymical relationship between society and animals, the simultaneity of congruity and difference; animals are like humans, but we are not like them.

Societies can usually accommodate the paradoxical status of animals through naming strategies, meat-avoidance or verbal taboos. However, the distinction is threatened in societies like Britain. The threats are of four main kinds. Firstly, in Britain at least, there is a high awareness of metonymy through pet-keeping. Secondly, advanced industrial societies practise a vast amount of highly sophisticated consubstantiality with meat-eating and vivisectional science, which is predicated on the use of animals as surrogate humans. Thirdly, people become aware of animals as metaphorical creatures by weekend visits to the countryside, when animals are seen in their apparently natural environment, leading a social life of sorts. Fourthly, the popular television wildlife programmes define animals both metaphorically (the programmes tell us of their social life) and metonymically (they always talk of the impact of humans on the animals and invariably voice a theme that 'we all live in the same world'). It is in countries like Britain, where animals are brought into the field of cultural experience *in an already socialised form*, that the horizon of humanity has to be redescribed through normative restraint which, once again, pushes the human and the animal apart.

The socialisation of animals is at its most reified and developed in advanced societies. Animals are fully accommodated within the compass of social life; they are economically and domestically metonymical, and visually metaphorical. The distinction by which humans can think humanity is blurred; since animals are already socialised, animals cannot be a discrete other against which humanity can be pragmatically reconfirmed. However, this difficulty can be avoided by two ploys: the greater tightening of socialisation or the taxonomic strategy of asserting moral relevance. The avoidance strategies of animal rights are indivisible from the consubstantiality of socialisation.

Think for a moment about who asserts animals' rights. Is it a laboratory rabbit, veal calf, or hunted fox? Not at all. Animal rights is exclusively asserted by society and it is intended to restrain human practices. It says that animals are morally the same as humans, and then asks humans to treat them as if they were human; it is up to us to struggle for animal rights because animals cannot fight for themselves. In other words, they are different. Animal rights classifies animals as non-moral objects which are metonymical to moral (human) subjects, and as a metaphorical society which is morally relevant since human society is morally relevant. Society thinks about animals to think about itself. If animals were not given rights, and it is crucial that it is humans who give animals rights, the classificatory distinctions between the human and the animal would be threatened with collapse.

The concentration of animal rights on mammals can be easily explained by this analysis. Singer, Regan, and Clark only unambiguously accept the moral relevance of mammals because only mammals are ambiguously close to humans. Animal rights contains a gradation of relevance which seems to dissolve amongst sea creatures, and it is no coincidence that sea creatures are the beings which are perceptually and geographically furthest from the human. Mammals are the animals which are most frequently metonymical to society, and with which humans are most closely consubstantial. The human/animal distinction is most likely to blur with mammals, and so they are the ones we must take most pains to distinguish ourselves from. Animal rights makes mammals *a part* of the human social system and *apart* from it; because they are congruous and incongruous, and therefore taxonomically ambivalent, their treatment must be subject to inhibition. The classificatory anomaly created by the perceptual fact that humans and dogs are similarly mammals is an interstitial taboo. The ritual avoidances of animal rights are an enactment of 'the discriminations by which . . . society and its cultural environment exist' (Douglas 1966: 170).

Animal rights confronts society with the biological reality that humans are a part of nature, that we are inextricably involved in the same world as dogs and pangolin, but tells us that we are different because we can be moral. Animal rights can be reduced to a ritual avoidance of touching animals; it helps society firmly delimit itself. More than a confrontation with the beast, animal rights is a classification of humanity.

The thesis has a Durkheimian ring. Perhaps the resonance is unavoidable given that this interpretation of animal rights relies on an anthropological tradition which is often reminiscent of the Durkheim of *The Elementary Forms of the Religious Life*. Certainly, Durkheim's thesis that religion is an expression of the autonomy of human society can be transposed to provide an immense advance in any understanding of animal rights. But the Durkheimian tradition contains two fundamental flaws; firstly, it sees society as a homogeneous solid, and secondly, it has difficulty explaining temporal change.

Durkheim saw the social terrain as the ultimate reality of human existence; it makes us fully human by restraining our innate urges and providing a framework of moral order. Now, since Durkheim assumed that outside of society all humans possess a common nature, so he believed that society must make broadly similar demands on all of us. Durkheim saw society as the site of all the individual's hopes and opportunities:

> It is that which raises him outside himself; it is even that which made him. For that which makes a man is the totality of the intellectual property which constitutes civilization, and civilization is the work of society. Thus is explained the preponderating role of the cult in all religions, whichever they may be. This is because society cannot make its influence felt unless it is in action, and it is not in action unless the individuals who compose it are assembled together and act in common. It is by common action that it takes consciousness of itself and realises its position; it is before all else an active co-operation. The collective ideas and sentiments are even possible only owing to these exterior movements which symbolize them. . . . Then it is action which dominates the religious life, because of the mere fact that it is society which is its source.
>
> (Durkheim 1915: 418)

Then it is action which dominates animal rights, because of the mere fact that it is society which is its source. A not wholly unsatisfactory thesis, but by no means the whole story. Society is not a homogeneous, internally frictionless solid. The perspective that religion is the self-understanding of society would lead to an assertion that all individuals should relate to animals in the same way; everyone should be a meat-eater or a vegetarian. Now this is patently inadequate. Certainly, animal rights may be interpreted as the other side of the rationalised socialisation of animals, and they jointly create a rigid classification of the properly human and social, but the two sides are in conflict. The very purpose of animal rights is to make all animals a taboo and thereby deny the moral and classificatory acceptability of factory farming, vivisection, hunting, and 'cruelty'. Rights and use are mutually repelling – and no doubt repellent – not attractive. Animal rights is not part of a single, holistic definition of humanity; it is one very specific definition of what it is to be really human and it scorns other definitions as abhorrent.

Lévi-Strauss, Douglas, and Edmund Leach also tend to understate historical change. They freeze analysis in time and assume that it is applicable at all times and in all places; consequently, Mary Douglas can interpret the rituals of the Dinka and the dietary codes of the book of Leviticus through the same perspective. However, sociologists should be wary of any such universalising project. On the one hand the ability to talk of modern African tribes and ancient religious texts in almost the same breath probably says more about Douglas's intellectual powers than any essential taxonomy, whilst it is important to recognise that taxonomy has not always existed in its present form. The interpretation of animal rights as a classification of the human must be supplemented with a historical dimension. Ideas of animal rights have not always existed, indeed in Britain they only started to be whispered in the eighteenth century. We must try to understand why.

Mary Midgley believed that a fish is always a fish, but she was wrong. A fish is only a fish if it is socially classified as one, and that classification is only concerned with fish to the extent that scaly things living in the sea help society define itself. After all, the very word 'fish' is a product of the imposition of socially produced categories on nature. Writers like Lorenz, Wilson, and Midgley are wrong; animals are indeed a blank paper which can be inscribed with any message, and symbolic meaning, that the social wishes. At its centre animal rights is a shimmering mirror; animals talk about humans, humans tell of animals. When we see a definition of one, we also see a classification of the other. The ethological-sociobiological tradition is woefully inadequate because it understands humans and animals as merely *natural* objects. The anthropological tradition is much better and profoundly important because it asserts that they are more fundamentally *social* objects. But there is a need to go further; humans and animals are not only social, they are also *historical* objects.

Chapter Three

CIVILISED ATTITUDES

The hypothesis is that the concept of animal rights is only marginally concerned with animals. More importantly, it is part of a social project to classify and define humanity. Animals are useful for humans to be able to think human. At the risk of lapsing into jargon, animal rights may be understood as a social ontology of social being. Moreover, it can now be seen that the philosophers, such as Peter Singer, Tom Regan, and Stephen Clark, begin to express doubts about the moral relevance of non-mammalian animals because it is only mammals which present a problem, a potential interstice, in attempts to classify the world firmly from a human perspective. It is probably obvious that one implicit assumption has run through the development of the hypothesis: all the writers who pretend to tell, or try to discover, the real truth of animals and humans are writing in bad faith. What society says of animals is part of the problem, not the answer. The supposed real truths display an astonishing tendency to turn out to be little more than social inventions. Has anyone recently seen a mermaid?

Of course, mermaids do not really exist. They were invented by frightened sailors who did not recognise a sea-cow when they saw one. However, those very mariners, and the people who listened to their tales, did believe in mermaids, and they worried about the significance of these half-human, half-animal hybrids. The existence of mermaids was as obvious as the pre-Copernican fact that the sun rotated around the earth. Clearly, any reliance upon naturalistic foundations cannot explain the social interpretation of animals and, more broadly speaking, the external world, and to dismiss accounts of mermaids, dragons or headless humans as mere yarns is to give voice to E.P. Thompson's famous 'enormous condescension of posterity' (Thompson 1980: 12).

But 'the social' or 'society' should not be treated in any reified way. This is where Lévi-Strauss, Douglas, and Edmund Leach must be qualified. They tend to operate in the shadow of Durkheim's position that the taxonomies which interpret and shape the relationship between humans and the natural world essentially constitute a structural unity and the self-understanding of society. Society is seen as a solidary whole in which all individuals practise and accept common beliefs. This internal consistency leads Lévi-Strauss and the others to assume that complex industrial societies are homogeneous and that an unproblematic 'social' can be reified into an overriding and determining reality. Lévi-Strauss feels able to compare industrialised, urban societies to the steam engine (Charbonnier 1969: 33–4). Meanwhile, Edmund Leach is aware that one society can use its classifications of animals as food or not food to condemn those of another society: '*Our* classification is not only correct, it is morally right and a mark of our superiority'. He continues to note that the French habit of eating frogs' legs 'provokes the English to refer to Frenchmen as Frogs with implications of withering contempt' (Leach 1964: 31). The observation is important, but Leach fails to extend it to the relationships amongst the English (or for that matter the French). His residual Durkheimianism causes a failure to see that some groups of Englishmen and women are witheringly called 'animals' by other Englishmen or women. Are football hooligans, for example, properly human like you and me, or are they little more than beasts who need to be caged?

Societies are not homogeneous solids that call into question the humanity only of outsiders; they are also typified by attempts to impose class-specific definitions of the human and properly social on the totality, and associated efforts to condemn the behaviour and views of others as rather beastly. Animal rights may well be one way society entrenches its own taxonomic centrality in contradistinction to the animal (by treating animals as things to be avoided if human-ness is to remain undiluted), but systems of classification, and indeed the ability of some people and not others legitimately to speak on behalf of the properly human and really social, are the product of social processes.

This assertion has been illustrated with great clarity by Keith

Thomas in *Man and the Natural World* (1983). The book is densely packed with historical evidence and has a powerful narrative drive. However, it is perhaps possible to summarise Thomas's underlying theme through use of the metaphor-metonymy framework, although without some of the more complicated knots tied by Lévi-Strauss. Thomas tells of the historical erosion of metonymical classification by metaphorical attitudes towards the natural world in England from 1500 to 1800. He argues that attitudes in the early modern period were unremittingly anthropocentric. It was agreed that humans, or perhaps more specifically men, were the centre and high point of life: 'in early modern England it was conventional to regard the world as made for man and all other species as subordinate to his wishes' (Thomas 1983: 51). Note that Thomas is saying that orthodoxy established the dominion of humans in a world that had already been made. In other words, the early modern period was certainly anthropocentric, but it also held to the belief that humans were part of the same system as animals and plants: the system created by God. The sense that the world was one vast system subordinate to humans was inevitably a largely ideational event, but Thomas suggests that it bolstered and made intelligible the close relations between social life and the natural world. He writes of

> the ancient assumption that man and nature were locked into one interacting world. There were analogies and correspondences between the species, and human fortunes could be sympathetically expressed, influenced and even foretold by plants, birds and animals. Hedgehogs, swallows, owls, cattle and cats, all gave out signs of a future change in the weather. Sailors watched for the stormy petrel, while the housewife used the cricket on the hearth as her barometer.
>
> (Thomas 1983: 75–6)

The metonymical awareness was profound, but Thomas has read too much Lévi-Strauss not to realise that, although early modern attitudes were simultaneously metonymical and anthropocentric, they also had to entrench the otherwise 'fragile boundaries between man and the animal creation' (Thomas 1983: 38). Crickets behaved as surrogate barometers probably because they could be allowed a privileged place on the hearth (they are so different), whereas if the same attributes had been seen in dogs or cats, the mammals would have been endowed with human characteristics and this, added to their ambiguous place in human social life, would have blurred the classificatory boundaries between the properly human and the properly animal.

Thomas is very perceptive on the logic behind the early modern taxonomies. He tells us that social life necessarily had to accommodate animals; after all, they occasionally shared the same house, were an obvious part of the largely agrarian life of the sixteenth century, and provided much of the motive power. There was little difference between the perceptions of the lord and the peasant since both lived relatively close to animals. Animals were everywhere, they were an inevitable part of our ancestors' lives, but a feature which God had made subordinate:

> In early modern England the official concept of the animal
> was a negative one, helping to define, by contrast, what was
> supposedly distinctive and admirable about the human
> species. . . . Animal analogies came particularly readily to the
> lips of those who saw more of animals, wild and domestic,
> than do most people today. The brute creation provided the
> most readily-available point of reference for the continuous
> process of human self-definition. Neither the same as
> humans, nor wholly dissimilar, the animals offered an almost
> inexhaustible fund of symbolic meaning.
>
> (Thomas 1983: 40)

Within this project of establishing animals as a distinctive other, virtually anything could be done to them so long as it did not threaten to undermine the clear and yet fragile boundaries which laid down the truth of human and social life. If anything, early modern attitudes contained a direct incitement to violence; aggressive behaviour towards animals was an active way for humans to define themselves as the centre of the universe and the zenith of God's work. The spatial blurring of classificatory difference was countered by active domination. The early modern period asserted a systemic unity of difference.

Keith Thomas concentrates on the processes behind the changing social and historical objectification of animals. The relationship with the 'not-human' moves from wanton domination to the situation where, he believes, by the beginning of the nineteenth century, animals were understood as, simply, animals, and therefore morally relevant. Thomas is in no doubt that prime importance must be given to industrialisation. 'This industrial order first emerged in England; as a result, it was there that concern for animals was most widely expressed' (Thomas 1983: 181). Concern could be expressed as the considerable dependence on animals' strength diminished; by the nineteenth century, horsepower was a measure of engines and machines, not horses. Animals were needed less, and they were worried about more. However, Thomas is a long way from falling into any economic or technological determinism. Certainly, he asserts the importance of industrialisation in stimulating change in attitudes towards the natural world, but industrialisation crucially involved the urbanisation of social life. The material context of the self-definition of humanity was fundamentally transformed between 1500 and 1800. In particular, the perception of metonymy collapsed; social life, that true domain of the properly human, retreated into the city and shortened its horizons. Instead of being at the very axis of the universe, Englishmen and women saw their urban life as merely one province amongst many others. By the nineteenth century, the universe had become a place of metaphor.

Alan Macfarlane has pointed out that Thomas is telling a rather old story: 'Weber's "disenchantment of the world" has occurred, Marx's alienation of man from the natural world is complete' (Macfarlane 1987: 79). Indeed, Thomas identifies many examples of the narrowing of social horizons and the detachment of humans from a divinely created, immutable natural order. By the nineteenth century, science had evidently proved that 'men were only beasts who had managed to better themselves' (Thomas 1983: 132), whilst astronomy raised the possibility that the earth was of little or no importance in the immensity of the universe. Geology showed that 'the earth and the species on it had not been created for the sake of humanity, but had a life and history independent of man' (Thomas 1983: 167, 168). We were learning that anthropocentrism was a self-flattering deception.

Urbanisation was also important because it led to the rise of the habit of pet-keeping. Thomas believes that pet-keeping is absolutely central in the history of human kindness towards animals. In the early modern period, animals were known to the extent that they told humans something (the stormy petrel warning, unsurprisingly, of storms), but by the eighteenth century pets were kept for their own sake. They tended to constitute a small-scale laboratory for budding behavioural psychologists: 'There is no doubt that it was the observation of household pets which buttressed the claims for animal intelligence and character' (Thomas 1983: 121).

The rise and incidence of pet-keeping seems to be closely associated with a decline in the functional requirement for animals and also with disposable income; after all, it costs money to keep an animal which has no economic value. The habit was firmly established by the sixteenth and seventeenth centuries and by then pets had become a 'normal feature of the middle-class household, especially in towns'. Indeed, all the typical features of modern-day pet-keeping, such as strong emotional bonds and the kinds of animals, can be identified as early as 1700 (Thomas 1983: 110, 117). It is important to note that pet-keeping was most prevalent amongst the urban middle class – that is, precisely the class that had the least strong direct relationship with animals. The bourgeois pet-keepers saw that cats and dogs at least had a reality independently of humans and, therefore, constituted a metaphorical world. At this point, Thomas makes some observations on the history of pet-naming which seem to run counter to those of Lévi-Strauss.

We know that according to Lévi-Strauss, and considerably simplifying his argument, human names are given to metaphorical animals, and nonhuman names to metonymical animals. Consequently, we talk of the bird Jenny Wren and the dog Rover. However, Thomas seems to suggest that the detachment of urban life from the natural world, along with the growth of scientific knowledge, demonstrated to the urban middle classes that the world was nothing more than a composite of a plurality of metaphorical systems. Pets could be safely named in a way that made them extensions of the social. Humans could become closer to their pets exactly because they were so far removed from them:

> The more the animal was doted on by the owner, the more likely was it to bear a human name. . . . [T]here was a recurring tendency, which in the eighteenth century became very pronounced, to give pets human names; and the shift was indicative of a closer bond between pet and human.
>
> (Thomas 1983: 114)

Ironically, the processes of spatial distanciation from animals caused the destruction of the old, ideational, classificatory division of life into the human and the animal. 'It is against this pet keeping background that we should view the growing tendency in the early modern period for scientists and intellectuals to break down the rigid boundaries between animals and man which earlier theorists had tried to raise' (Thomas 1983: 122). To put this into Lévi-Straussian terms, pets were recognised as one small part of the larger metaphorical system of animals, and precisely because animals were observed and known to be so deeply metaphorical to humans, exactly because anthropocentrism was undermined by industrialisation and urbanisation, some animals could be accommodated as an extension, a metonym, of the human world. In the old days, animals were treated differently because they were the same; now they are treated the same because they are different.

In England, it was the intellectuals and the urban middle class who first suggested that animals were morally relevant. Thomas explains the paradox why it was those groups which had the least first-hand knowledge of animals that were the most enthusiastic speakers for compassion and rights. They were the agents and protagonists of a taxonomy which saw humanity as just one small part of a potentially infinite thing. As they sat by the fireside, examining fossils and stroking the dog, they could see that anthropocentrism was a myth; their science laid the foundations for a new, objectively true classification of the universe. Meanwhile, the rural population carried on its old ways; it still had a direct, personal relationship with animals, it retained a stake in the anthropocentric attitudes without which the definitions of human and animals in the rural world would collapse. The stage was set for mutual incomprehension and hostility. Not least, the 'men of science' attacked the vulgar language of the yokels:

> by eroding the old vocabulary, with its rich symbolic
> overtones, the naturalists had completed their onslaught on
> the long established notion that nature was responsive to
> human affairs. . . . In place of a natural world redolent with
> human analogy and symbolic meaning, and sensitive to man's
> behaviour, they constructed a detached natural scene to be
> viewed and studied by the observer from the outside, as if by

peering through a window, in the secure knowledge that the objects of contemplation inhabited a separate realm, offering no omens or signs, without meaning or significance.

(Thomas 1983: 89)

In the seventeenth and eighteenth centuries, battle was joined between a country and work-based anthropocentric classification, and a town and leisure-based system which accepted the purposeless boundlessness of the universe. Perhaps Mary Midgley belongs in a Georgian drawing-room. The systems of classification were antagonistic, yet both represented the human need to establish firmly the ontological basis of humanity and society.

The urban middle class was the enthusiast for compassion and the protagonist of the Romantic view of nature. It was the defender of a humane sensibility, and attempted to ensure that its definitions were accepted as the truth. It formed bodies like the Society for the Prevention of Cruelty to Animals to extend its model of the treatment of animals to people like butchers or coach-drivers who remained anthropocentric (Thomas 1983: 186). It also expressed distaste with 'the warlike traditions of the aristocracy' such as hunting which were based on wanton dominion of nature (Thomas 1983: 183). Thomas concludes that 'In practice, it was almost impossible to reflect on animals without being distracted by the conflicting perceptions imposed by social class' (Thomas 1983: 184). The Durkheimian position that attitudes towards animals reflect the self-definition of a homogeneous society has been exploded. Different social groups define their humanity, and establish what it is to be properly human in different ways; and from their perspective any other classifications seem to blur the human/animal distinction. And so members of the RSPCA and other reforming movements condemned certain treatments of animals as 'beastly', not because they were intrinsically cruel, but simply because they could not be accommodated within the taxonomic ontology of humanity.

In Thomas's analysis, animal rights would become intelligible as the product of, initially, the urban middle class observing animals' existence independently of humans and establishing such metaphorical awareness as the basis of a moral and aesthetic sensibility which repudiated the coercive metonymy of anthropocentrism. Indeed, by the late eighteenth century any sign that animals were treated as metonyms in any way other than the most kindly had to be disguised.

> Killing for food was now an activity about which an increasing number of people felt furtive or uneasy. The concealment of slaughter houses from the public eye had become a necessary device to avoid too blatant a clash between material facts and private sensibilities.
>
> (Thomas 1983: 300)

Some individuals did not even think that concealment went far enough; their interpretation of animals as a separate part of the universe was such that any trace of anthropocentric metonymy was denied. They became vegetarian. Thomas ends his analysis with an open problem: the progress of industrialisation and the consolidation and acceleration of urbanisation were processes which simultaneously subjugated the natural world and yet distanced humans from it; the town dwellers found their new abilities increasingly abhorrent. The dilemma which has plagued us since the nineteenth century has been 'how to reconcile the physical requirements of civilization with the new feelings and values which that same civilization had generated' (Thomas 1983: 301).

Interestingly, Keith Thomas's understanding of the development of a compassionate sensibility towards nature as the product of the detachment of social life from animals, his notion that the world was disenchanted in this way, as humans observed animals from a greater distance, is very similar to a sociological statement of scientificity. Norbert Elias's paper 'Problems of Involvement and Detachment' (1956) contains a definition of scientific knowledge which broadly compares to Thomas's explanation of the rise of a metaphorical perspective on, and kindness towards, animals. Both tend to say that objective, true knowledge is only produced by social subjects who are detached from the object they are trying to understand. In the 1956 essay at least, Elias's prose is leaden, his sentence construction baroque, but the underlying theme seems to be relatively straightforward.

Elias contends that scientific inquiry attempts 'to find the inherent order of events as it is, independently not of any, but of any particular observer' (Elias 1956: 228). If the scientist is to generate knowledge tending towards the truth, she or he must be detached from the object of study. The scientist must control any involvement. Scientificity is rooted in objective observation. However, Elias believes that complete detachment from the object is impossible; the scientist can only attempt to ensure that personal commitment is balanced by scientific objectivity. After all, Elias writes, natural scientists have been taught by bitter experience that too much involvement 'is liable to jeopardize the usefulness which their work may have in themselves or for their own group' (Elias 1956: 229).He associates science with the withdrawal of humans from the objects of study, a thesis which bears direct comparison with Keith Thomas's explanation for the growth of a non-anthropocentric world picture. According to Thomas, the English began to observe and truly understand animals once they had moved into towns and developed a system of classification which detached the social and human from the animal and natural. In other words, Thomas is implying that people were more kind to animals as involvement diminished, as involvement was weakened by detachment. The urban middle class understood animals more adequately, with a more detached observation than the country yokels or landed gentry who were still involved with animals on a daily basis. As Elias might put it, the town dwellers comprehended animals with a greater scientificity.

Did Thomas know Elias's essay when writing *Man and the Natural World*? Certainly, Thomas was aware of other parts of Norbert Elias's work, and believed it important. Elias's most significant contributions to sociology are the two volumes of *The Civilizing Process – The History of Manners* and *State Formation and Civilization* – which were originally published in 1939 but wallowed in the dustbin of history until the 1970s. (An outline of the reception of Elias's work is offered in Goudsblom 1977.) In a lecture on laughter in Tudor and Stuart England, Thomas stated that Elias's 'important' work 'richly deserves an English translation' (Thomas 1977). When a translation of *The History of Manners* was, indeed, published in 1978, Thomas offered a rather cautious welcome, although he did think that historians had a great deal to learn from Elias's concentration on manners (Thomas 1978). It seems reasonably fair to speculate that *Man and the Natural World* is at least in part a historian's response to Elias's lead. Attention must now turn to Elias; his work might add a great deal of sociological weight to Thomas's seemingly plausible interpretation of the changing relationships between society and animals.

Elias's theory is based on the assumption that humans have to learn, and be taught, how to be social individuals, That pedagogic dialogue is itself fashioned by social relationships. For Elias, social relations are highly dynamic; they change over time in the wake of the increasing concentration in the state of the use of violence and, also, the growing complexity of the social interdependencies in which each individual is caught. Elias rejects any tendencies that sociology might entertain towards grand theory (Parsons is explicitly chided: see the 1968 introduction to Elias 1978a), or the Leibnizian monad. He sees a crucial connection between the patterns of individuality and the patterns of social relationships in which individuals live. The dynamism of that nexus is the civilising process. (For Elias's own fine summary of his sociology, see Elias 1982, Part 2.)

Elias illustrates the meaning of the civilising process with the *example* of the moral and intellectual development of a child. Elias is not suggesting that the process of a child's development is a strict analogy to the process of civilisation. The illustration is merely heuristic. He tells us that a child is ruled by natural passion and is only concerned with pleasure, or at least the avoidance of displeasure. The child defecates, sleeps, and tries to eat at will, and protests when those pleasurable activities cannot be carried out. However, as the child grows older, hedonism increasingly conflicts with the demands of other people; the child cannot eat when it wants and, moreover, it must learn that eating only happens at certain times of day. The child has to become more refined, pleasures must be inhibited, and children who remain like babies and swing from laughter to tears simply because they cannot have what they want must learn to 'grow up'. Everything must be moderated and pacified, controlled and restrained. There is a social demand for the *civilisation* of affects. The child must learn to play a socially acceptable role, it must learn that it cannot be violent. The heuristic connection between the learning process of the child and the civilising process in the history of society is, for Elias, quite plain: 'the individual, in his short history, passes once more through some of the processes that his society has traversed in its long history' (Elias 1978a: xiii). This self-restraint and social constraint – I had to learn to restrain myself, and my teachers taught me constraint – constitutes the 'specific direction' of the civilising process. It is the process whereby 'the more animalic human activities are progressively thrust behind the scenes of men's communal social life and invested with feelings of shame' (Elias 1982: 230). Elias suggests that in much the same way a child grows into a sophisticated adult, since the early Middle Ages Western European societies have become ever more complex. He observes a trend from a condition of fractured societies to today's regulated and pacified nation-states.

Is Elias saying that outside of society, humans are just animals? Is he saying that, naturally, we just respond to our basic urges? Is he merely a sophisticated sociobiologist? No, Elias is not. He is certainly very scornful of any Lorenz-Wilson approach to under-standing human action. They seek to reduce all behaviour to a lowest common denominator, identified as either species survival or the evolution of genes. Against this methodology, Elias raises the formal objection that humans and, moreover, humans in society, are far too complex for any reductionist interpretation:

one cannot comprehend the functioning and structure of systems which embody a higher level of organization and control alone in terms of others which are less highly organized even if the former are the descendants of the latter. While men function partly as other animals do, as a whole they function and behave in a way no other animal does.

(Elias 1956: 248)

He also objects that Lorenz is too prone to generalise about human behaviour. Elias agrees that Lorenz is a careful observer of greylag geese or sticklebacks, but points out that Lorenz is remarkably reticent to extend such care to understanding humans (Elias 1978b: 178). Moreover, Elias believes that individuals are always and everywhere implicated in webs of social relationships. Although it is possible to read Elias through Hobbes, and arguably quite legitimate to do so, Elias does not similarly hold to an idea of the pre-social human living in a state of pure nature.

However, anticipation of Elias's much-vaunted 'process sociology' can be found elsewhere, most obviously in Freud's speculations on the history of civilisation, but it is also frequently reminiscent of Durkheim's notion of moral density. The example of children demonstrated Elias's belief that we are all driven to satisfy instinctual pleasures, but those drives are increasingly hemmed in, and subject to restraint, as the social networks in which we participate extend and become more complex. We have to become more civilised as we become more involved in highly complicated social relationships, and we become more involved simply because we become dependent on more people. Individuality is shaped by the social division of labour. The thesis is derived from Elias but it could easily come from Durkheim, who suggested that the division of labour in society increases, 'as there are more individuals sufficiently in contact to be able to act and react upon one another'. The frequency or density of reactions provides the basis for a moral system compelling each individual to play an orderly, ordered role (for Durkheim, see Giddens 1971: 78–9).

The great advantage of Elias's work is that it opens up the history of these profoundly linked 'sociogenetic' and 'psychogenetic' transformations. Elias would tell us that animal rights, and kindness to animals, are a product of humans' social life, of civilisation and human embarrassment at our own animality.

Elias believes that in the medieval period, individuals behaved in what we would call a childlike way in childlike societies (although the behaviour patterns of the time were entirely suited to the medieval social context). In these historical figurations (Elias's concept for the societal 'webs of interdependence' which are also the framework of personality formation – see Elias 1978b: 15), 'emotions are expressed more violently and directly'. A comparison of the medieval period to the present reveals that there were 'fewer psychological nuances and complexities in the general stock of ideas. There are friend and foe, desire and aversion, good and bad people' (Elias 1978a: 63).

During this period, Elias continues (and it is difficult to summarise Elias without making his work sound like a 'Just So' story), violence and war were a common state of affairs. There were many warriors who sought to increase their domination and power at the expense of their neighbours. The use of violence was diverse, warriors faced few social restraints; they lived a life geared towards the satisfaction of pleasure. Peasants were murdered, women were raped, cottages were burnt by local warrior lords who could seek pleasure in any way they wanted. The meaning of life was found, not in metaphysics, but bloodshed. Indeed:

no punitive social power existed. The only threat, the only
danger that could instil fear was that of being overpowered in
battle by a stronger opponent. Leaving aside a small elite,
rapine, pillage, and murder were standard practice in the
warrior society of this time. . . . Outbursts of cruelty did not
exclude one from social life. They were not outlawed. The
pleasure in killing and torturing others was great, and it was
a socially permitted pleasure.

(Elias 1978a: 194)

Might was right. However, this situation, in which there was no
monopoly on the use of violence and personalities were concerned
only with immediate gratification, was transformed as some
warrior lords gained local superiority and others were killed. The
geography of social life, which was originally splintered with many
small fiefdoms, started to centralise as a diminishing number of
lords were able to assert authority over increasingly large areas of
land. The lord became the master of a central court, and the other
lords within his reach had to curry favour to maintain their social
position. Already, with the movement towards state formation,
some individuals were having to think beyond immediate
pleasure, were having to construct a deferred and deferential
personality. They were having to rely on civilisation rather than
aggression to guarantee status.

Moreover, money developed as the new way of gaining things.
Courtiers had to maintain their place at court; otherwise the lord
who now controlled the local use of violence might launch his
army against them. They had to buy goods rather than just take
them from a peasant. The division of functions deepened; there
were buyers, sellers, and manufacturers. However, the greater use
of money led to its devaluation. Elias argues that in the fifteenth
and sixteenth centuries, the process of the monopolisation of force
in the courts rapidly accelerated as the only courts able to maintain
their domination and prestige were those which, through trade or
taxation, could control more money. After all, what was the point
of being a dignitary in a court that was freezing cold in winter, and
only had second-rate wine, when the one 20 miles away could
afford the finest clarets? The old courts with fixed incomes fell
under the sway of the single state which had efficient tax
inspectors and control of the main trade routes. Only one state

61

could maintain itself; the legitimate use of violence was further concentrated and ever larger areas of social life were pacified. The division of functions lengthened again; yet more individuals had to perform services rather than oppress or be oppressed, and the increasing use of money stimulated the growth of a new trading class, the bourgeoisie (Elias 1982: 201–25).

Elias is quite plain that these transformations in the development, the sociogenesis, of nation-states have a profound impact on the personalities of the individuals living in societies where the division of functions is deepening. Elias writes:

> From the earliest period of the history of the occident to the present, social functions have become more and more differentiated under the pressure of competition. The more differentiated they become, the larger grows the number of functions and thus of people on whom the individual constantly depends in all his actions, from the simplest and most commonplace to the more complex and uncommon. As more and more people must attune their conduct to that of others, the web of actions must be organized more and more strictly and accurately if each individual action is to fulfil its social function. The individual is compelled to regulate his conduct in an increasingly differentiated, more even and more stable manner.
>
> (Elias 1982: 232)

The individual must ensure that his or her behaviour is utterly predictable. Otherwise the complex webs of interdependency would be threatened. If the individual cannot control his or her manners, their place in society is threatened. We become embarrassed about our bodily functions, we try to restrain our urges, lest we offend society. We try to be civilised, in accordance with the historical-processual conditions we live in, and deny all else as animal. Elias continues in a rather breathless sentence:

> The closer the web of interdependencies in which the individual is enmeshed with the advancing division of functions, the larger the social spaces over which this network extends and which become integrated into functional or institutional units – the more threatened is the social existence of the individual who gives way to spontaneous

impulses and emotions, the greater is the social advantage of those able to moderate their affects, and the more strongly is each individual constrained from an early age to take account of the effects of his own or other people's actions on a whole series of units in the social chain.

(Elias 1982: 236)

The individual enhances social advantage, and controls spontaneity, by forming a 'wall of deep-rooted fears'.

The social position of warriors depended on strength. Little ashamed or embarrassed them. However, as the division of labour deepens, individuals are ever more tightly involved in webs of interdependency. In Durkheimian terms, the moral density of society thickens, and individuals learn that to guarantee firmly the social position without which life is untenable, they must restrain their emotions and bodily behaviour. Now, the standing and prestige of a specific group in the division of functions is undermined by pressure from the lower classes. Since courtiers had made their own behaviour and manners the yardstick of civilised behaviour, the emergent bourgeoisie modelled their own attitudes and bodily control on courtly codes. This imitative trickle down from above relatively lessened the prestige of the courtiers, whose criteria of civilisation were now little different from those of the 'lower orders'. A compulsion towards an ever greater refinement of manners, a further advance of civilisation, and a further 'pushing behind the scenes' of everything and anything reminiscent of human animality was set in train. The threshold of embarrassment and repugnance advanced (Elias 1978a: 100–1). The process of civilisation is the process of humanity distancing itself from the animal. Humans 'in the course of the civilising process, seek to suppress in themselves every characteristic that they feel to be "animal"' (Elias 1978a: 120).

The Eliasian method would see animal rights as a system which, firstly, denounces violence because aggression is the preserve of the nation-state, and, secondly, voices an embarrassment about the 'animal' dimensions of human life which civilisation tries to suppress. For Elias, kindness to animals would be a historical phenomenon which reflects the social repudiation of beastliness. It is useful to compare this definition with the one stimulated by Lévi-Strauss, Mary Douglas, and Edmund Leach. The anthropologists suggest that the human/animal classification is originally rooted in the perception of the natural world and the taxonomic ordering of that perception. Consequently, the 'animal' is a material a priori in so far as it is the living object perceived as not human, but the precise meaning of the concept 'animal' is something to be decided by social acts and the place of the perceived body in the taxonomic code. The 'animal' is a concept which is only meaningful because it is the structural opposite of the human.

Elias is different. For him, the labels 'human' and 'animal' indeed refer to something immutable – spontaneous behaviour and the control or otherwise of aggression – but the meaning of the labels is subject to a processual transformation. Earlier I used Lévi-Strauss and those working under his influence to generate a rather complex dialectical interpretation of animal rights, but Elias helps us see that the structures which the anthropologists use to understand human/animal classifications might themselves be historical constructs.

But the questions are these: is Elias's historical sociology useful for understanding modern classifications? Is his theory as good as it claims? Elias has engaged in discussions which do provide hints for an interpretation of animal rights through the civilising process, and it would seem that one of the most influential statements of the need for kindness to animals does lend him support. If Elias is right it should be possible to find statements which condemn cruelty to animals on the grounds that such unregulated conduct is illegitimate violence and attacks social interdependency. It should be easy to find reflections of Elias's claim that 'The monopolization of physical violence . . . imposes on people a greater or lesser degree of self-control' (Elias 1982: 239). Indeed it is.

In 1750–51, William Hogarth published *The Four Stages of Cruelty*. The prints told of the progress of the slum child Tom Nero from torturing animals and beating his horse as a coachman, to murdering his mistress and, finally, as a not yet dead victim of the hangman, being handed over to the surgeons for research. The story is a classic statement that humans should be kind to animals. It is encountered again and again in eighteenth- and nineteenth-century moralising (Lansbury 1985: 53, Thomas 1983: 150–1), and was even taken up by Kant as an illustration of his maxim that 'Our duties towards animals . . . are indirect duties towards humanity' (Kant 1930: 239). Hogarth's plates reverberate with the contradiction that whilst they are ostensibly an attack on cruelty, they really involve an impassioned plea for fairness and predictability in social relations. Hogarth presents

> a vision of men as victims and perpetrators of cruelty, distinguishable only as they are dominated or themselves able to dominate others. . . . If animals are victimized by cruel humans, humans are habitually – and not merely ultimately – victimized by barristers and . . . physicians, the professional groups to whom tradition attributes the most callous self-interest.
>
> (Paulson 1975: 61)

The moral tale fits neatly into Norbert Elias's civilising process. Cruelty towards animals engenders anxieties, but the basis of condemnation is not any declaration of the moral relevance of animals; instead it is a fear that the torture of animals indicates a possibility that violent behaviour will erupt in normally pacified social spaces. Animal rights becomes a simple rationalisation of anxiety.

Elias's own work contains two further illustrations which are particularly important if it is hoped to understand statements of the moral relevance of animals from the perspective of the civilising process: meat-eating and cat-burning.

Elias's account of the history of European meat-eating in *The History of Manners* suggests that it is useful to interpret animal rights, or at least the vegetarian strand of it, as an advance of the threshold of shame and repugnance. He points out that in medieval meat-eating entire dead animals, or large parts of them, were taken to upper-class tables where the meat was carved. However, by the seventeenth century the French had ceased to carve at the table. Why? Elias admits that part of the explanation may be the decreasing size of households (fewer people need less meat), but believes that the civilising process is far more important. The civilising process involves people suppressing any behaviour which may be defined as animal: 'They likewise suppress such characteristics in their food' (Elias 1978a: 120).

This direction is quite clear. From a standard of feeling by which the sight and carving of a dead animal at the table are actually pleasurable, or at least not at all unpleasant, the development leads to another standard by which reminders that the meat dish has something to do with the killing of an animal are avoided to the utmost. In many of our meat dishes the animal form is so concealed and changed by the art of its preparation and carving that while eating one is scarcely reminded of its origin.

(Elias 1978a: 120)

The observation is surely valid. In many respects the meat we eat is barely associated with an animal: 'the distasteful is *removed behind the scenes of social life*' (Elias 1978a: 121). Through the hiding away of intervening stages, and the repudiation of the animal and animal-like cuts of meat, it is very difficult to make the connection between a cow in a field and a beefburger. Civilised humans – and remember, we are only civilised because of the fact of the deepening social division of labour and monopolisation of violence – find it repugnant to be reminded of the extreme violence and release of self-restraint by the butcher which lies behind something as commonplace as a meal.

Modern individuals would find many of the meat-centred habits of medieval courtiers quite repellent. We would be reminded of the animalic connotation of meat consumption, and for Elias at least, there is every reason to assume that in the future our habits will be viewed with similar disgust.

There are even *des gens si délicats* . . . to whom the sight of butchers' shops with the bodies of dead animals is distasteful, and others who from more or less rationally disguised feelings of disgust refuse to eat meat altogether. But these are forward thrusts in the threshold of repugnance that go beyond the standard of civilized society in the twentieth century, and are therefore considered 'abnormal'. Nevertheless, it cannot be ignored that it was advances of this kind (if they coincided with the direction of social development in general) that led in the past to changes of standards, and that this particular advance in the threshold of repugnance is proceeding in the same direction that has been followed thus far.

(Elias 1978a: 120)

By this interpretation, George Orwell's mockery of vegetarians merely shows his inability to see beyond 1984. Is one right to think that, behind the qualification, Elias is suggesting that the advance of feelings of shame and repugnance will eventually lead to widespread vegetarianism? Elias interprets vegetarianism as the systematisation of food dislikes and aversions and, possibly, places it in the vanguard of the processual development of manners. (Stephen Mennell, one of Elias's more enthusiastic admirers, understands vegetarianism in much the same way; see Mennell 1985.)

The discussion on meat concentrates on the hiding away of any reminders of the animal, whilst Hogarth's melodrama of Tom Nero is a morality tale for a regulated society where the state has established a monopoly of the use of violence. The case of cat burning brings the two parts together. The example is taken from French history, but it will eventually help us understand Anglo-Saxon attitudes.

Elias's first reference to cat burning is wonderfully dry: 'In Paris during the sixteenth century it was one of the festive pleasures of Midsummer Day to burn alive one or two cats' (Elias 1978a: 203). The cats were pushed into a sack or basket which was hung from a scaffold over a bonfire. As the sacks began to burn they fell into the fire, burning the cats alive. The crowd, which often included the king and queen, could listen to solemn music whilst laughing at the cries of the animals. Elias believes that this habit, this sport, is an especially useful illustration of the civilising process, because 'the joy in torturing living creatures shows itself so nakedly and purposely, without any excuse before reason' (Elias 1978a: 204). His point is that cat-burning was a source of enjoyment in the sixteenth century because social life had not been thoroughly pacified and, moreover, because personality formation involved a less rigid structure of shame and repugnance than it does today. The 'normal conditioning' of sixteenth-century France permitted a far greater satisfaction of immediate pleasures than the standards of normality which presently prevail in societies with deep divisions of functions. For us, cat-burning is cruel and abominable; for them it was hilarious. Indeed, Elias seems unable to avoid expressing his own distaste: 'it shows an institution in which the visual satisfaction of the urge to cruelty, the joy in watching pain inflicted, emerges particularly purely, without any rational justification and disguise as punishment or means of discipline' (Elias 1978a: 203). It is precisely this horror of cat-burning and the inability to understand it which, for Elias, demonstrates the efficacy of the civilising process.

He would argue that cat-burning was identified as distasteful with the advance of the threshold of repugnance, which was itself a reflection of the fact that individuals had to regulate their conduct more and more. For Elias, individuals are products of their society: 'What we take entirely for granted . . . had first to be slowly and laboriously acquired and developed by society as a whole' (Elias 1978a: 69). We take it for granted that cats should not be burnt, but only because we are the products of a process which made that obviousness a necessary foundation of a regulated, predictable, and safe social life. If our societies were not so complex, if moral density were not so compelling, perhaps we too would build scaffolds and push a box of matches into the eager hands of the monarch. Cat-burning is now seen as brutal, indeed as 'animal', but only because since the sixteenth century Western European societies have processually advanced in civilisation, only because we thoroughly repudiate any traces of animality in ourselves. No doubt, Elias would explain the decline of bear-baiting in much the same way. (It is certainly how he understands the historical changes in English fox-hunting; see 'An Essay on Sport and Violence' in Elias and Dunning 1986, but for doubts about the 'Essay' see Tester 1989.)

Elias cannot fully understand cat-burning. Indeed he rejects any excuse that cat-burning might have been rationally justifiable. It is merely an illustration of the fact that in the sixteenth century as compared with the twentieth, Frenchmen and women were able to be more violent, could enjoy more vicious pleasures, all simply because there was no social requirement not to. The meaning of cat-burning is a lack of restraint. That is all.

But is it? So far, Elias has been given an enthusiastic reception. Now doubts need to be raised. Robert Darnton has also looked at the French habit of torturing cats; his interpretation is very different from the one Elias offers and implies grave flaws in the entire project of the civilising process (Darnton 1985). Elias fails to recognise that cat-burning, -skinning, or -hanging might, actually, have been redolent with meaning in pre-modern times; might have had a far deeper social meaning than just the relatively free play of aggression.

Darnton's story concerns an event in a printer's shop in Paris in the late 1730s. The shop was owned by a bourgeois whose wife had a number of pet cats. The cats were allowed to eat at the master's table whilst the apprentice printers ate scraps from the master's plate. For the printers, and the apprentices in particular, this was a violation of the Golden Age of artisan culture when, it was believed, masters and workers ate and lived together in a republic founded on professional pride. However, by the early eighteenth century the realities of the print shop diverged sharply from the myth. The apprentices 'were treated like animals while the animals were promoted over their heads to the position the boys should have occupied, the place at the master's table' (Darnton 1985: 83). The printers decided to retaliate; they massacred the cats.

Now Elias's analysis would be predictable. The printers killed the cats because they were prone to a relatively free play of emotions; not free enough to kill the master and his wife, to be sure, but still so unrestrained as to be able to massacre animals. Meanwhile, the fondness of the bourgeois for cats would be adduced as proof of their civilisation and ability to control their emotions far more than the classes beneath them. Elias would concentrate on the social history of aggression. This is not good enough. Darnton makes the point that the important feature in the cat massacre was not the death of the cats but the entertainment it gave the workers. The printers thought their actions absolutely hilarious. A lack of embarrassment which we now find abominable? No. A set of cultural meanings around cats that we cannot understand because our culture differs from that of pre-industrial Europe? Yes.

Darnton clearly shows that the cat massacre was not an example of a low threshold of repugnance, nor an inability to restrain aggression. Elias would presumably have us believe that cats were killed simply because cats were available, but according to Darnton, the massacre had very deep and complex social meanings. Cats were killed because the killing of cats had profound ritual value. The very fact that we cannot understand why the events were so funny is a clue that 'the violent rituals of artisans belong to a world that seems unthinkable today' (Darnton 1985: 105). Unthinkable: because we do not know the taxonomies that make it thinkable, not just because it is abhorrently violent.

Unthinkable, simply because we do not know how to think it.

Norbert Elias reduces Midsummer cat-burning to an unintelligible act of violence and cruelty. However, Darnton argues that it can be understood if it is placed in the full context of a cultural system in which 'cats bore enormous symbolic weight . . . the folklore was rich, ancient, and widespread' (Darnton 1985: 95). Elias has abstracted his example and reduced it to the lowest intelligible denominator, violence, and therefore totally missed its cultural significance. Eighteenth-century people would have agreed that cats 'are good for staging ceremonies' (Darnton 1985: 91–2) because they saw that cats were taxonomically anomalous, and therefore dangerous. Cats were said to possess the deliberation that was the true preserve of humans, and it was thought that 'Witches transformed themselves into cats in order to cast spells on their victims' (Darnton 1985: 93). Moreover, cats occupied an anomalous place in the house (they were nonhuman extensions of the human family) and were especially associated with female sexuality. We have already seen that the apprentice printers resented the fact that cats were treated like humans. The importance of cats resided in their multiple ambiguity; they were classified as animals but also had special features that transcended that classification. They were interstitial, they were magical. As Darnton says 'the men of the Old Regime could hear a great deal in the wail of a cat' (Darnton 1985: 95). Especially if it was a wail of pain; they heard the reimposition of the order of the world as it should have been rather than actually was. Killing cats was funny because it was also comforting and a direct attack on the harbingers of danger. It reasserted the indivisible humanity of all humans.

The point is that the cries of a cat meant a great deal to *the men of the Old Regime*. What does a miaow mean today? Not very much. And why? Because the taxonomic structures which shape and mould the relationships between animals and society, which define what a cat is, are different. This is what it means to say that animals are a historical object; they are used to understand the meaning and basis of humanity, but the structures which shape that use are themselves historical. They are discontinuous over time.

Obviously, Thomas and Elias would disagree. They want to concentrate on the continuities of a process. This leads Elias to dismiss some past behaviour as beyond rational explanation when, in fact, for the historical participants it was saturated with meaning. Ultimately, Elias wants to understand *their* cat-burning in *our* terms. He makes no attempt to understand it in theirs. Certainly, cat-burning lacks a rational justification, but twentieth-century definitions of rationality are not necessarily the same as eighteenth-century definitions. The emphasis on continuity also bedevils Keith Thomas's work, and leads him to the odd position of arguing that whilst attitudes towards nature and animals changed in England between 1500 and 1800, 'The truth is that one single, coherent and remarkably constant attitude underlay the great bulk of the preaching and pamphleteering against animal cruelty between the fifteenth and nineteenth centuries' (Thomas 1983: 153). It is difficult to know how attitudes can simultaneously remain 'remarkably constant' whilst changing. Of course, Thomas emphasises how the process of urbanisation stimulated a concern with cruelty and kindness, but if it did not stimulate the original ideals, where did they come from, and why? (See also Macfarlane 1987.)

However, perhaps Thomas can be right on both counts. Perhaps some attitudes were constant, but could it be that their position and meaning in the structures of classification changed radically? Perhaps it is the case that animal rights, as a full-blown moral idea and not just idle speculation, is only possible in the context of one specific taxonomic system. Certainly, attitudes might in them-selves demonstrate a continuity, but that might be far less relevant than any discontinuities in the overall structures within which they operate. It is much like saying 'Trees have green leaves'. The comment is correct, but it means different things for different trees at different times of the year. The continuity of the statement hides a more fundamental discontinuity of meaning. As Michel Foucault wrote when he was looking at ideas which evidently remained continuous from one era to another: 'Several themes, principles, or notions may be found in the one and the other alike, true: but for all that, they do not have the same place or the same value within them' (Foucault 1986: 21). It is this version of history, history as the discontinuity of the classifications which make us and our world, that I believe must inform any sociology of animal rights in modern Britain.

Chapter Four

A PIG'S LIFE

The distorted wails of murdered cats echo from the eighteenth century, but the echo is unclear, and we must strain our ears if we want to detect its meaning. The pained miaows are as unthinkable as the squeals of a fourteenth-century pig. In 1386 a court in the Normandy town of Falaise tried a sow which had bitten and torn the face and arms of a human child who subsequently died. The pig was found guilty of the offence. After the trial, which followed the proper procedures for a murder charge, the pig was dressed in human clothes and taken to the town square where it was publicly 'mangled and maimed in the head and forelegs', before being hanged. The sentence was carried out by the public executioner, a grizzly craftsman and no mere butcher, who was given a new pair of gloves. The legal process cost the town a total of 10 sous and 10 deniers. To commemorate the event, a fresco was painted in the local church of the Holy Trinity. However, in 1820 the church was whitewashed and the painting lost (Evans 1906: 140–1). The trial was not unique; animal trials were a frequent occurrence in Europe until the middle and end of the eighteenth century.

In April 1989, two Rottweiler dogs savaged to death an 11-year-old girl in Strathclyde, and then attacked the woman who tried to save her. The next month, a 5-year-old boy was attacked by three Rottweilers in Birmingham; he was dragged from his bicycle and needed twenty-one stitches in the wounds. The response of fourteenth-century French jurists can be guessed; they would have tried the dogs and then publicly executed them. The twentieth-century response was rather different. The dogs were taken away and humanely 'put down' out of anyone's gaze. Meanwhile, attempts were made to prosecute the owners of the

Rottweilers and pressure mounted for the introduction of a national dog licensing scheme. After all 'It's not so much the dogs that should attract opprobrium as their owners' (*Guardian* 1 June, 1989).

For Norbert Elias, the different treatments of the sow and Rottweiler would be clinching proof of the civilising process. He would emphasise the hiding away of the basically retributional act of slaughtering the murderous animal and, indeed, the restraint needed by the human who actually did the killing. Elias would stress the shortening of the time scale of execution; from mangling, maiming, and hanging to a single injection. Elias would explain the transition through the increasing need to restrain emotion and protect the webs of social interdependency. Unfortunately, this misses the point that the punishment of the pig was not a wanton act of aggression. Certainly, violence was involved, but E.P. Evans, the chronicler of animal trials, is right to point out that 'Here we have a strict application of the *lex talionis*, the primitive retributive principle of taking an eye for an eye and a tooth for a tooth' (Evans 1906: 140). The key words are 'strict' and 'primitive'. The trials are *now* seen as primitive because they are unthinkable and, let us be honest, more or less unintelligible, but strict because the violence was not as free as Elias might believe. The Falaise pig-killing comes from the earliest days of the civilising process Elias examines, and yet one of the remarkable features is the exceptional restraint involved. The sow was only maimed in a way which directly mirrored the injuries it had inflicted on the child. Nothing else was permitted – a far more restrained pattern of behaviour than Midsummer cat-burning which remained popular at least two centuries later. Either the French became less restrained or the 'quite clear' direction (Elias 1978a: 120) of the civilising process is simply the result of the forced induction of historical events into a preconceived conceptual frame. Whatever the Eliasian response, the story of the civilising process cannot be accepted without a far greater *critical* development than it has so far received. The clues for understanding animal trials, and how we have moved from hanging to humane killing, are provided in two facts; firstly, the trials and prosecutions ceased in the latter part of the eighteenth century; and secondly, we do not really understand them anyway.

Robert Darnton says that the inability to get a joke should be the starting place for understanding (Darnton 1985: 82). E.P. Evans seems to have thought so as well. His book on animal trials is amongst the oddest pieces that the sociologist of the relationships between animals and society will come across; it is necessary to pinch oneself and remember that this is not a Borgesian gloss on some manuscript delivered by a member of a shady sect. Evans confronts the evidence squarely. He shows that the trials were not a farce. The full panoply of pre-modern legal ritual was used. Indeed, Bartholomew Chassenée, one of the leading jurists in sixteenth-century France, made his reputation as counsel for some rats which were accused by the ecclesiastical court of Autun of 'having feloniously eaten up and wantonly destroyed the barley-crop of that province' (Evans 1906: 18). Chassenée managed to have the charges dropped on the legal technicality that the rats could not safely travel to the court because they would be ambushed and murdered by their arch-enemies, cats (Evans 1906: 19).

Evans cites similar cases from Britain, Germany, France, and Italy, and ends up utterly bewildered. The whole tone of Evans's book is that of a confident, early twentieth-century scholar looking back incredulously at the absurd behaviour of earlier times. He covered his inability to get the joke with a fairly crude cultural positivism (Cohen 1986: 16). But the analysis contradicted the positivism; to be sure, animal trials are absurd and abominable from a twentieth-century perspective, but they were saturated with symbolic and cultural meaning when they were carried out. The fascinating part of Evans's account is the failure of his positivism.

The broad thesis that can be extracted from Evans's work is that animal trials attempted to reassert the immutable order of the world, and the primacy of humanity in the God-ordained scheme. The trials were based on the equation of an eye for an eye and, since God had ordained this rule and applied it to all creation under human dominion, all creatures were subject to it. Rats could be prosecuted for eating barley because they were usurping the place of humanity (only humans grow crops) and, therefore, upsetting God's order of things. For Evans, the trials ceased as the advance of rational knowledge showed theological anthropocentrism to be a myth: 'This crude and brutal conception of justice is the survival of a primitive and barbarous state of society' (Evans

1906: 181). Indeed, the positivist critique of religion knows no bounds; 'The divine government . . . still corresponds to the ideals of right and retribution entertained by savage tribes and the lowest types of mankind' (Evans 1906: 182). Animal trials ceased because they were seen to be a superstitious myth, and we do not understand them because we are rational. We know better. Evans covered his incomprehension with abuse.

So, for Evans the fact that animal trials ceased during the eighteenth century would be entirely accidental. It would just be a result of the growth of science in that period. But there is more to the eighteenth century than science; it was also the era when claims for a moral treatment of animals began to be expressed in something greater than a purely speculative way. In an important statement of animal rights published in the late nineteenth century (which will be discussed later), Henry Salt provided a very valuable bibliography of some of the most important declarations of the moral relevance of animals, from which it would seem that Hogarth's condemnation of cruelty was not unique. In the first edition of his book, Salt mentioned twenty-seven books or pamphlets published in Britain before the late nineteenth century, of which thirteen were issued between 1742 and 1800, the rest being spread through the next century (Salt 1980: 135–66). That is, animal trials fell into wide decay in Europe, and of course Britain was involved in the decline, at precisely the time when people started to worry about whether animals made moral claims.

It is very easy to bring these two tendencies together in a relationship of cause and effect; animal trials stopped, and animals were worried about, because of the rise of humanitarianism. A reassuring idea, but it is little more than an assertion, and not an explanation. Certainly, it can be accepted that claims of animals' moral importance were one part of a widespread and new humanitarian sentiment, which would also include anti-slavery, penal reform, and so forth. But where did the sentiment come from? Put another way: Why humanitarianism? And why humanitarianism *then*? E.P. Evans would no doubt point to rationality, but rationality is morally ambivalent. After all, Auschwitz can be seen as a masterpiece of rationality. Keith Thomas might be more helpful. He would – does – suggest that the new sentiment arose with urbanisation; social life was geographically and ideationally removed from a regular encounter with animals, and was thus able to view them more objectively. Urbanisation destroyed anthropocentric blinkers. A similar story is told by James Turner, who contends that humanitarianism and compassion were 'an antidote to the growing competitiveness and increased individual autonomy of a modernizing world' (Turner 1980: 81). This concentration of material events might explain when, but it does not explain why. The cause and effect coupling is made too easily and there seems to be little more than an assertion that because humanitarianism *did* arise at the time of urbanisation, it *must* have appeared then.

Humanitarianism and compassion are products of human knowledge. They are solely events of the systems of classification which are the foundation of moral relationships, and which attempt to make the world intelligible as it is experienced from the city. The question which must be asked is, then: what was happening in knowledge, in classification, in the eighteenth century? What is the source of the inability to get the joke of hanging a sow? The answers to these questions go far deeper than just a resort to science or reason; after all, they were themselves only made possible because there was a space and role for them in the social ordering of perceived things.

According to the anthropologists, and for that matter Keith Thomas, the world is perceived by a society or humanity which seeks to make the universe intelligible and define the truly human place in it. Consequently, anthropocentrism is the product of perception (which is variously mind- or historically dependent). Unfortunately, the reasoning is circular since it presupposes an anthropocentric subject who is able to perceive the world anthropocentrically. (This is especially a problem for Leach, and is perhaps rooted in the anthropological assumption of the 'unity of humanity'; see Leach 1964 and 1982: chap. 2.) Now, whilst the anthropological project does have considerable value, caution must be taken to avoid the trap of circular reasoning. The knowledge of animals which shapes all social relations with them is not an unmediated reflection of biology, and similarly an effort should be made to move away from a latent foundational anthropocentrism in any discussion of 'humanity.' Just as it is the classificatory ordering of perceived things which defines the animal, the full insight of the thesis should be reversed;

classification also creates the human. It certainly creates the humanitarian human.

Not all things are thinkable. Certainly, the capital punishment of a pig or the grim laughter of cat-killers seems a little odd nowadays. But no doubt Bartholomew Chassenée would be equally bewildered by our humanitarianism which causes us to blame the owner if a Rottweiler savages a child. The reason is quite simple; animal trials are abominable and disgusting, and are dismissed as an example of the unrestrained aggression or superstitiousness of the past, because they threaten

> [A] breaking up of all the ordered surfaces and all the planes with which we are accustomed to tame the wild profusion of existing things, and continuing long afterwards to disturb and threaten with collapse our age-old distinction between the Same and the Other.
>
> (Foucault 1970: xv)

The passage is by Michel Foucault. It tells how he felt after reading a story by Borges which set out a taxonomy of animals including categories such as 'embalmed','fabulous', 'included in the present classification'. Perhaps the list could have included 'those tried in court', or 'causing humour as they died.' Foucault says that he laughed at Borges's list but without really getting the joke because what 'is demonstrated as the exotic charm of another system of thought, is the limitation of our own, the stark impossibility of thinking *that*' (Foucault 1970: xv). Why is it impossible to think some things? How does our thought limit our perception of the world?

We can only think *this* and not *that* because our thoughts and perceptions are not free. They are determined by structural rules which have changed historically. Animal trials are unthinkable, but animal rights is not, because modern systems of classification rest on different rules than those which informed the understanding of the worthies of Falaise.

Michel Foucault's gleeful acceptance of the possibility of the dissolution of 'our age-old distinction between the Same and the Other' has a pictorial counterpart in the work of René Magritte, who wanted to put the real world on trial, by painting a giant apple floating above a mountain range, or a leaf that transforms itself into a bird (Gablik 1985). Foucault and Magritte were aware of the affinities of their work; see Foucault 1983: 57–8). But Foucault's project of prosecuting the 'age-old' is ironic. The book from which the quotation is taken, *The Order of Things*, indeed all Foucault's work, involved an attempt to show that presently obvious distinctions are not timeless at all, rather they are historical. He obviously agrees with Lévi-Strauss that the objects apprehended in perception only take on meaning through a socially confirmed ordering which establishes the taxonomic boundaries of the Same. However, Lévi-Strauss anchors the coherence of order on 'constraints specific to the functioning of the human mind. These constraints determine how symbols are formed, and explain their opposition and how they connect' (Lévi-Strauss 1987: 103–4). A leaf-bird is incongruous because it violates the mind-dependent ordering of external reality. Meanwhile, Mary Douglas and Edmund Leach would probably stress the interstitial position of an animal which is also a plant, and explore how its magical or polluted properties reinforce the self-definition of society.

Foucault's work is important because it shows that the contemporary order of things, the modern understanding, is based on rules of knowledge which are a relatively recent historical phenomenon. The knowledge which structures our understanding, and establishes the basis of moral relationships with externally real objects, such as animals, has not been the same throughout time. The sets of rules (Foucault's *episteme*), which make knowledge, morality, the definitions of the Same and the Other, possible, do not reveal a simple processual advance as Elias or Thomas might like us to believe. On the contrary, the rapid decline of animal trials and the contemporaneous rise of compassion lead any analysis of the relationships between animals and society to acknowledge 'the fact that within the space of a few years a culture sometimes ceases to think as it had been thinking up till then and begins to think other things in a new way' (Foucault 1970: 50).

Animal rights is a feature of such a 'new way of thinking'. The stimulus for a moral investment of the social treatment of animals comes from the appearance of a historically new set of foundations for the ordered understanding of animals, and not from any more objective knowledge of them at all. We blame the owners of Rottweilers rather than the dogs themselves, and we do not execute sows, because our understanding and classification of animals is different, not because it is better.

Despite the impression we may have of an almost
uninterrupted development of the European *ratio* from the
Renaissance to our own day . . . the system of positivities was
transformed in a wholesale fashion at the end of the
eighteenth and beginning of the nineteenth century. Not that
reason made any progress: it was simply that the mode of
being of things, and of the order that divided them up before
presenting them to the understanding, was profoundly
altered.

(Foucault 1970: xxii)

Note the date. Foucault identifies changes in the structure of
knowledge at the end of the eighteenth century, and we already
know from Keith Thomas and E.P. Evans that this period also
experienced fundamental transformations in the social treatment
of animals. Both Thomas and Evans tell the story of the disenchantment of the world; Thomas emphasises the decline of the
anthropocentrism which sought God's justification whilst Evans
more simply identifies the overthrow of superstition. But these are
little more than surface occurrences. If Foucault's lead is followed,
if we dig deep into knowledge and try to discover its *archaeological*
foundations, it will be possible to see that worries about the moral
claims of animals were unlikely before the late eighteenth century.

In *The Order of Things*, Foucault identifies three coherent
epistemological orders in the history of Western thought: the
Renaissance, the Classical, and the Modern (which he calls the Age
of Man). However, the book contains a never-quite-stated sense
that Foucault is trying to usher the Death of Man and herald a new
era in the ordering of the wild profusion of objects. What was the
status of animals in these different eras of knowledge?

For the Renaissance, the period that extended to the late
seventeenth century, the universe was something without depth. It
was a vast reservoir of resemblances. The words which designated
things also bore the imprint of those things, and to say the word
was, in some way, to conjure the essence of the object.
Consequently, the social knowledge of an animal had no
privileged status; indeed neither did the animal itself. All
knowledge was directly comparable to a quality which the animal
really possessed. During the Renaissance:

When one is faced with the task of writing an animal's *history*,

79

it is useless and impossible to choose between the profession of naturalist and that of compiler: one has to collect together into one and the same form of knowledge all that has been *seen* and *heard*, all that has been *recounted*, either by nature or men, by the language of the world, by tradition, or by the poets.

(Foucault 1970: 40)

Now, in this system, full knowledge is only possible to the extent that everything it is possible to say about an animal has been collected. The saying had as much validity as the seeing since words were indivisible from the thing they signified; and so mermaids could be as real as mice, and the Borgesian taxonomy which made Foucault laugh might have been possible.

This picture of knowledge has been encountered before. It is broadly the world of symbolic meaning which Keith Thomas says was undermined by urbanisation and objective observation (Thomas 1983: 89). Foucault is right to point out that the Renaissance scheme, where the bestiary which contains all fact and fable is the site of truth about a creature, is essentially a self-enclosed system which doubles back on itself in endless, unchanging repetition. The ordering and understanding of objects attempted 'to discover . . . the primitive text of a discourse sustained, and retained, forever' (Foucault 1970: 62). However, Foucault fails to draw out the theological dimension which Thomas believes was so important. Certainly, Renaissance thought tried to establish the eternal knowledge of animals, but in the very act of collecting all the necessary evidence, in writing all the words, the Renaissance was also emphasising the centrality of humans in a system which must have been divinely created. (How else could words be known to have a magical connection with things?) Foucault's Renaissance *episteme* is much the same as Thomas's anthropocentrism. Simply by knowing animals, the distinctive uniqueness of humans was confirmed; animals could not know all *this*. Only humans could try to know the truth.

However, where Keith Thomas rather simply juxtaposes anthropocentrism with non-anthropocentrism, Foucault sees a Classical *episteme* during the eighteenth century. What Thomas understands to be just decline and replacement is shown by Foucault to be a coherent, analytically separable, period in its own right. However, Thomas should not be simply subordinated to

Foucault. One of the serious difficulties with *The Order of Things* is how it tries to avoid any confrontation with the question of why one structure of knowledge was replaced with another. Foucault tends to refer vaguely to 'an erosion from outside' (Foucault 1970: 50), but never quite spells out what this means. Thomas does; he is right to stress the radical importance of urbanisation in changing social perceptions of the natural world. Yet Thomas assumes that urbanisation necessarily led to the rise of compassion; he does not explain why it did. With his concentration on the structures of knowledge, which attempt to order the perception and understanding of urban life as much as natural objects, Foucault can, although the process of urbanisation is more important than Foucault wants to admit. It constituted a new set of circumstances that had to be made intelligible.

The Classical *episteme* can be understood as an ultimately unsuccessful attempt to order a simultaneously urban and rural social life. Animals had no independent being during the Renaissance; to say their names was to say them. Animals resembled themselves, and only humans could know this because God had given them a special place in the world. However, Classical taxonomy tried to accommodate a double perception of animals as objects which were simultaneously seen to be separate from the properly human (which was increasingly equated with urban life), whilst retaining a wealth of symbolic meaning in the countryside. In other words, animals were at one and the same time the Same and yet the Other. This difficulty was reconciled through a system which attempted to establish firmly the basis of being human by stressing the different *within* the same. Animals might well be similar to humans, but they remained radically different. This complex interpretation was confirmed by the establishment of the table:

> To the Renaissance, the strangeness of animals was a
> spectacle: it was featured in fairs, in tournaments, in fictitious
> or real contests, in reconstructions of legends in which the
> bestiary displayed its ageless fables. The natural history room
> and the garden, as created in the classical period, replace the
> circular procession of the 'show' with the arrangement of
> things in a 'table.' What came surreptitiously into being
> between the age of the theatre and that of the catalogue was

81

not the desire for knowledge, but a new way of connecting things both to the eye and to discourse. A new way of making history.

(Foucault 1970: 131)

The eighteenth-century enterprise of compiling vast catalogues which could establish the connection between objects again reinforced the centrality of humanity since only humans could draw up the necessary taxonomic tables, because only humans could use language. Although the Classical age still believed that words were linked to things, it saw the link in terms of representation rather than the resemblance of the Renaissance (Foucault 1970: 132). The natural history of the eighteenth century was only necessary to the extent that words and things were no longer indivisible, to the extent that the word 'dog' no longer necessarily resembled a four-legged creature. Words merely represented; and so the individuals who could catalogue and control words became the only ones who could properly know. The old believers in symbolic metonymy became little more than superstitious fools. There is undoubtedly a connection between this new knowledge and the conflict between urban and rural interpretations of animals.

The point is, however, that by equating humanity with language and the control of words, Classical classification put all natural objects on the same level, as things which had to be known. Any one creature was simply one instance, one Other, within a far greater similitude of things. The tables and catalogues were the privileged sites of order which forced all creatures into its grids. The mythology was stripped away from animals and instead they became physical bodies. Knowledge was rooted in observation, and now, with the emphasis on grids and linear progressions, the tables and catalogues necessarily assumed some starting place which was the point of departure for any ordering of things. That place was filled by the human body, which was thus pushed aside; there was nothing that the human body could be catalogued against. It was the indivisible Same.

Classical knowledge conceived of the world as an already existing order which was represented and made intelligible by the careful observations of the natural historians. The project involved 'undertaking a meticulous examination of things themselves for the first time, and then of transcribing what it has gathered in smooth, neutralised, and faithful words' (Foucault 1970: 131). The demand to order the empirical is most clearly reflected in Linnaeus's attempt to impose orderly names on things which reflected their vegetable or animal structure. In this project, the assumption of the human body as in some way irreducible and always the same was absolutely vital. According to Foucault, in the Classical system of classification:

> it becomes possible to describe certain fairly complex forms on the basis of their very visible resemblance to the human body, which serves as a reservoir for models of visibility, and acts as a spontaneous link between what we can see and what we can say.
>
> (Foucault 1970: 135)

The physical differences between humans and animals were condensed into degrees of similitude to the human body. The catalogue was a tale of metaphor within metonymy. Although Foucault seems loath to do so, it is important to note that such a perception of visible bodies was only fully voiced by the more educated, town-dwelling members of society. Keith Thomas has shown that the towns and cities were the home of science. No doubt Linnaeus and his fellow cataloguers mocked the 'yokels' who continued to believe that animals possessed symbolic meanings.

The Parisian cat-murderers were operating within the Classical system of classification. A cat massacre was a doubly viable protest against the actions of humans. The cats were the possessions of the print shop owner and his wife, and were also understood through the tables of knowledge to be relatively similar to humans. The printers were exploiting the linearity of Classical knowledge and telling the bourgeois that they were the real victims of murder. The cats were different enough to be morally and legally irrelevant, but similar enough to make a violent point very clearly. The laughter of the printers was certainly a reflection of their delight and relief in reimposing clear barriers between the human and the animal, but they laughed because they were also quite literally getting away with murder. We no longer laugh because we no longer compile catalogues of similitude. Moreover, as the massacre shows, the moral position of animals within the Classical system was ambivalent at best. Certainly, Thomas mentions a number of writers in the eighteenth century who believed that animals were worthy of compassion, or who made a case for vegetarianism, but it is reasonable to suggest that their views were little more than speculation and fairly unimportant before the final years of the century.

Classical classification contained the seeds of its own destruction. Quite simply, the search for the Different within the Same fell into the trap of putting a question mark against the efficacy of any criteria of visible similitude. The human body was seen as a yardstick of measurement, the site of the Same *par excellence*. But in purely empirical terms, a plant or a parrot is so different that any sameness is rather minimal. The flat table was seen to have a cracked underside, much as when a piece of wax is pressed against a coin; one side is flat and the same, but the reverse is marked and uneven. Classical knowledge contained a possibility that 'the teeming profusion of similitudes, the clearly defined order among the empirical multiplicities' would escape all structural coherence and fall into unintelligibility (Foucault 1970: 237). The concern to order the empirical world was turned on its head. In the modern *episteme*, which developed in the late eighteenth and early nineteenth centuries: 'The visible order, with its permanent grid of distinctions, is now a superficial glitter above an abyss' (Foucault 1970: 251). That abyss is, in the most powerful sense, unthinkable.

The modern *episteme* avoids the Classical difficulty of undermining the central category of the Same by denying the importance of the visible world. Instead, the modern system creates an order of things by concentrating upon the Same behind the Different. Now, Linnaeus would have noted that human beings need to breathe to live, and his method of the linear table would have told him that, similarly, all the other objects of the natural historian's concern should have their own form of breathing. He would create an ordering of animals and plants in so far as they differed from the human. Modern classification follows a contrary path. Although it acknowledges difference, it manages to avoid the threat of disorder by reinventing the standard of similitude.

It matters little, after all, that gills and lungs may have a few variables of form, magnitude, or number in common: they resemble one another because they are two varieties of that non-existent, abstract, unreal, unassignable organ, absent from all describable species, yet present in the animal kingdom in its entirety, which serves for *respiration in general* . . . What to Classical eyes were merely differences juxtaposed with identities must now be ordered and conceived on the basis of a functional homogeneity which is their hidden foundation.

(Foucault 1970: 264–265)

The modern *episteme* pays heed to the nature of living creatures, but their bodies are far less important than the similarities of their organic structure. Fishes and humans are comparable despite their incongruities because they similarly embody 'respiration in general'. There are obvious links with the assumptions of the philosophers of animal rights. Peter Singer, Tom Regan, and Stephen Clark accept that animals are visibly different from humans, but they demand a recognition of the 'fact' that animals and humans share a sensual organic structure. Indeed, this is the heart of Singer's assault on speciesism, and the basis of Tom Regan's rights theory. The moral question operates at a remove from superficiality and attempts to develop an order founded upon abstract categories of social knowledge and perception. The fascinating dimension of animal rights is how the commitment to organic structure, which could potentially include even plants, is tempered by the visibility of species which is otherwise denigrated. They want to deny the importance of the visible, but are only really concerned with the animals which are most like us.

Obviously, Singer, Regan, and Clark would admit to this restriction and see it as evidence that humans do, indeed, act morally when we perceive similitude. We know that the organic structure of mammalian animals is comparable to the structure of humans and so we modify our behaviour. As Foucault suggests, 'Animal species differ at their peripheries, and resemble each other at their centres; they are connected by the inaccessible, and separated by the apparent' (Foucault 1970: 267). For Foucault, the sentence sums up how modern classification understands animals and humans; it is also the understanding used in animal rights. The moralists are not prepared to accept that this ordering of things is attributable only to changes in the deep structures which shape morality. Despite the beliefs of the protagonists, animal rights is not a knowledge of the irreducible being of animals at all.

Now, the point to note about modern classification and its denigration of the visible world is how it pushes the keys for understanding into a realm of quasi-transcendental categories. No animal suffers 'in general', a concept which is only intelligible in the context of the knowledge which created it. The modern *episteme* restates the Renaissance and Classical assertion of the centrality of humanity. Of course, the concentration on humans should not cause any great surprise in view of the theses of the anthropological literature. But the anthropological category of a unified 'humanity' is beginning to crack. If the main principles which order the world are not open to ready apprehension, they can only be known by individuals who do or can participate in the discourses of knowing. Foucault's own analysis tends to preclude or ignore a recognition that modern systems of classification contain different social spaces, but by the nineteenth century the proper human was she or he who was aware of the transcendental categories of order in contradistinction to those who only knew what they saw or did.

The modern *episteme* makes a practical fracturing of 'humanity' possible (a fracture anticipated in the story of the Parisian cat-killers). Indeed, it also contained the possibility that the visible world would be denied to such an extent that any unity would become secondary to abstract categories of things 'in general'. The threat of classificatory anarchy was overcome, and indeed all things in general and all the degrees of being human were reconciled by a turn to an even greater abstraction. The modern period is the era of *life*:

> The classification of living beings is no longer to be found in the great expanse of order; the possibility of classification now arises from the depths of life, from those elements most hidden from view. Before, the living being was a locality of natural classification; now, the fact of being classifiable is a property of the living being.
>
> (Foucault 1970: 268)

The notion that life is the basis of classification which is represented in quasi-transcendental abstractions from organic structure falls into a serious taxonomic trap. In the Classical period, Sameness was the point of departure of a search for Difference; to be sure, animals might have been placed on a table which stressed humanity, but they were visibly distinguishable. The modern *episteme* elides the distinction. Humans and animals become mere physical forms of an abstract something behind them, an abstraction which is the keystone of knowledge: Life. The difficulty for ordered classification is that humans and animals are similarly living organic beings. Humans become objects to be classified like any other beasts.

Fortunately, the abyss of the indistinct is avoided by the very act of making humans an object of study. Who were the subjects who made humans an object like other animals? Other humans. Humans are given a special position as the living object which is also the subject that knows life. The anthropological-discursive figure of 'Man' is at one and the same time a part of the system of animals, and apart from it.

> Man's mode of being as constituted in modern thought
> enables him to play two roles. he is at the same time at the
> foundation of all positivities and present, in a way that cannot
> even be termed privileged, in the element of empirical beings.
> (Foucault 1970: 344)

Humans are the animals who know they are different. Georges Bataille was aware of the problems opened up by the dual status of the human. Bataille writes with more than a little irony:

> Man's equivocal attitude toward the wild animal is more than
> usually absurd. Human dignity does exist (it is, apparently,
> above all suspicion), but not on one's visits to the zoo – as
> when, for instance, the animals watch the approaching
> crowds of children tailed by papa-men and mama-women.
> Man, despite appearances, must know that when he talks of
> human dignity in the presence of animals, he lies like a dog.
> (Bataille 1986: 23)

The position of animals as representations of Otherness which help firmly classify the Sameness of human beings is in this sense historical. The deployment of animals as species which are different but organic living beings which are the same goes to the heart of modern taxonomy. The ambiguous status of 'Man' is the historical basis for the moral principle of animal rights. It is certainly the classificatory principle implicit to the theories of Singer, Regan, and Clark. The distinction between humans and animals is simultaneously clear and blurred; animal rights is one way in which the ambiguity can be confronted and reconciled. The animal has a mundane social meaning as the visibly different body of a similarly living organism, and that daily meaning is shaped by a complex historical context.

The ambiguity of 'Man' provides a full explanation for the rise of compassion in the late eighteenth century. People started to worry about the social treatment of animals to the extent that life was identified as the basis of knowledge and made the main principle for the order of things. Classification demanded behaviour which would respect the similitude of all living organic structures regardless of any visible distinctions, whilst also maintaining the privileged status of humanity as the only historical subject able to know life. We should act differently precisely because we can; animals can be the same only in so far as we can be different humans. Now, although this situation lies at the heart of contemporary moral practices, it would be naïve to think that the moral ideas simply grew from modern knowledge like fruit from a tree, and just waited to be plucked by Singer and the others. Animal rights might well be coherent, or at least a useful umbrella term, in the late twentieth century, but that unity has not always existed. Unity had to be created and it only gelled in the late nineteenth century. It drew on roots which reflected the curious status of 'Man' as the subject who is an object.

Historically it is possible to identify two demands for a moral treatment of animals which play on the paradox of the human as a different kind of animal. (Of course, these are my own analytical categories. They cannot be found in the past *per se*.) They can usefully be called the Demand for Difference, and the Demand for Similitude. The Demand for Difference was the first to appear by the space of a few years and, as the label implies, it was an attempt to enhance the privilege of being human through a project of the social extirpation of animality. During the eighteenth and nineteenth centuries, the term 'animal' became a pejorative label which could be applied to humans who seemed to be little more than objects ruled by their natural passions and urges. The Demand for Difference played on an attempt to make humans more subjective and responsive to things which *only humans could know*, primarily the abstract principle of life. Animals were useful because they were a stick with which to beat social unruliness and 'beastliness'. Without the ordering of social life, humans would be mere beasts. The Demand involved attempts to create orderly and regulated social relationships through discipline and policing. This involved animal welfare laws and the formation of surveillance organisations such as the RSPCA. The Demand for Difference attempted to make humans subjects, by controlling the objectivity of animality.

The Demand for Similitude followed a radically alternative path. It emphasised the extent to which all organic beings, regardless of 'the more obvious signs displayed on the surface of bodies' (Foucault 1970: 229), were all linked as living things, and therefore of a comparable classificatory status. The Demand for Difference stressed the uniquely human and the properly social. The Demand for Similitude was associated with the idea that humans should live in accordance with the dictates of natural, organic being. It condemned society and attempted to show how the repudiation of the organic had caused a decay of life.

Both Demands were concerned to applaud life, and both accepted it as the key concept around which the classification and understanding of the world should revolve. But their definitions, and the practices they implied, restated the epistemological ambiguity of human being. Is the human a privileged subject who is separated from nature, or is the human an object who should glory in organic life? Was the basis of classification to be visible difference or invisible congruity? The present-day disputes between the protagonists of animal rights and vivisectionists and meat-eaters show that it is still impossible to give a universally true answer to these questions, but this has not stopped everyone trying. The disputes will probably continue until either we can be certain about the final basis of what it is to be human, or until the day when 'Man' is finally buried.

All of this is to delve deeply into historical processes. At least in *The Order of Things*, Foucault was happy to paint with broad brush-strokes. The important thing was the outline, and he tended to assume simply that classificatory systems applied equally throughout the social. He rather assumed a solid society which would not discredit a Durkheim. However, certainly for the purposes of an investigation of animal rights, such an assumption should not be made. Different people relate to animals in different ways, and indeed the historical Demands for Difference and Similitude were voiced by antagonistic social groups. The humans who were the subjects of classification were not the same people as the humans who were the objects. Not least, the Demand for Difference was associated with attempts by 'administrators, teachers and "social scientists"' to impose *their own* criteria of what it was to be human on those whom *they* saw as still disordered and prone to animal passion (Bauman 1987: 67). It invariably involved the urban bourgeoisie (that is, the historical human subjects) trying to impose discipline on the urban working class (namely, human objects). Hogarth's story of Tom Nero gives a fine illustration. Earlier, I mentioned that Tom Nero was a slum-dwelling threat to social order. Hogarth's young animal torturer was wearing the arm-band of the foundling school. Nero was identified with the urban working class, which was thus portrayed as a group which should be forced to accept regulation and made to control its animality. Indeed, the late eighteenth-century attack on cruelty to animals was a highly complex event. Zygmunt Bauman has drawn attention to a curious fact:

> The concentric assault on 'bloodsports' such as bull-baiting and cock-fighting has been widely documented by the enthusiastic recorders of moral progress; what they failed to note, however, was the fact that the most prominent among the attackers were the very classes who made sport synonymous with hunting and collective, ritual killing of animals.
>
> (Bauman 1987: 64)

The identification of a historical Demand for Difference can explain why many of the great moralists of Georgian England found bull-baiting repugnant and fox-hunting edifying, and indeed, how many of today's supporters of animal welfare laws eat meat without feeling any sense of a contradiction. Meanwhile, the Demand for Similitude was developed by people who believed that attempts to confirm human difference could only lead to a denial of the essential life-respecting goodness of humanity. It was a radical critique of the urban society which had been established by the early nineteenth century, and wanted individual practices of Similarity rather than a social imposition of Difference. The two Demands developed independently, and when they did coincide they were at best disinterested with the visions of each other, if not openly hostile.

The discontinuities in the history of Western thought are the background to the specific struggles of social groups and the attempts to found morality on either the uniquely human or the abstractly natural. The struggles operated on the site of the unstable status of 'Man' and in their different ways attempted to establish a proper classification of the distinctions between the human and the animal. They are the precursors of today's statements of animal rights.

An exploration of the conditions and practices which make some things thinkable can certainly explain the decline of animal trials. Certainly, the trials ceased when compassion developed, but the two tendencies are not associated in anything other than the most trivial sense. Animal trials were possible until the end of the Classical period. Linnaeus and the others wanted to compile a vast catalogue which would finally classify the unchanging things of nature. The tables imposed social and human definitions throughout the natural world and, specifically, brought animals within the domain of the law. An animal was legally relevant if it violated taxonomy and performed an act which was properly reserved for humans. After all, the Classical era saw all things as ultimately congruous. Earlier, animal trials were a feature of the Renaissance because it was thought that the places taken up by humans and animals should resemble the ordinations of God's word; an animal could be punished if it did something which God had forbidden. (For both the Renaissance and Classical understanding, it is useful to remember Mary Douglas's account of purity and danger; see Douglas 1966.)

The Renaissance and Classical periods concentrated on the visibility of the animal body performing an incongruous (dirty, disordered) act. The systems of classification reasserted their order through the inscription of their categories on the animals' bodies. However, modern taxonomy subsumes all organic beings within the more fundamental category of life, and identifies similitude in terms of abstract concepts. One of these would be the ability to suffer. The Falaise pig-executioners inflicted pain on the pig; the squeals of the animal were an audible representation of the reimposition of order on the world. But within a system that stresses life, pain takes on a new meaning. It becomes a signification of organic death and is, thereby, turned into something to be feared (for more on the fear of pain see Turner 1980). A knowledge founded on life cannot deliberately inflict pain or death, and modern classification also says that animals are objects, they cannot be legal subjects. Modern law is based on the assumption of subjectivity and responsibility, and only humans who demonstrate subjective will and intentionality are accepted as responsible (hence the plea of insanity, see Foucault 1977, 1978.) Animals were ejected from the courts by two burly warders. One told them that they were not guilty because they were not responsible for their own actions, whilst the second wore soft gloves lest the animals' organic life be harmed.

The death of animal trials says something more. Keith Thomas argued that compassion developed, and attitudes towards nature changed, to the extent that town-dwellers saw that the anthropocentric understanding of things was inadequate. He emphasises the decline and restriction of social knowledge over animals. But the story should be of its *extension*. Animals have been a point for the deduction of human being since the eighteenth century simply because they live. The point is, however, that life, the category which links all beings regardless of visible differences, can only possibly be known by the subjects of knowledge. And only humans can be subjects. Classification may well centre on the invisible being of life, but the knowledge of life is uniquely human. Thomas is wrong to say that our eighteenth-century ancestors learned a new modesty.

Harriet Ritvo would agree that Thomas is mistaken. She also believes that a new power was gained over animals in the final years of the eighteenth century. Indeed, she suggests that since that period, the British have been able to turn animals into a submissive and unthreatening metaphorical society which mirrors idealised images of intra-social exploitation and domination (Ritvo 1987: 3). Ritvo identifies the privilege which *all* humans exercised over *all* animals. The point is significant. Animals were indeed subordinated to the social, they were made a metaphor, but such a thesis does not acknowledge that animals simultaneously remained metonymical, nor that some people were classified beneath the hounds or horses of the rich and the knowledgeable. Animals continued to be potentially consubstantial with us, and it is exactly the privileged knowledge of that potential which is worked out in the deliberations over the proper and moral treatment of animals.

The Demand for Difference and the Demand for Similitude were two early attempts to come to terms with the new, difficult importance which humans perceived that they had in the late eighteenth century. The Demands were entirely products of transformations in the social apprehension of animals and the place of humanity in the world. Humanitarianism is about being human, not being kind. The proud moral certainties and obviousnesses which presently guide the relationships between animals and society, and which pretend to say so much that is true, are nothing more than social-historical constructs. And the story of their invention can be told. It is possible to tell why the joke of murdering cats is not funny any more, or why the Falaise pig execution was whitewashed from history, like the fresco.

Chapter Five

A DIFFERENT KIND OF BEAST

Shortly before their ship completed the journey from Surinam to Bordeaux, Candide and the old scholar Martin could be found trying to reconcile their knowledge of the world with the teachings of Dr Pangloss:

> 'Do you think', said Candide, 'that men have always massacred each other, as they do to-day, that they have always been false, cozening, faithless, ungrateful, thieving, weak, inconstant, mean-spirited, envious, greedy, drunken, miserly, ambitious, bloody, slanderous, debauched, fanatic, hypocritical, and stupid?'
> 'Do you think', said Martin, 'that hawks have always eaten pigeons when they could find them?'
> 'Of course I do', said Candide.
> 'Well', said Martin, 'if hawks have always had the same character, why should you suppose that men have changed theirs?'
> 'Oh, but there's a great difference', said Candide; 'for Free Will . . .'
>
> (Voltaire 1947: 96)

But what about Free Will? Is it the foundation stone which makes humans a different kind of animal? According to Hobbes, it just lets people massacre each other and be precisely those things which Martin said were as natural and pleasant as a hawk eating a pigeon. By the late eighteenth century, a life without social regulation was a very dangerous thing, as Tom Nero had found out. Individuals have to practise their humanity, and become social; and if they do not do it from choice, if they persist in acting

94

like unthinking hawks, they have to be made to be different.

The necessity was rooted in the modern taxonomic systems which developed towards the end of the eighteenth century, and made humans simultaneously subjects and objects of knowledge. Candide was right to identify a fundamental distinction between humans and hawks, just as Martin could validly argue that there was no distinction at all. They could both be right because it was possible that they were talking about different humans; Candide of the educated Pangloss and the bountiful Lady Cunegonde, Martin of the miserable pickpockets he had met once at Saint Germain's Fair. Modern taxonomy implicitly assumes that some people are sufficiently separate from hawks that their knowledge and behaviour establish the criteria of what it is to be properly human. And those standards could be ruthlessly imposed on other humans who were not seen to be sufficiently civilised and, therefore, indistinguishable from animals. The wealthy, town-dwelling bourgeoisie denounced the beastly unruliness of the animal lower orders. After all, Tom Nero's story was a warning that, without social discipline and order, 'We are like that. The allegiances that make the human world human must be beaten into our heads' (Ignatieff 1984: 50).

This is the nub of the Demand for Difference, one of the eighteenth- and nineteenth-century responses to the ambiguous classificatory position of 'Man' as the privileged, free representative of a common and compelling life. The Demand for Difference attempted to overcome the confusions which the ambivalence might have created by involving a thorough repudiation of the place of 'animality' in the province of what was truly human and properly social. Unsurprisingly, it could only be fully voiced by those social groups for whom animals were themselves utterly objective and, therefore, an invariant demonstration of all that humans should not be. The Demand for Difference was an exclusively urban concern and supported by the knowledgeable arbiters of taste and virtue. Of course, the 'animal' which they wanted to seek out was not actually some trace of a common mammalian ancestry which could creep out if people were not on due guard, or indeed duly guarded. It was simply that which the creators of morality did not themselves do. The 'animal' is the label applied by the bourgeoisie to a social other as part of a crusade to make them the same, or at least to transform them from evidently objective, wild brutality to docile acquiescence. The Demand tried to make everyone respect an abstract category of life which could only be known by certain social groups, by those who 'knew best'.

Ironically, one of the most important statements of the Demand for Difference seems to suggest that the key consideration is the degree of congruence between humans and animals. In 1789, Jeremy Bentham published his thoughts on the need for a utilitarian moral and legal code. He noted that the ability of non-human species to experience happiness, and their interest to avoid pain, had 'been neglected by the insensibility of the ancient jurists', to such an extent that they were merely treated as things (Bentham 1960: 411). He speculated that

> The day *may* come, when the rest of the animal creation may acquire those rights which never could have been withholden from them but by the hand of tyranny. The French have already discovered that the blackness of the skin is no reason why a human being should be abandoned without redress to the caprice of a tormentor. It may come one day to be recognised, that the number of the legs, the viliosity of the skin, or the termination of the *os sacrum*, are reasons equally insufficient for abandoning a sensitive being to the same fate. What else is it that should trace the inseparable line? Is it the faculty of reason, or, perhaps, the faculty of discourse? But a full-grown horse or dog is beyond comparison a more rational, as well as a more conversable animal than any infant of a day, or a week, or even a month, old. But suppose the case were otherwise, what would it avail? the question is not, Can they *reason*? nor, Can they *talk*? but, Can they *suffer*?
> (Bentham 1960: 412)

Bentham is straddling the double figure of 'Man'. He is saying that as organic structures, regardless of the appearances of species, humans and animals can be classified together on the basis of the general ability to suffer. Bentham is proposing that classificatory similitude extend into moral equivalence. This dimension of the passage is fastened onto by the heralds of moral progress; it has been suggested on the strength of the quotation that 'Bentham was the first moralist to insist on the rights of animals' (Baumgardt 1952: 308). Peter Singer also welcomed Bentham's statement, and his work on animal liberation often reads as little more than an exegesis on these few sentences which were only a part of a footnote to the main argument.

However, it is right to point to the originality and importance of Bentham's questions, but the passage is rather more subtle than 'moral progress' approaches admit. Certainly, Bentham is shouting out that if animals can suffer they are taxonomically and therefore morally comparable to humans, but between the shouts he is whispering something very different. Quite simply: who is asking the question of animal suffering? Jeremy Bentham. And who will answer it? Bentham's colleagues who know the truth of animals. The utilitarian approach is only secondarily concerned with any general categories that lump humans and animals together. It is more fundamentally an announcement of human privilege. Let us look at the quotation again; it fully subordinates animals to the benevolence of those humans who 'know best'.

It is well known that in utilitarianism, which Bentham helped invent, an action or a rule is moral if it increases the sum of happiness in the moral community, immoral if it decreases it. The movements of happiness can be known and calculated. Now, Bentham is obviously suggesting that in the future these calculations might have to be expanded to include animals. (Presumably, writers like Singer would identify today's animal rights as that once future time.) The only important question is whether or not animals can suffer; they should be included within the moral circle if it is known that they can. But Bentham's position did not cause a turn to any more or less common-sense notion of suffering in general, linking all organic beings. His argument is not: if we suffer, so do they. On the contrary, it is: if we know they can suffer we should not hurt them, a problem that can only be resolved to the extent that we have a privileged knowledge only we can act upon. Imagine that I am kicking a dog. Bentham does not believe that it has an inalienable right not to be kicked; instead he is saying that if I know the dog suffers I should not kick it because I am knowingly causing it to be unhappy. He is appealing to my ability to know what is best for the dog and change myself accordingly. The whole point of Bentham's case is my special ability to become a different kind of being.

He was sure that the privileged, if ultimately unsteady, figure of 'Man' could discover the hidden truths of nature. Bentham did not doubt that knowledge could help society distance itself from animals, and thus know their real and secret vitality. Bentham saw the development of morality as a guide to how far humans' potential privilege and radical difference had been advanced. He speculated only that the day *might* come when it is realised that animals should be pulled into the orbit of morality. There is nothing inevitable about this, no necessity. All he identifies is a process which depends entirely on the enhancement of the unique knowledge possessed by some people. Morality is made into something dependent on the orderly understanding and classification of animals regardless of what visible signs might imply.

The notion has a social impact. If moral behaviour relies on the possession of the knowledge which uses general categories to classify humans and animals as similar (in suffering, pain), then those who demonstrate the greatest regard for animals are, by definition, the most knowledgeable. I kick a dog because I do not know it suffers. I simply rely on the visible distinction between me and it. However, you condemn my actions since you do indeed know of its pain. You know that all organic beings are linked through the abstraction of life. You know better than I; and so you lavish affection on your poodle, and try to do something about my disgusting beastliness. After all, to you I am barely human. The allegiances which shape society have not been beaten into my head. Kindness to animals reflects the existence of a properly social individual.

Such a reading helps align the comments on animals to Bentham's interests with legislation. He is simultaneously proposing an extension of moral enfranchisement and a tightening of social discipline. Bentham wanted to extend freedom and applaud the uniqueness of 'Man', but he also believed that the freedom to be human was only possible if society was turned into a regulated and regulative set of relationships. 'In an unequal and increasingly divided society, this was the only way to expand liberty and fortify consent without compromising security' (Ignatieff 1978: 212). Bentham was a thinker of his time; he believed that humans were indeed similar to animals, but he also believed that society and knowledge could make them different. His writings reveal a determination to guarantee and firmly guard the privileges of 'Man'. Bentham wanted to embrace animals whilst exterminating animality.

Kant agreed: 'We can judge the heart of a man by his treatment of animals' (Kant 1930: 240). Bentham argued that we have an obligation not to cause an animal to suffer only if we know we are hurting it. Although the individual is rather incidental in all this (it could easily be replaced by a brick wall or a piece of paper), at least it makes claims of some sort in itself. Kant disallowed even this:

so far as animals are concerned, we have no direct duties. Animals are not self-conscious and are there merely as a means to an end. That end is man. We can ask, 'Why do animals exist?' But to ask, 'Why does man exist?' is a meaningless question. Our duties towards animals are merely indirect duties towards humanity.

(Kant 1930: 239)

Kant continued to suggest that we be kind to animals 'for he who is cruel to animals becomes hard also in his dealings with men' (Kant 1930: 240). Kant leaves us in no doubt that, for him, humans are utterly different from animals. Indeed, he was prepared to reverse the categorical imperative and make them a mere means to our ends. As such, Kant allowed the morality of vivisection on the grounds that although the scientists certainly act cruelly, their actions are perfectly justifiable, 'since animals must be regarded as man's instruments' (Kant 1930: 240). Bentham did not preclude the possibility that vivisection would eventually be defined as immoral.

Kant's position was derived from Hogarth's melodrama. This is the clue to Kant's real concerns. Kant follows Hogarth and assumes that it is the urban poor and working class who are cruel to animals and, therefore, not up to the full measure of being human. If a person can be judged by their treatment of animals, then Tom Nero and his ghastly ilk are little more than violent beasts. People like Nero should be watched and coerced because 'Tender feelings towards dumb animals develop humane feelings towards mankind' (Kant 1930: 240). After Hogarth made the engravings, foundling schoolchildren and coach-drivers did not have tender feelings towards animals and they could not be expected to be tender, orderly, and moral in social relations. (Interestingly, the coach-drivers of Paris were also feared and hated; see Papayanis 1985.) Like Bentham, Kant wants discipline and the attenuation of human differences from the animals, to ensure the status of 'Man' as the only consciously social being. Also, like Bentham, Kant assumes that only some people are sufficiently a part of society to be able to govern cruel and beastly coach-drivers.

Kant explicitly makes the connection between social order and humanity. He told of Leibniz who evidently once observed a worm. After he had made his discoveries from the worm, Leibniz placed it back on the tree he took it from 'so that it should not come to harm through any act of his'. He was pushing even beyond the limits of contemporary animal rights. It is doubtful whether Singer, Regan, or Clark would be morally concerned with a worm. Kant comments that Leibniz 'would have been sorry – a natural feeling for a humane man – to destroy such a creature for no reason' (Kant 1930: 240). Two things are significant in the example. Firstly, Kant is clearly equating knowledge with humanitarianism; Leibniz would have been sorry had he harmed the worm because he knew his natural feeling. Secondly, Kant gave the illustration in a series of lectures on ethics; it was deliberately meant to play a part in the moral instruction and formation of those who would be the knowledgeable. Humanitarianism is not an abstract concept which simply takes hold of us; we must endeavour to be humane, and humanity can only be known by those who are fully social and well regulated, just like Bentham or Kant. Those people who do not know better are inhuman. They are cruel and something less than human. They are beasts.

These two philosophical ideas, which clearly play on the modern taxonomic ambivalence of 'Man' had a deep social impact. Bentham's stress on knowledge led to a notion that compassion towards animals reflected the prestige and status of the 'lady' and 'gentleman'. Meanwhile, Kant's position that duties to animals are properly indirect duties to humans and society contributed to the development of policing organisations which could ensure their respect. The positions combined in a system where the knowledgeable and kindly (the bourgeoisie), the proper humans who lived a fully social life, disciplined the the cruel treatment of animals carried out by the beastly and unruly (the hard-hearted, beastly, human brutes). Those who were sufficiently different tried to make other social groups different as well. As one anonymous correspondent to the *Gentleman's Magazine* said in April 1791, the legislature should 'empower the humane to awe the hard-hearted by the dread of penalty'. The writer went on to declare: 'What a source of enjoyment might the affluent possess', if they bought the animals they saw suffering at the hands of the cruel ('B' 1791: 336).

The humane and the hard-hearted were identified as two different social groups with contradictory attitudes towards animals. The one was applauded as kind, the other scorned as cruel. Cruelty is the dark, necessary, other side of kindness. It can only be identified by those who are not cruel, who are gentle and compassionate. Now, if the legislature does indeed permit coercion of the cruel and the relief of animals, the new power could only be carried out by humane and affluent people who are themselves kind. The hard-hearted are so lost to humanity, and so ignorant, that left to themselves they cannot understand the error of their ways. The naming of cruelty requires a *pathos of distance* (Nietzsche's phrase; see Nietzsche 1956) by which socially acceptable concepts and behaviour can be opposed to the bad. During the eighteenth century, a process of distanciation can indeed be observed. Of course, it was importantly rooted in the urbanisation of social life, and the turning of towns into the place where questions of humanity and society were resolved, but there was also a related process of the wealthy and knowledgeable withdrawing from activities which they used to share with other groups. The trend was particularly strong in animal-related sports. The use of animals to think human being shifted from metonymical coercion to metaphorical compassion.

It might be thought that feelings of revulsion towards recreations involving animals would be particularly significant in the lofty tale of moral progress and compassion. Yet the decline of the sports tells a slightly different story. A quite astonishing number of animals must have died in the name of sport in the years before about 1850. The English had been ingenious in devising new ways of inflicting pain, or more likely death, on animals. There were many recreations which gave widespread pleasure: except for the cock which was made to fight or had stones thrown at it, or the bull which was baited by dogs. Indeed, the sports 'retained a degree of favour, or at least sufferance, from the governing class, and many gentlemen . . . actively patronized cock-fighting and sometimes even bull-baiting. Blood sports had not yet come to be widely regarded as cruel or disreputable' (Malcolmson 1982: 20). But they soon did. By the early nineteenth century, the activities were regularly denounced by gentlemen who had previously enjoyed them, and were all but unknown by 1850. This remarkable shift in morality reflected the increasingly consolidated urban life of the bourgeoisie and their classification of others, whether human or animal, as things to be known and regulated rather than played with. Their detachment led to a new morality. As they withdrew from some pleasures, they tried to impose their urban and class-specific definitions of order and human being throughout society. If the rich and knowledgeable no longer enjoyed bear-baiting, neither should anyone else.

Keith Thomas gives a fine example of the withdrawal. After a vigorous campaign, the annual Eton ram hunt was discontinued after 1747, 'nearly a hundred years before the reformers managed to suppress the proletarian Stamford bull running' (Thomas 1983: 186). Thomas makes little of the century-long gap, and seems to think that it simply highlights the success of humanitarianism in one struggle and its relative failure in another. However, the example says rather more. The pleasure of killing animals stopped at Eton before Stamford as part of the general withdrawal of the wealthy and powerful from activities which were previously common and shared. Just as the parents of the Eton pupils believed that only they and their class were the representatives of human being in its purest form, they asserted that participation in the corrupt delights of the 'lower orders' could only dirty them. The problem was that the urban population did not know how to enjoy itself without threatening the destruction of the human world. Only the bourgeoisie and aristocracy could be allowed any leisure, because only they knew how to behave. Social discrimination and taxonomic differences were indivisible.

Various cases were made to explain why relationships with animals should not be cruel. The bourgeoisie avoided cruelty on the grounds that its compassionate urban knowledge also avoided animals (except when they were pets and therefore surrogate humans which were obviously so different that they presented few taxonomic difficulties), and also because they were the prestigious subjects of social and moral certainty. They were the only people who could know the abstract categories which made the world intelligible, because only they had convincingly overthrown anthropocentric and theological myths. Meanwhile, the urban working class had to be made more orderly and properly human;

it had to be disciplined and made to behave in an utterly regular way which posed no threat to society. If the working population did anything which might 'harden the heart', it was seen to edge into the province of the brute. The workers could become something less than fully human and, therefore, a threat to all social and taxonomic coherence. They were mere objects, and the problem was how to make them human enough for their social role:

> Reasoning and remonstrance are vain; a severe reprimand is treated with insolence; and, should corporal punishment be inflicted, it is to be feared that the brute, who calls himself a man, may, on the first opportunity, wreak his vengeance on the unoffending quadruped.

> (R——Y 1800: 848)

The answer was 'distributing *gratis* to poor families where there are children, some small publication on the subject' (R——Y 1800: 848). In other words, appeal to the remaining shreds of humanity to make them humane.

But this was not the only answer to the bourgeoisie's difficulty of making sure that the human beasts of the working class were more orderly and responsible than hawks or pigeons. In the eighteenth and nineteenth centuries, the Demand for Difference was made by two methods which reconciled the taxonomic oddity that although 'Man' might well be special 'he' is not that special. The methods were amongst the first and most compelling attempts to moralise the relationships between animals and society, and took the form of legislation and surveillance. They involved a forceful expulsion from social relations of whatever the bourgeoisie defined as animal or brutish.

Between 1800 and 1835, the wider social debate about the morality of ways of treating animals led parliament to debate eleven anti-cruelty bills. All failed except for an Act of 1822 to Prevent the Cruel Treatment of Cattle, and the Cruelty to Animals Act which criminalised animal-baiting. For us, the mechanisms which led to the bills' enactment or rejection are relatively unimportant, but the debates they caused are absolutely intriguing. The ideas which the members of parliament used to justify their arguments were quite consistent over the years. Both the protagonists and opponents of anti-cruelty measures relied on the same trusted themes. Consequently, it is not necessary to look at all the debates in detail. It is reasonable to concentrate for the most part on just two classic cases: firstly, the speech with which Lord Erskine presented a bill to the Lords in 1809 'to prevent malicious and wanton cruelty to animals'; and secondly, an attempt by the Irish landowner Richard Martin to establish a parliamentary select committee in 1824 'to inquire, whether the practice of Bear-baiting, and other cruel sports, has a mischievous effect on the morals of the people'.

Lord Erskine's speech of 1809 was not a masterpiece of brevity (as his fellow lords noticed), but it was fascinating because he explicitly reflected on both the privileged and unprivileged dimensions of 'Man'. Erskine was in no doubt that all people should accept the moral claims which animals make. He believed that humans and animals are similar organic structures, but humans are, or at least can be, special because they can be subjects of their own intentions. Erskine began with the Christian orthodoxy that God 'gave to man his dominion over the lower world', with 'dominion' meaning a moral trust (Erskine 1809: 554). Our moral duties are recognised through the similarities of organic structure and the knowledge created by the taxonomic principle of life.

> For every animal which comes in contact with man, and whose powers, and qualities, and instincts, are obviously constructed for his use, nature has taken the same care to provide, and as carefully and bountifully as for man himself, organs and feelings for its own enjoyment and happiness. Almost every sense bestowed upon man is equally bestowed upon them; seeing, hearing, feeling, thinking; the sense of pain and pleasure; the passions of love and anger; sensibility to kindness, and pangs from unkindness and neglect, are inseparable characteristics of their natures as much as of our own.
>
> (Erskine 1809: 555)

The turn away from visible distinctions, and towards abstract categories of similitude, led Erskine to the moral proposition that animals 'are created indeed for our use, but not for our abuse' (Erskine 1809: 555).

However, Erskine did not believe that all humans necessarily have to acknowledge animals' moral claims simply because we are no better than they are. On the contrary, he emphasised God's dominion and announced that humans could, crucially, change themselves. The House of Lords was especially important because its laws could establish 'the grand efficacious principle' of anticruelty:

> as a spontaneous rule in the mind of every man who reads it
> – which will make every human bosom a sanctuary against
> cruelty – which will extend the influence of a British statute
> beyond even the vast bounds of British jurisdiction, and
> consecrate, perhaps, in all nations, and in all ages, that just
> and eternal principle which binds the whole living world in
> one harmonious chain, under the dominion of enlightened
> man, the lord and governor of all.
>
> (Erskine 1809: 557)

The classificatory ambiguity of 'Man' and the potential for disorder implicit to modern knowledge is clear. 'Man' is at one and the same time bound to all living beings and yet the governor of all. The social point, of course, is that the enlightened were less tightly bound to the animal than the unenlightened, something proved by the fact that they were already 'a sanctuary against cruelty'. Erskine and the other bourgeois were so deeply shaped by things which only humans could do (namely, intentionally repudiate cruelty) that they saw themselves as the standard of the properly human and the fully social. Political and taxonomic status extended into a campaign to make the social others more human by making them less cruel. Classificatory and social order are two sides of the same coin. Anti-cruelty legislation drums social allegiances, forces human being, into our heads: 'The moral sense . . . cannot but have a most powerful effect upon our feelings and sympathies for one another' (Erskine 1809: 556).

Erskine told the Lords that if cruelty is 'habitually indulged in, on beings beneath us', it 'destroys every security of human life, by hardening the heart for the perpetration of all crimes' (Erskine 1809: 570). Cruelty is wrong because it undermines social order. He was using the story of Tom Nero, which Kant had written up. He argued that cruelty is something which can be known fairly readily 'because nature has created a standard in the human heart, by which it may be surely ascertained' (Erskine 1809: 569). This simple belief that cruelty is associated with a capacity of the human heart, and a knowledge of it, gives the argument profound social implications. Cruelty is linked to ignorance (a lack of the ability to ascertain), to a lack of humanity. It was a badge of social position:

> These unmanly and disgusting outrages are frequently perpetrated by the basest and most worthless; incapable, for the most part, of any reproach which can reach the mind, and who know no more of the law, than that it suffers them to indulge their savage dispositions with impunity.
>
> (Erskine 1809: 553–4)

The savages were not a loose collection of individuals. Erskine was worried about the 'violence and outrages committed by the lower orders of the people', and wanted humane (humanising) legislation directed only at them (Erskine 1809: 556).

Throughout his speech, Erskine poured contempt on the working population. At best they were stupid, at worst a threat to humanity. In either case there was a need to inculcate a finer regard for social order amongst them. Interestingly, Erskine mentioned a bill of 1800 which tried to make bull-baiting illegal. He thought it unfortunate that the bill said little about the right of the bull not to be abused, but applauded its 'very laudable objects of human policy', which were 'to put an end to sports which led away the servants and the labourers of manufacture and husbandry from the service of their masters' (Erskine 1809: 559–60). Quite simply, the 'masterless men' of the early nineteenth century could not be trusted to be human(e).

The effort to make the 'lower orders' of the working class more controlled and controllable was extended to inform another pressing demand. There is no reason to think that Erskine was not sincere in his belief that cruelty to animals implied cruelty to humans, but it is important to remember that he put the idea before the House of Lords in the wake of revolution. He wanted to be sure that the mob would not turn from the Bastille to Newgate, and tried to enforce the moral codes which would make a British repeat of 1789 more difficult. The Hogarth-Kant story had taken a very tight and frightening grip. 'The times in which we live . . . have read us an awful lesson upon the importance of preserving the moral sympathies'. It was imperative that the beastly lower orders should be made moral, and the Lords should never be found 'neglecting the cultivation of the moral sense, the best security of states, and the greatest consolation of the world'

(Erskine 1809: 570). Similarly, in the 1800 bull-baiting debate, the extremely worried Sir William Pulteney introduced the proposals by claiming that

> The reasons for such a notion as this were obvious. . . . The practice was cruel and inhuman, it drew together idle and disorderly persons; it drew from their occupations many who ought to be earning subsistence for themselves and families. It created many disorderly and mischievous proceedings and furnished scenes of profligacy and cruelty.
>
> (Quoted in Moss 1961: 14)

For Erskine and Pulteney, cruelty to animals made plebeians less squeamish about decapitating the monarch, whilst the urban workers should be living a life of labour; they could not be allowed to enjoy bull-baiting when they should be working to keep their families. Crocodiles wept. (However, Darnton shows that the connection between cruelty to animals and violence to humans was sometimes more than rhetorical; see also Archer 1985.)

Erskine's exclusive concern with how the urban working class related to animals was recognised at the time. Windham, a long-standing opponent of anti-cruelty legislation, said that 'The bill, instead of being called A Bill for preventing Cruelty to Animals, should be entitled, A Bill for harassing and oppressing certain classes among the lower orders of the people' (Windham 1809: 1036). Windham's mockery did not mean that he was less concerned with order than Erskine. Windham merely felt that cruelty to animals was too trivial for legislation and that the bill overstated its case. He believed that Erskine was creating a morality 'in which men were to become virtuous at others' expense' (Windham 1809: 1031). For Windham, all humans were privileged in so far as animals were subordinate, and as the behaviour of country gentlemen proved 'cruel sports did not make cruel people' (Windham 1809: 1025*). He broke with the Kantian line assumed by Erskine and also harked back to Classical classification in which all humanity was afforded a special status, and where visible distinctions rigidly defined the human and the animal. Windham did not understand the categories which are the basis of modern moral connections between the sufferings of an animal and the pains of a person.

Although the 1809 bill was lost, the arguments kept their

currency. They were recycled by Richard Martin in 1824. Martin's speech is interesting as it quite clearly states which social groups need to be more human and less animal. Attention will also be paid to a short Commons debate in May 1823 which vividly revealed attitudes towards the morality or otherwise of different relationships with animals.

Richard Martin earned the nickname 'Humanity Dick' for his efforts to legislate against cruelty. Evidently, the efforts make due to him 'the gratitude of all decent folk' (Moss 1961: 14). Martin was at the fore of the early nineteenth-century efforts to introduce a moral component to the treatment of animals, and it is not unreasonable to suppose that his speeches summarise the most compelling arguments for the relevance of animals. It is interesting then that Martin was mostly concerned to crush 'the amusement of the lowest rabble' (Martin 1824: 488). He was worried that 'cruel sports, if persevered in ... deteriorate and corrupt the morals of the people' (Martin 1824: 487). Presumably, the deterioration was obvious since it turned 'people' into a barely human 'lowest rabble'.

Martin's case for animals' moral claims was broadly similar to the one made by Erskine. Although animals do not make moral claims in the same way as humans, they claim protection. Animals should be treated kindly because it is a denial or a corruption of humanity to treat them in any other way. The precise social slant of this perspective is clear in the following passage. Remember, Martin was asking for the establishment of a select committee to investigate the humanity of bear-baiting and similar sports. *Parliamentary Debates* records his position:

> If animals could be contended to have no right to the
> protection of man, he still should contend, that the sports
> which were the object of his motion ought to be suppressed,
> as tending to corrupt morals, and endanger good order; and
> it was on this ground that he particularly founded his motion.
> He would tell the House, that the persons who were collected
> together at the bear-baitings, and badger-baitings were the
> lowest and most wretched description of people. They were
> the horse-butchers of the vicinity of the metropolis, the
> butchers' boys, the coal-porters – those were the description
> of people who frequented the bear-pits.
>
> (Martin 1824: 487)

The sports were cruel and disorderly on two counts; firstly they brought together social groups who should otherwise remain quite separate (Hogarth had earlier shown this mingling in *The Cock Pit*), and secondly they brought together animals and not-proper humans (boys; dirty, bloody labourers). The sports were disgusting because they blurred social distinctions and dissolved human-animal boundaries, in a violent celebration of blood. The argument was also beautifully circular in a way which enhanced the prestige of people like Richard Martin; the sports were disorderly (both socially and taxonomically) and attended by the lowest rabble. Therefore the poor urban workers were a cruel threat to all order, all social allegiances, if left to themselves. Martin and his friends were privileged because, unlike the beastly humans, they were detached enough to be able to see, and do something about, the spiral of brutality.

The circle of disorder–workers–cruelty permitted an aggressive onslaught against the popular activities which were held to give spleen to the beast within, whilst at the same time heralding the virtues of hunting. For Martin it was quite impossible that obviously humane, compassionate, knowledgeable people could be at all cruel. The rather tortured explanations why working-class bear-baiting was a repugnant abomination, whilst bourgeois fox-hunting was thoroughly acceptable, were drawn out by one of Martin's staunchest allies, a Mr J. Smith. Smith made it clear that subjective 'Man ' had to coerce the beast-humans who were objects of their passions. In particular, the activities of the urban working class had to be crushed because:

> those who frequented them were the lowest, the most
> unfortunate and the most ignorant of the populace. . . . [T]he
> practices . . . were injurious to the real comforts and
> happiness of those people. If they examined individually the
> history of those who attended these cruel sports, they would
> find them persons totally uneducated, that was, as to any
> moral or religious knowledge.
>
> (Smith 1824: 491)

The bear-baiters did not bear the stamp of humanity. Fowell Buxton knew 'the case of a boy, who, from attending at dog-fights, and mixing with the society there, became perverted to every useful purpose in society' (Fowell Buxton 1823: 435) – a contention which rather begs the obvious question: whose useful purposes? Fowell Buxton was telling the Commons that children are as innocents; they could not be expected to know better. Consequently, those with the knowledge to prevent the young falling into the pits of animality had a moral responsibility to legislate the iniquitous human brutes out of existence.

However, children whose bourgeois parents went fox-hunting were in no such moral danger. As Martin asked the Commons with some perplexity:

> When hon. gentlemen said, that bear-baiting and badger-baiting were to be compared to fox-hunting and partridge-shooting, he would gravely admonish those gentlemen how they might hurt their own popularity when they said that they could not put down these cruel sports without putting down the field-sports, in which they delighted. It was making them out to be as cruel and as monstrous as those monstrous wretches the bear-baiters. Those who sported on their own manors, or fished in their own streams, were a very different sort of men. He had known men as humane as men could be who followed the sports of the field.
>
> (Martin 1824: 487)

Privileged social groups simply cannot be cruel, or at least so Martin told his fellow privileged members of parliament.

The contours of the legislative path of the Demand for Difference should be plain from the speeches by Erskine and Martin, neither of which managed to introduce new measures. Although both declared that animals have rights which create human obligations, they were more concerned to tackle any practical acts which seemed to knock 'Man' off 'his' already shaky pedestal. In particular, they believed that disgusting, cruel, immoral behaviour was the preserve of the urban working class, simply on the grounds that the mass had not been educated to know better, whereas the bourgeoisie had been. Moreover, only the rich and knowledgeable could know the basis of being, because only they were rational subjects; they applauded animal rights because morality reflected their confidence that they were in every important respect uniquely human.

But speeches to parliament or the passing of new laws are one thing. Making sure that the ignorant monsters really become properly human through either coercion or consent is quite another. The legislation had to be supported by policing. The surveillance was carried out by the voluntary anti-cruelty societies. Although the Royal Society for the Prevention of Cruelty to Animals has been the most famous and effective of the societies which police the workers to make sure they do not relapse into beastliness, it was not the first such body. In 1809 a Society for the Suppression and Prevention of Wanton Cruelty to Animals was founded in Liverpool. The group did not enjoy any success, probably because at the time the city had no police force nor magistrates who could impose the little anti-cruelty legislation in existence (for an account of the Liverpool society see Moss 1961: 20–1). The London-based Society for the Prevention of Cruelty to Animals was not formed until June 1824 at the ironically named Old Slaughter's Coffee House. It became the Royal Society in 1840. The meeting at Old Slaughter's was the product of another meeting which had been held there in 1822. The SPCA was established with something more in mind than a simple moralising of the urban working class; it also wanted to show them the religious law. Indeed, one historian has suggested that the SPCA was 'predominantly evangelical in origin and aim' (Harrison 1967: 99).

Evangelism had an immense impact on the Society. In 1821, before the first coffee house meeting, a notice had been placed in the *Gentleman's Magazine* which was virtually identical to one the Reverend Arthur Broome had placed in the *Monthly Magazine*. The announcement stated that a person

> actuated by a compassionate regard for the sufferings of the brute species, and lamenting in common with every feeling mind, the wanton cruelties which are so frequently practised with impunity, earnestly suggests the formation of a Society, by whose united exertions, some check may be applied, if practicable, to an evil which is equally repugnant to the dictates of humanity, and to the benevolent spirit and precepts of the Christian religion.
>
> (Clerus 1821: 386)

Sympathisers were invited to write to an address near Paternoster Row in London. In 1832, the adherence to the 'Christian religion' led to a purge of the SPCA's eccentric Jewish secretary, Lewis

Gompertz (Fairholme and Pain 1924: 24). Moss unconvincingly rejects charges of anti-Semitism (Moss 1961: 28). The evangelical sentiments which Broome drew upon had been in circulation for many years, and had been stated in a sermon by the Reverend James Granger as early as October 1772.

In many ways, Granger anticipated Erskine and Martin. He too believed that cruelty demonstrated inadequate humanity in specific sections of society. His sermon was 'not only . . . for such as have the care of horses, and other useful Beasts; but also for Children, and those concerned in forming their heart' (quoted in Fairholme and Pain 1924: 8). Granger used the authority of the pulpit to launch a direct attack on the behaviour of the workers who continued to work and live near animals. Granger was exploiting Nietzsche's pathos of distance (that is, his distanciation and unambiguous distinction from animals). If mere words could call forth brimstone and damnation, the Reverend would have probably succeeded when in an exceptionally fierce onslaught against the cruelties practised on horses by the sermon's fictional addressee, T.B. Drayman, he declaimed:

> If thou breakest any more whips about him, and respect thy horrid oaths, wishing thyself 'damned and double-damned' if thou are not revenged of him, I shall take care that thou be punished by a Justice of the Peace, as well as thy own master, in this world; and give thee fair warning, that a worse punishment waits for thee in the next; and that damnation will certainly come according to thy call.
>
> (Quoted in Fairholme and Pain 1924: 8)

Granger was denounced as a lunatic after delivering the sermon, and although his preaching was condemned 'as a prostitution of the dignity of the pulpit' (Fairholme and Pain 1924: 8), he had made serious points. He was only speaking to the workers who still handled living animals; Granger was calling on them to change themselves but, if they would not, he was sure that the magistrates, who were presumably already distanced from direct encounters with animals, would impose discipline. Granger's sermon voiced the hostility of urban and rural understandings of animals. He is telling Tom Drayman that God's children who have a fully awakened heart do not do certain things. It is also worth noting that Granger is talking to Drayman in much the same way as

Drayman would talk to his horse. Throughout the relationship is subject to object, namer to named. The authority which the pulpit gave Granger and his true religious knowledge emphasised his privileges; Drayman was much the same as an animal. Granger did not sympathise with the working class. Sympathy was reserved for the poor animals; the brutal humans just needed to be coerced and judiciously watched.

The opprobrium experienced by Granger did not deter other religiously minded reformers. Four years later Humphrey Primatt published *A Dissertation on the Duty of Mercy and the Sin of Cruelty to Brute Animals*. The essay was saturated by modern classification and was committed to looking behind the visible world to discover the secret, abstract linkages between things. Indeed, Primatt went so far as to say that all appearances are quite irrelevant because 'Nature never intended these distinctions as foundations for right of tyranny and oppression' (quoted in Salt 1980: 141). Instead, he relied on the ability of social knowledge to transcend the purely visible and develop an awareness of beings as living organic structures. Primatt wanted this ability to be the foundation of the moral principle 'do unto others as, in their condition, you would be done unto' (quoted in Salt 1980: 142). However, Primatt retained his belief in the distinctiveness of 'Man'. Certainly cruel relationships with animals ought to be 'decreed to be as illegal as they are sinful', but the appeal was not based on a belief that humans should recognise their living congruity with animals. It was simply so that 'we should not hear of so many shocking murders and acts of inhumanity as we now do' (quoted in Fairholme and Pain 1924: 10–11).

Arthur Broome happily dusted off the ideas of Granger and Primatt. The SPCA was eventually formed by a group of evangelists, parliamentarians, and the wealthy who responded to the magazine notices. At the inaugural meeting Fowell Buxton told the gentlemen that they had come together, not only

> to prevent the exercise of cruelty towards animals, but to spread amongst the lower orders of the people, especially amongst those to whom the care of animals was entrusted, a degree of moral feeling which would compel them to think and act like those of a superior class.
>
> (Quoted in Fairholme and Pain 1924: 55)

He might well have added: 'To think and act as we tell them'.

The first meeting decided that the Society should follow a dual policy of self-improvement through moral education and surveillance and punishment. The strategy continues to this day, although moral education has been transformed into advertising. The SPCA wanted to be sure that the cruel debasement of humanity would be reflected upon and condemned. As Granger might have put it, the Society tried to make the urban workers repent their oaths, and be sure of damnation in this world and the next. Two committees were formed. The first was made up of parliamentarians and clergy. It was 'appointed to superintend the Publication of Tracts, Sermons, and similar modes of influencing public opinion'. Amongst the first publications were Humphrey Primatt's essay and Lord Erskine's speech to the House of Lords. However, it is perhaps the second committee, made up by Fowell Buxton, Richard Martin, and an assortment of the worthies of London, which is most interesting. It was 'appointed to adopt measures for Inspecting the Markets and Streets of the Metropolis, the slaughter houses, the conduct of Coachmen' (Moss 1961: 23). The first committee presupposed the potential subjectivity of all humans. It assumed that through reading and contemplation the cruel and beastly could change; they could become more human and less animal by becoming more humane. However, the second committee had little faith in reformed slaughterhouse workers. Instead it believed that they had to be forced to be human. It wanted to make their cruelties quite visible by pulling them out of the dark pits of inhumanity and into the radiant, pure light of the humane law.

The evangelists had never been slow to take matters into their own hands if they encountered cruelty. Richard Martin personally walked around Smithfield Market trying to find offences punishable under his Act. He brought the first prosecution under it when he accused a horse-dealer and a butcher of beating a horse. In 1824 he employed an inspector to carry out the patrols, and at the same time Arthur Broome employed a man named Wheeler to do a similar job. Wheeler was so enthusiastic that in his first six months he secured sixty prosecutions (Fairholme and Pain 1924: 40). The SPCA tried to consolidate these random individual initiatives by setting up its own police force to carry out surveillance.

In 1832 the Society employed two inspectors (then called constables) who were paid 10 shillings a week plus rewards for convictions. By 1855 there were eighty constables and 120 in 1897. The police imagery was not confined to the title 'constable'. In 1856 the Society's officers were issued with uniforms 'similar to those in use by the Police'. For some reason, the uniform's coat also had the letters 'P.C.' and a number embroidered on the collar (Harrison 1973: 795). The relationship with the real police force was so close that in 1881 the Wigan constabulary sought the help of an RSPCA inspector and former officer to help crush a riot (Harrison 1973: 795). The inspectors concentrated on urban areas and frequently incited the wrath of those they were policing; in 1839 Constable Piper was killed after trying to suppress a cock-fight in Hamworth. Of course, acts of workers' resistance were just more grist to the mill of their inhumane unruliness. The inspectors were under considerable pressure after December 1851 when the Society introduced a scheme whereby the officer with the fewest monthly convictions was dismissed. This implies an exceptionally intrusive surveillance. No doubt the inspectors were fired by evangelical enthusiasm, but they also had the dull, compulsive knowledge that if they were not diligent, they would be dismissed. The impact of the policing is shown by the number of convictions for cruelty: 1,357 in the decade 1830–39, rising dramatically to 71,657 in 1890–99 (Harrison 1967: 102). Clearly, it is better to explain such a remarkable increase by the greater effectiveness of surveillance rather than a simple increase in the number of illegal acts. The RSPCA continues to rely on surveillance carried out by officers who dress like the police.

The surveillance and legislative paths of the early nineteenth-century Demand for Difference represented the efforts of the bourgeoisie to impose its classifications and definitions of 'proper' human being on all social groups. The definitions were the morality of a class which had appropriated to itself the virtues of kindness and compassion, and the knowledge of a class which believed that animality was a quality behind the visible, and therefore lurking in humans as much as hawks or cats. For the bourgeoisie it was possible that the urban working class might not have had the 'allegiances which make human life human' drummed into its collective head since it remained relatively congruous with animals. The coach-driver was obviously a beast; after all, he worked with them. Meanwhile, the fox-hunting, fishing, and shooting enjoyed by the country gentleman was obviously not cruel because he was merely using his social possessions. The one social group was so different from animals that it could kill them, the other was so similar that it could only be cruel. Essentially, the anti-cruelty concerns of the Demand for Difference boil down to one simple message: real men and women (like us) do not do that (as you do).

The 'lady' was identified as the person *par excellence* who could practise humanitarianism and inculcate greater humanity. After all, Hannah More believed that there were 'peculiarly feminine' qualities which were the leading edge of the moral regeneration of the nation (Hall 1979). The 'ladies' were busy in every sphere of philanthropic activity, and, indeed, between 1790 and 1830 their involvement increased dramatically, although they avoided the magnificently named City of London Truss Society for the Relief of the Ruptured Poor (Prochaska 1974). The campaign against cruelty to animals was fully a part of the general picture. When the early Liverpool society was reformed in 1834, it was 'chiefly under the auspices of ladies' (Moss 1961: 21), whilst in 1870 the RSPCA established a Ladies Education Committee under Baroness Burdett-Coutts and Mrs Smithies. They formed the Bands of Mercy which tried to promote humanitarianism amongst urban schoolchildren (Moss 1961: 198). 'Ladies' also gave 470 of the RSPCA's 739 nineteenth-century legacies (Harrison 1967: 108).

The 'ladies' were *noblesse oblige*, indeed all the rich and know-ledgeable felt a duty to do something about the dissolution of humanity which the working class threatened. Part of the obliga-tion involved legislation and surveillance, but it should not be forgotten that the bourgeoisie also changed itself. It quickly with-drew from participation in cruel sports and also made sure that it never had to kill animals personally. Meat simply appeared as a commodity placed on the dinner table, and even the animals killed for sport were never touched by clean, humane hands. For example, in fox-hunting, the killing is usually carried out by dogs or, if a human is needed, by a landworker (Tester 1989). Whilst the working class just took part in undoubtedly violent and bloody recreations, and daily mingled with animals, the bourgeois practised his or her unique, human(e) subjectivity from a safe distance. Cruelty

hurts the feelings of speculative individuals, who cannot help
shuddering at the misery they are frequently obliged to be
witness to; but which, to shew the difference between
cultivated and uncultivated minds, proves a fruitful source of
high gratification to the illiterate and vulgar bulk of mankind.

(Humanus 1789: 17)

This writer continued to criticise hunting and horse-racing, but his
general argument would have been popular in the riding saddles
of the shires. The hunters would have defined themselves as
'speculative individuals' who knew and demonstrated their obligation to avoid cruelty, and thereby avoid the animal. But this did
not mean that the gentle and compassionate had to be thoroughly
kind. Ironically, they could be exceptionally violent without falling
into the trap of cruelty.

The bourgeoisie was confronted with a serious taxonomic
difficulty. Some visibly human beings could be like animals; the
urban working class was potentially interstitial in classification
and revolutionary in politics. The response was to turn all
activities which were not 'properly human' (that is, accepted by the
knowledgeable) into immoral pollutants. The brutes who carried
out awful acts were to be either shaped into humane beings
(reclassified) or, simply, got rid off (made taboo). The writer who
signed himself 'Humanus' advocated the following punishment
for a wealthy man he once saw crudely geld a horse. The
punishment is not cruel because it is being carried out by proper
humans who are reasserting social and moral order, and indeed
the miscreant deserves punishment because he had forgotten the
noblesse oblige expected of him:

Had I been an absolute prince . . . I would first have fulfilled
the *lex talionis*; I would next have extended this wretch
between four stout drayhorses, in opposite direction; I would
have racked him to death, and finally have gibbeted him as a
feast for birds of prey. It is hard there should be no law for
brute animals, when they carry so large a proportion of
representatives to every legislative assembly.

(Humanus 1789: 17)

And this in a letter preaching kindness! Mr Humanus's point is
that the horse owner should have known better, and if a bourgeois

does this, what can be expected of the 'illiterate and vulgar bulk'? The punishment was not especially immoral because it was advocated in the name of humanity. The human beast was to be extirpated from society in a beastly way: 'the social map projected by their crusade led humanitarians to treat groups they castigated for cruelty almost as exiles from the human community' (Ritvo 1987: 134).

One of the basic forms of the 'human community' was, and remains, the nation. The bourgeoisie possessed the knowledge and clout to be able to claim to speak on behalf of the country. Their human being was indivisible from being humane, and their ideal of compassion became such a key component in the construction of 'Englishness' that today we are apparently a nation of 'animal lovers'. The corollary is that people or societies which do not love animals as we do, who are not kindly and compassionate, must be less than human. Ideas of animal rights could become part of a cultural imperialism if not racism. Lord Erskine touched on the theme in his 1809 speech when he said parliament should pass a law which would be 'consecrated' in 'all nations, and in all ages' (Erskine 1809: 557), whilst a correspondent to the *Gentleman's Magazine* asserted that 'no people are more alive to the emotions of pity than the English' ('B' 1791: 334). The domestic implications of the association between bourgeois compassion and Englishness fitted in very neatly with the denial of the immutable human-ness of the urban working class; the workers were turned into an inferior and dangerous enemy nation within. Harriet Ritvo has made similar observations, but for her the advocates of kindness and compassion only denied the place in national virtue of 'those who violated the concerns of what was often called "humanity" in at least a rhetorical sense' (Ritvo 1987: 130). Certainly, rhetoric was involved, but the exclusion was also very real and diligently enforced. The exclusion of the urban working class from the community of those who could speak for England was not mere word play. It was a social reality.

The Demand for Difference, which emphasised the uniquely human, and rejected all else as beastly, is reminiscent of nothing so much as Nietzsche's comment that:

> it was the 'good' themselves, that is to say the noble, mighty, highly placed, and high-minded who decreed themselves and

their actions to be good, i.e. belonging to the highest rank, in contradistinction to all that was base, low-minded and plebeian. It was only this *pathos of distance* that authorised them to create values and name them . . .

The basic concept is always *noble* in the hierarchical, class sense, and from this has developed, by historical necessity, the concept *good* embracing nobility of mind, spiritual distinction. This development is strictly parallel to that other which converted the notions *common, plebeian, base*, into the notion *bad*.

(Nietzsche 1956: 160–2)

How did the plebeians respond? Their sports had been outlawed, their behaviour had been put under the control of legislation, and they were watched by the RSPCA. It would be nice to think that they offered some resistance (although not too nice for animals), but they did not. Apart from punching a few RSPCA inspectors they acquiesced in the new moral codes and accepted that, perhaps, their relationships with animals had indeed been less than human. Now their sports are virtually forgotten. Just as the Falaise clergy whitewashed the fresco of the pig execution, so the idyll of England's green and pleasant land has no place for the bear-baiters or cock-fight enthusiasts, nor indeed for the coach-driver who had to beat the horses if his bourgeois passengers were to be on time for their appointment. Gunter Grass has realised the rather nasty political implications of this kind of analysis. One of Grass's characters planned deliberately to outrage the Berlin bourgeoisie by burning his pet dog. As the character reasoned:

A burning dog will shake them. Nothing else shakes them. They can read all about it and gape at pictures through a magnifying glass, or have it right under their noses on TV. All they say is: bad bad. But if my dog burns, the cake will fall out of their faces.

(Grass 1973: 116)

The working class plays little or no constructive role in the history of animal rights and the attempts to make the relationships between animal and society more moral. Quite simply, the first stirrings of anti-cruelty legislation, and the early protection societies, were unsure that the working class was sufficiently distant from 'brute creation' for anything but the harshest persuasion to work. The Demand for Difference was about bourgeois attempts to consolidate a noble national identity after its own image and with a passive urban population. It hoped to create different women and men by opening up a moralising space in their dealings with animals. The Demand for Similitude was also a bourgeois morality, but it did not agree that humans should glory in their difference from the beast.

Chapter Six

A SIMILAR NATURE

For the legislators and preachers of the Demand for Difference, society was the only sure guarantee of an orderly and disciplined human life. Humanity was a beleaguered garrison; it was infiltrated by the Trojan horses of beasts hiding in human bodies, and surrounded by a potentially threatening nature. Things were not as they seemed. Animals and animality were 'burdened with disturbing and nocturnal powers', and were permanently 'escaping from the general laws of being as it is posited and analysed in representation' (Foucault 1970: 278). Individuals like James Granger, Richard Martin, and, later in the nineteenth century, Baroness Burdett-Coutts knew that they were totally divorced from any traces of the brute in their lives and attitudes, and they were confident that their kindness and compassion to animals demonstrated how human(e) they really were. But they were presented with the difficulty that some groups of people did not represent humanitarianism and instead just gave free, violent rein to the wild beast within. The urban working class diluted its human being by mixing with animals and not upholding bourgeois definitions of social respectability. And if the workers were not fully social, neither could they be fully human. The bourgeoisie imposed the burden to humanise the lower orders upon itself.

Such was the late eighteenth- and early nineteenth-century Demand for Difference. Its guiding light was shown in a report of an event in Sunderland in 1822. On 28 May, Simon Thornton went to watch a bull-baiting. His enjoyment was short-lived. The crowd was so great that Thornton was pushed to the ground and broke his leg. Complications set in and he died after a few days. The local intelligentsia was in little doubt that the 'cruel torture' of the bull-baiting had inflamed the unruly passions of the denizens of Sunderland to such an extent that they changed into an inhumane mob. Simon Thornton died because the allegiances of social life had not taken a sufficiently forceful hold. The bull-baitings were 'the disgrace of the vulgar, and are indications of a barbarous spirit which can only be eradicated by knowledge which rouses the finer feelings, and instills a sense of duty to every animated being' (Sykes 1973: 147). The duties which individuals should recognise in their dealings with animals are the duties to know the 'finer feelings'. Animals have rights, as without them it would be impossible for humans to be fully social and properly human. Knowledge and the knowledgeable play a critical role; humanity is only possible with a pedagogy of compassion. The knowledge which makes us humane also vanquishes nocturnal nature.

The Demand for Difference played on the strand of modern classification which emphasised the specialness of some individuals (those who lived an entirely social life separate from animals), and how different the others could or should become. The Demand flattered the self-esteem of the bourgeoisie, who imposed it with force and vigour. It was a moral and a cultural crusade as much as an event in the history of making things intelligible. But although the force of the Demand was intense, it was not dominant to the exclusion of all else. Given the difficult status of 'Man', that was impossible. Erskine, Martin, and Fowell Buxton would have agreed with the suggestion that 'the whole progress of the human species removes man constantly farther and farther from his primitive state', but they would have been horrified as they read on: 'the more we acquire new knowledge, the more we deprive ourselves of acquiring the most important knowledge of all' (Rousseau 1984: 67). Here was someone who was directly contradicting the claim of the Demand for Difference that knowledge was good because it underlined the uniqueness of 'Man'; someone with the audacity to declare that the problem of 'Man' is not insufficient sociality. On the contrary, the difficulty is the too tight inhibition of 'Man' by society. The pretence that 'Man' was wholly special was being questioned.

Even before the English bourgeoisie had developed the main props of the Demand for Difference, Jean-Jacques Rousseau had anticipated its understanding of human being, and turned it back on itself. Rousseau drew on the second strand of 'Man' in modern knowledge. It denied difference and, instead, pushed 'Man' into the realm of the organic, living objects of knowledge. Rousseau stressed the notion of 'Man' in nature and denigrated 'Man' in society. Unlike Granger, Bentham, and Kant, Rousseau believed that the human heart was not naturally hard and brutish; rather it had been made so by social life. Consequently, the urban working class was only prone to cruelty because it was trapped in a coercive and oppressive society. Cruelty was not attributable to a too weak participation in social relationships. Rousseau was suggesting that 'Man' could only be made a stable figure if the arrogant attempts to enhance Difference were rejected, and if it was accepted instead that nature was a condition of morality and a guide to the right.

Rousseau became particularly aware of the natural, 'which men have polluted, while pretending to be anxious to purify it', after the third child he had with Thérèse Levasseur was left at the orphanage, like all its brothers and sisters, perhaps to become a Parisian Tom Nero. It is easy to imagine what Granger would have made of Rousseau's rejection of his children; he would have probably preached a fiery sermon against the downfall of French family life. But Rousseau denied that his action revealed a brutal man. His defence is interesting because it equates moral sensibility with nature in a way which directly contradicts the Bentham-Kant equation of sensibility with society. They would say that only an ignorant person would reject a child. Rousseau agreed. His defence seems to be precisely the fact that he did not know better. He was proud that he was as innocent dealing with children as he was dealing with the French aristocracy. Rousseau gloried in his position as a social outsider:

> If I had been one of those low-born men, who are deaf to the
> gentle voice of Nature, in whose heart no real sentiment of
> justice or humanity ever springs up, this hardening of my
> heart would have been quite easy to understand. But is it
> possible that . . . my natural goodwill towards all my
> fellow-creatures, my ardent love of the great, the true, the
> beautiful and the just; my horror of evil of every kind, my
> utter inability to hate or injure, or even to think of it; the
> sweet and lively emotion which I feel at the sight of all that is
> virtuous, generous, and amiable; is it possible, I ask, that all
> these can ever agree in the same heart with the depravity

which, without the least scruple, tramples underfoot the
sweetest of obligations? No! I feel and loudly assert – it is
impossible . . . I may have been mistaken, never hardened.

(Rousseau 1931: 8)

The protagonists of the Demand for Difference would have never
told the world that they might be moral and mistaken at the same
time. For them, morality was truth; it was doubly right. Rousseau followed the unprivileged interpretation of 'Man' and asserted that
too much knowledge merely hid morality. According to Rousseau,
the right and the good was indivisible from the natural, and individuals might only be properly human to the extent that they
reconciled themselves with their similitude to all other living organic
beings. From the perspective of the Demand for Similitude, society
and social expectations are simply a pollution of the pure truth of
nature. Rousseau would have argued that attempts to make everyone ever more social were both dangerous and absurd since privileged 'Man' was a mere degeneration from natural, Similar 'Man'.
The true basis of human being, and the right relationships between
animals and society, can be discovered if individuals live naturally.
The question is: what was Rousseau's picture of natural 'Man'?

According to the *Confessions*, Rousseau started his contemplation
on natural human being whilst preparing the *Discourse on the Origins
and Foundations of Inequality among Men* in 1753. He was staying for
seven or eight days at Saint Germain, a holiday which Rousseau
recalled as one of the happiest times in his life. Whilst Thérèse and
the other women paid for the stay and, inevitably, carried out all
the chores, Rousseau went for walks in the forest. On the strolls he
developed a picture of real 'Man' in the state of nature:

I buried myself in the forest, where I sought and found the
picture of those primitive times, of which I boldly sketched
the history. I demolished the pitiful lies of mankind; I dared
to expose their nature in all its nakedness, to follow the
progress of time and of the things which have disfigured this
nature; and, comparing the man, as man has made him, with
the natural man, I showed him, in his pretended perfection,
the true source of his misery.

(Rousseau 1931: 39)

It is hard to imagine a statement which would offend the

assumptions of the Demand for Difference more deeply. Rousseau is saying that society is disgraceful. It is social life, and the imposition of social order, which make people miserable, passionate, and unruly. Social obligations are a pretence, natural bonds are the truth. If we lived in the state nature intended, we might well be naked and less well housed, but we would be infinitely happier and healthier. Rousseau bewailed the fact that 'reason has succeeded in suffocating nature' (Rousseau 1984: 70).

In much the same way as he felt he had grasped pure nature on the solitary walks in the deserted forests near Saint Germain, he felt that any true understanding of 'Man' must also try to appreciate 'Man' without society. Rousseau removed the history of civilisation and progress and found: 'an animal less strong than some, less agile than others, but taken as a whole the most advantageously organized of all' (Rousseau 1984: 81). 'Man' was simply one beast among many, almost unrecognisable as the ancestor of the mannered and sophisticated Parisians Rousseau had to mingle with. 'Man' in the state of nature was the Noble Savage, who rummaged through plants for food, drunk at a stream and slept anywhere that was vaguely shaded. This was all 'Man' wanted and to this day really needs: 'behold, his needs are furnished' (Rousseau 1984: 81).

The Noble Savage only ate the food which was naturally provided and easily digested. Rousseau reduced 'Man' to an organic being which was healthy to the extent that it ate natural food in a natural way. 'Man's' ability to cook sumptuous meals had only caused illness, because 'Man' is really no more free to eat anything than any other animal. All creatures should be guided by their biological constitution. Classification through organic being and abstraction from the empirical told Rousseau all he needed to know about the food of the Noble Savage:

> Animals that live only on vegetation all have blunt teeth, like the horse, the ox, the sheep, the hare, while voracious animals have sharp teeth, like the cat, the dog, the wolf, the fox. As for the intestines, frugivorous animals have some, such as the colon, which are not found in voracious animals. It appears therefore that man, having teeth and intestines like the frugivorous animals, should naturally be classified in that category.
>
> (Rousseau 1984: 143)

This is a thoroughly modern statement and a fairly clear example of how modern knowledge permanently undermines any privileges humans might give themselves. Of course, it was methodologically inevitable that Rousseau would end up with a picture of 'Man' as a natural structure, totally removed from any social excrescence, but the statement is important. Rousseau went beyond the manifest, indeed he believed that any classification derived from appearance was totally inadequate. Rousseau took a discursive scalpel to the body and discovered that 'Man' is not unique. Teeth and intestines prove that we are much the same as sheep and hares. Any other taxonomy is just an arrogant lie, and health and happiness are impossible if we do not eat the things dictated by our inner constitution. Meat and morality are incompatible.

The classification of 'Man' with animals relied on greater evidence than the indicators of what we should eat. It also drew on the number of young, which 'provides a further reason for taking man out of the class of carnivorous animals and putting him among the frugivorous species' (Rousseau 1984: 146). There is no trace in this account of the high, knowing, universal legislator whom Lord Erskine applauded; now we are merely nipples. Rousseau pointed out that vegetable-eating animals rarely have more than two young at a time, whereas meat-eating animals invariably do. He observed that it is also rare for women to give birth to more than two children at once, and so, again, humans and frugivorous animals are put in the same category, and intelligible in the same way. Evidently, it is fairly easy to explain why plant-eating animals have fewer young than the meat-eaters. Frugivores spend nearly all day gathering their food (think of sheep in a field; all they do is eat). They spend so long eating that they do not have time to feed a lot of offspring. However, wild carnivorous animals 'taking their meals almost in an instant, can more readily and more frequently pass between their young and the hunt' (Rousseau 1984: 146). It is worth noting that all the animals which Rousseau says are similar to humans have been successfully domesticated and tamed. He linked 'Man' to the animals which are known to be different through daily relationships, and the animals which are taxonomically different happen to live furthest away in the wild. Rousseau is making an interesting play on metaphorical and metonymical relationships with animals (compare with Leach 1964).

Similitude is multiplying rapidly. 'Man' has the organic structure of a frugivorous animal, therefore health is impossible given a socialised meat diet. Humans have no more young than domestic animals, therefore we cannot possibly be wild hunters. Naturally, we are as savage as a sheep. Organically 'Man' is peaceful, healthy, and caring, only different from the animals because 'he' has degenerated from natural goodness by creating society through cooperation and greedy claims of ownership which people were 'simple enough to believe' (Rousseau 1984: 109).

The idea of the Noble Savage had far-reaching taxonomic implications. If 'Man' was really an animal, then animals could be versions of 'Man'. Indeed 'Rousseau's savage man was truly an orangutan' (Wokler 1978: 117). Rousseau believed that explorers had given proof of the links between 'Man' and animals in their memoirs, although they had not entirely realised that the animals 'were in fact real savage men . . . still found in the primitive state of nature' (Rousseau 1984: 155). Rousseau supported his thesis with a number of accounts of the relationships which orang-utans and some other animals had allegedly had with humans. Apparently, in 'the forests of Mayomba in the Kingdom of Loango', the fruit- and nut-eating pongos often sat in a quiet circle around a fire left by humans, whilst in the Congo they frequently raped women and girls (Rousseau did not seem to realise that sexual assault is not very peaceable). One orang-utan was known to have drunk from a pot: 'Afterwards it wiped its lips politely. It lay down to sleep, its head on a pillow, covering itself with so much grace that one would take it for a man in bed' (Rousseau 1984: 156). The rather relaxed language implies that Rousseau was quite unconcerned about the degree of similitude between humans and animals. The similarities were things of amazement, not abhorrence. Moreover, because Rousseau believed that the taxonomic and organic links had only been hidden by social pretensions, he was implicitly suggesting that we should try to become more like orang-utans. He created the possibility that we should give up meat-eating and violence if we want to live truly. 'Man' is not special any more.

Indeed, if the orang-utan was a human in a pure state of nature, if humanity was a difference of degree and education rather than kind, it was also possible for humans to be like animals if they had remained outside society. Richard Martin might have sympathised with the idea a little, but where his natural human was Hobbes's murderous beast, Rousseau's was a gentle innocent; a beast we should approach rather than annihilate. The possibility was not accepted kindly. In the 1760s some joker wrote a letter and signed it: 'ROUSSEAU, jusqu'à ce jour . . . Citoyen de Genève, mais à présent, ORANG-OUTANG' (quoted in Wokler 1978: 114). However, Lord Monboddo did champion Rousseau's insight in Britain, and tried to confirm it.

Like Rousseau, Monboddo believed that humans in the state of nature are mere animals. The orang-utan was a surviving relic of 'Man' before the development of society. Rousseau relied on hearsay and speculation to develop his idea of the Noble Savage, but Monboddo believed that he had actually spoken to one who lived on a farm near Berkhampsted. In June 1782, Monboddo met Peter the Wild Boy, who was then about 70 years old. Evidently, Peter had been found by George I on a hunting expedition in Germany, brought over to England, and given a King's pension. Peter had been sent to school but could only say his own name and 'King George'. Monboddo thought that Peter was a living anomaly, after all: 'His face is not at all ugly or disagreeable; and he has a look that may be called sensible and sagacious for a savage' (Monboddo 1785: 113). In 1751 Peter had wandered away from the farm and somehow ended up in Norwich prison as a vagrant. On 27 October, the prison burned down. Peter's behaviour caused some astonishment; he did not try to run away but just stared at the blaze. Had someone not come to rescue him he 'would probably have perished like a horse in the flames'. The incredulity towards fire merely proved that 'he seems to be more of the Ouran Outang species than of the human' (*Gentleman's Magazine*, vol. 21, November 1751: 522).

Monboddo thought that Peter straddled the human and the animal in more than just behaviour. Peter's diet and moral goodness were also natural.

> He never was mischievous, but had always that gentleness of nature which I hold to be characteristical of our nature, at least till we become carnivorous, and hunters or warriors. He feeds at present as the farmer and his wife do; but . . . when he first came to Hertfordshire . . . he then fed very much

upon the leaves of cabbage which he eat [*sic*] raw. He was
then . . . about fifteen years of age, walked upright, but could
climb trees like a squirrel.

(Monboddo 1785: 113)

Peter was somewhere between a meat-eating human warrior and
a cabbage chewing man-squirrel. Monboddo decided that Peter
was a human, and indeed asserted that all the other 'savages' found
in Europe since the Middle Ages were as well. Monboddo also said
that Peter was not an idiot; his lack of speech was simply due to the
fact that he had not needed to talk because he had not lived with
other people during the years of language learning. He was not
mentally incapable. The same was true of Peter's posture.
Although Peter now walked upright, he only did so because he had
copied other humans. When he was alone in the forest, Peter used
all fours. Peter was a person who had not been made social. For
Monboddo, as indeed for Rousseau, he was an indication of
humans' true, natural goodness which is indivisible from a warm
animality.

Peter had not been taught to be human. Even in his old age he
was fit, healthy, and fearless. But if Peter was outside of society and
therefore an animal, what would happen if the most human
animals were socialised? Monboddo thought he knew. A good and
patient teacher 'could have taught the Oran Outan in Sir Ashton
Lever's collection, who learned to articulate a few words, so as to
speak plainly enough' (Monboddo 1785: 114). 'Man' and beast are
seen in exactly the same light. The only difference is how society
has changed our good, natural behaviour into something
questionable and worrying. Although Peter was a member of the
human species, he had no more privilege than a caged ape. Peter
died in 1785, and was still treated by most people as rather less
than a real and proper human. His obituary notice treated him as
a mere oddity, and ended with the recollection that 'A half-length
figure of him was for many years exhibited at Mrs Salmon's in
Fleet-street' (*Gentleman's Magazine*, 55, March 1785: 236). Mrs
Salmon probably dusted the figure down and gave it pride of place
in the window.

Animals and 'Man' were taxonomically similar things and
understood in much the same way. Jean-Jacques Rousseau had
managed to undermine any appeals for human uniqueness, but it

129

was the very 'Man' Rousseau who was saying this. All human privilege had been denied, but humans still had to be different enough to be able to deny it. Rousseau's position edges into the other figure of 'Man' when it argues that humans perceive natural similitude to animals through an awareness of difference: 'The savage, living among the animals and placed from an early stage where he has to measure himself against them, soon makes the comparison' (Rousseau 1984: 87). Lévi-Strauss saw a great deal of insight in this sentence when he argued that humans use animals to think their humanity (see Lévi-Strauss 1966). Perceptual blurring is made the stuff of a distinction; humans might perceive shared animality but they also see the human species as a separate group within all animals. Rousseau drew parallels between human and animal bodies as living organisms 'which nature has given senses', but believed humans to be slightly different: 'man participates in his own actions in his capacity as a free agent. The beast chooses or rejects by instinct, man by an act of freewill' (Rousseau 1984: 87).

So, humans possess innate freewill which can be employed to the end of self-improvement, and can therefore choose to make animals a basis for the definition of human being. Naturally, the differences between species are morally irrelevant. The bestowal of meaning only happens when 'Man' begins to take advantage of freewill and creates fictitious moral attributes, which define who or what should be treated as other. Rousseau sadly confessed that only humans are able to choose who is the same and who is the other. The orang-utans of the Congo were 'Men' in the state of nature who had not had the opportunities to develop their potential for language and progress. They knew no false morality nor bounds to their compassion. They still lived a natural life, whereas Western Europe had travelled along a path of ironic improvement.

The quest for progress, the consolidation of 'Man's' separate society, has caused only inequality and an avoidance of the natural law. Since humans are naturally passive and gentle, any other treatment of animals must be a contradiction of our true being. Natural law relies on a general knowledge of organic life and runs alongside the argument that humans' natural diet is entirely frugivorous. Rousseau tells us that the Noble Savage would never harm a creature except where self-preservation was at stake, because natural compassion extends to all life. Humans are naturally compassionate and only forget duties towards animals if they have been made selfish by society:

> By these means, we can put an end to the age-old dispute as to whether natural law applies to animals, for while it is clear that animals, being devoid of intellect and free-will, cannot recognize this law, yet by reason of the fact that they share, so to speak, in our nature by virtue of the sensitivity with which they are endowed, it follows that animals ought to have a share in natural right, and that men are bound by a certain form of duty towards them. It seems, in fact, that if I am obliged to refrain from doing any harm to my neighbour, it is less because he is a reasonable being than because he is a sentient one; and a quality which is common to beast and man ought to give the former the right not to be uselessly ill-treated by the latter.
>
> (Rousseau 1984: 71)

Natural law establishes individual duties towards animals. If only we try to clarify the sentiments which social definitions of otherness have distorted, we will find a 'natural aversion to seeing any other sentient being perish or suffer' (Rousseau 1984: 70). Humans must accept similitude with animals; anything else is a mendacious weakening of organic life. Similitude establishes the principle that 'the perceiving animal identifies itself more intimately with the suffering animal. Now it is clear that this identification must have been infinitely closer in the state of nature than in the state of reason' (Rousseau 1984: 101). We do not pity animals precisely because we are social; if we lived a natural life we would treat animals naturally.

These are the main themes of the Demand for Similitude. Whereas the Demand for Difference presupposed the uniqueness of 'Man' and only looked at organic structures as objects of knowledge, the Demand for Similitude involves a thorough critique of the apparent world. It rejected both the importance of classification by appearance, and the position that society produces truth. Moreover, where the case for Difference required attempts by some social groups forcibly to change others in a project of total social reform from above, the Demand for Similitude led to other goals. Rousseau wants us to take off the suffocation of society and breathe the fresh air of natural law and natural diet. He wanted 'Man' to be true to nature and thereby be true to 'him'self: 'the savage lives within himself; social man lives always outside himself; he knows how to live only in the opinion of others' (Rousseau 1984: 136). The individual who tries to regain the glorious state of nature would not care at all for the scorn or contempt of the privileged social humans who are only concerned with their standing in the eyes of everyone else. Rousseau seems to say that it is good, because it is natural, to go against the requirements and allegiances of society. In particular it is right that we should be compassionate towards animals and accept that we and they are really much the same. Human difference (freewill and the capacity for self-improvement) has only caused a decay of life. The goal was not to simply demolish society and start again at Year Zero. Whilst the individual should aim to be true in relationships with all organic beings, the social project of the *Discourse on Inequality* was rather more dramatic. It involved a political revolution which would realign existing civilisation with the natural law: 'For it is manifestly contrary to the laws of nature . . . that a handful of people should gorge themselves with superfluities while the hungry multitude goes in want of necessities' (Rousseau 1984: 137).

Rousseau's hints that the relationships between animals and society should be shaped by a moral recognition of organic similitude, and their association with a revolutionary political agenda which would have horrified the protagonists of the Demand for Difference were taken up avidly in Britain.

Joseph Ritson was born in Stockton in 1752 and died in London in 1803. He was a barrister, collector of ballads, author, and enthusiast for the French Revolution. He was also quite exceptionally bad tempered and notorious for his pedantic attention to detail. Ritson rarely did things half-heartedly. After visiting France in 1791 he insisted on being called Citizen Ritson, became an atheist and, in 1793, set himself apart from nearly everyone else in Britain by adopting the Republican calendar. During the 1780s he developed a very idiosyncratic and erratic method of spelling which seems to defy any logical consistency (Lee 1896: 328). Unlike Rousseau, he also practised what he preached. Ritson agreed that 'Man' in the state of nature was frugivorous, and so he gave up meat: 'To this depressing diet he adhered, in the face of much ridicule, until death, and it was doubtless in part responsible for the moroseness of temper which characterised his later years' (Lee 1896: 327–8). Ritson's arguments are contained in his 1802 book, *An Essay on Abstinence from Animal Food, as a Moral Duty*. It owes obvious debts to 'the sensible and eloquent Rousseau' (Ritson 1802: 26).

It has been said that the *Essay* 'bears marks of incipient insanity' (Lee 1896: 330). Ritson hoped to prove the physical and social need for a vegetable-based diet. Although his discussion often complemented Rousseau's, Ritson relied on a remarkably differ-ent method of enquiry. Rousseau never pretended that his state of nature was anything more than an ideal invention with little historical accuracy. He denied any biblical notion that 'Man' was a Noble Savage before the Flood, and openly told his readers that 'One must not take the kind of research which we enter into as the pursuit of the truths of history, but solely as hypothetical and conditional reasonings' (Rousseau 1984: 78). Not surprisingly then, all the talk of orang-utans tended to be restricted to notes and kept away from the main story of the *Discourse*. Rousseau offered a hypothetical history which made it easy to criticise the present. Ritson's method was very different, and emphasised the evidence which Rousseau made into footnotes. Ritson believed that the diaries and memoirs of explorers contained accounts of humans who still lived in the state of nature, and he compared them all in a cross-cultural, anthropological method. The Demand for Difference played an important part in attempts to construct an English identity which might justify imperialism, but Ritson made the Demand for Similitude into a taxonomy which had no place for special identities. England was not the home of unique 'Man'. It was just one place amongst many others where people happened to live and deal with animals. All is the same, nowhere is different.

Joseph Ritson opened his argument with the suggestion that 'Man . . . in a state of nature, was, if not the real orang-utan of the forests and mountains of Asia or Africa at the present day, at least, an animal of the same family, and very nearly resembleing it' (Ritson 1802: 13–14; this passage and all the others from Ritson keep the original spelling). He supported the claim by mentioning many cases of orang-utans being mistaken for humans (Ritson 1802: 18–19) and blurred any immutable human-animal distinctions even more when he spoke of the human children like Peter who had been raised by animals (Ritson 1802: 22–5). The point was obvious. Humans and animals are essentially the same, and similitude is only hidden by movement away from the state of nature into society.

Ritson made the taxonomic case which Rousseau had also mentioned, that 'It seems . . . that, the teeth and intestines of man being like those of frugivorous animals, he should, naturally, be ranged in this class' (Ritson 1802: 41). 'Man' outside of society is comparable to an orang-utan, and therefore humans' natural state must be like that of the apes. Because orang-utans are neither cruel nor meat-eaters, humans should not be so either. Ritson combined organic structure and empirical observation to undermine the claims for classificatory primacy which could be based on merely physical distinctions. Visible privileges were utterly trivial, since all living creatures were more importantly 'participateing of feeling, of seeing, of hearing, of imagination and of intellection, which each of them hath received from nature for the acquireing of what is agreeable to it, and the avoiding of what is disagreeable' (Ritson 1802: 94).

Ritson went so far as to imply that the only things Europeans did represent was decay and illness. He compared the inhabitants of the urbanised parts of Europe to the people who lived in other cultures, and concluded that the greatest enthusiasts of social progress and knowledge were physically the weakest. And the cause of their bodily decay? Contempt for the healthy, natural, vegetable diet which remained central to eating elsewhere. Indeed, the high infant mortality rate in London was solely due to the corruption of health caused by meat-eating (Ritson 1802: 147). Ritson was saying that the degree of human society can be measured by what is eaten; the more meat, the less natural; the less vegetable, the more social. Consequently, the most socialised classes should also be the least natural. There is an interesting coincidence with the Demand for Difference, although the arguments quickly move apart again. Richard Martin would have agreed that he and the other members of the urban bourgeoisie were detached from anything natural, but where the knowledgeable legislators of Difference were proud of their entirely social existence, Ritson repudiated it. What Difference saw as good, Similitude denounced as bad. As Ritson said in a passage which again pushes humanity into the multitude of animals:

> It is, in fact, perfectly ridiculous and absurd to pretend that
> animal food is absolutely necessary for the support of so
> comparatively diminished and feeble a being as man, while
> the largeëst, strongest, and most powerful, which require
> sustenance in proportion to their bulk and vigour, the horse,
> the bul, the camel . . . are supported entirely by vegetable
> substanceës.
>
> (Ritson 1802: 81–2)

Meat-eating was responsible for far more than just physical ruin.
It also led to mental illness. Dr Cheyne had proved to Ritson's
satisfaction that 'real lunacy, madness, and a disorder'd brain, can
possiblely be accounted for from no other natural cause but a meat
regimen of diet' (Ritson 1802: 159; for more about Cheyne, see
Turner 1984).

Ritson blamed meat for everything. All cruelty and injustice
began when 'Man' was arrogant enough to try to hide similitude
with animals. 'The slave trade, that abominable violation of the
rights of nature, is, most probablely, oweing to the same cause; as
wel as a variety of violent acts, both rational and personal, which
are usually attributeëd to other motives' (Ritson 1802: 89). The
consumption of meat is so incompatible with our morally good
organic structure, that it inflames any aggressive passions and can
ultimately lead to cannibalism (Ritson 1802: 124). The Demand
for Difference would have either defended the slave trade on the
grounds that blacks are inadequate humans, or condemned it
through claims for moral enfranchisement. Ritson followed a
more basic path. Slavery, as well as murders and wars, only happen
because civilised humans started to eat meat; therefore they can
only stop if we all stick to a vegetable diet. He seems to be saying
that eating animals is illicit consubstantiality; it is a pollution of
human being and can only cause dirty and profane behaviour. One
kind of dirtiness is cruelty to animals. We should be kind towards
them, firstly because the vegetable diet makes us passive, and
secondly because of natural similitude:

> As the use of animal flesh makes man cruel and barbarous,
> and to take delight in pain and torture, whence the fondness
> of the Romans for the shews of fighting gladiators, and

wild-beasts, the Spaniards and Portuguese, for their
bul-feasts, their inquisition, and *auto da fè*, the Neapolitan for
his *fiesta da cocagna*, and the Engleishman for his bul- and
bear-baitings, his cock-fights, his boxing matches, his
pleasures of the chase &c. so the abstinence from that habit
has an immediate tendency to soften the manners, and
dispose the mind to receive uncommon satisfaction from the
exercise of gentleness and humanity toward the minuteëst
objects of creation.

(Ritson 1802: 206)

This passage tips over everything which the Demand for
Difference took for granted. The kind heart is now nourished by
leeks and swedes rather than legislation and surveillance. The
proper human is the person who lives a natural life shaped by
obligations of organic structure, not urban politics.

Ever since Hogarth had created the story of Tom Nero, it was
widely accepted that violence to animals led to violence towards
humans, and Ritson agreed. But where Hogarth blamed the
existence of Nero on the insufficient enforcement of social regulation, Ritson cursed the meat which hardened and corrupted
humanity. He even suggested that the fox-hunters and
partridge-shooters would be keen to start hunting 'poor people for
their pleasure', if there was not a law to stop them. After all, the
Dutch hunted Hottentots in South Africa, and the extermination
of the Aborigines in Australia by the British colonists would have
only proved Ritson's claim (Ritson 1802: 234). According to the
Demand for Difference, society makes us human and humane. For
the Demand for Similitude, society makes us brutish murderers.
Cruelty to animals is no longer an offence against social sensibilities; it is a crime against nature, justice, and 'a feeling and
reflective mind' (Ritson 1802: 88).

Joseph Ritson believed that a return to the natural vegetable
diet would be totally beneficial. It would make us more healthy,
and make our relationships with other people and animals far less
aggressive. It would put us back in touch with true human being.
All we need do is recognise that we cannot hide from the compulsions of organic structure any more than horses or hares can. A
turn to the state of nature would create kinder, gentler people who
would respect the similitude of all life. The knowledgeable

bourgeoisie wanted to make the urban working class more like itself. Ritson ignored intra-social relations and, instead, wanted each individual to play a part in reconciling human life with its anthropological basis.

The argument was not very popular, and Ritson's essay stimulated a lively debate in the *Gentleman's Magazine*. One correspondent said that the book 'contains the greatest mixture of blasphemy and nonsense I have ever seen' (Censorinus 1803: 915). Another was more magnificently angry:

> Perceiving that Mr Ritson's eccentric, if not absurd, publication, condemning the use of animal food, has been made more attention to in your . . . Magazine than, probably, most of your readers will be of opinion such a work deserved . . . I must observe, that this newly broached doctrine, or rather this old one attempted to be new revived, proves the author to be as ignorant of Nature, as he is deficient in argument. . . . [I]f these animals were permitted to increase *ad infinitum*, their necessary consumption of vegetable food must be so great as not to leave this slender-witted would-be reformer even a cabbage, to enable him to put forth his silly lucubrations.
>
> (RER 1804: 297–8)

Clearly, this correspondent was writing across the ambiguities of 'Man'. He thought it was silly that a human being should be made so radically like animals. Even one of Ritson's supporters, who quoted the *Essay* in his own book, felt that although the case for kindness to animals was good 'Mr R's book contained many things of a less defensible nature with respect to moral opinions' (Pratt 1803: 1030).

The correspondent charged that Ritson was trying to revive an old set of ideas. He was right. Many passages in Ritson's essay are similar to the views of Pythagoras and Plutarch, and of course Rousseau was also fond of Plutarch. Pythagoras and Plutarch wrote in the Neoplatonist tradition that all animate beings possess a soul which is one individual moment of a universal One. All life was linked through the spirit regardless of biology. Since the soul is universal, it can exist in any physical form and, indeed, the Neoplatonists believed that it transmigrated from human to animal bodies (see Wallis 1972). Now, this idea can have an impact on the way society treats animals. If all life is linked by the One, and if the spirit is prior to any individual, then it must be the case that there is a right way of life. In particular, if all humans and animals are always and already metaphysically identical, there is a case for meat avoidance and compassion. If we are cruel to animals, or eat them, how can we be sure that the soul we are harming is not that of one of our close relatives? Plutarch made it clear that the need to avoid animals either as meat or things to hit was rooted in the taxonomic difficulties created by the universal spirit. He also made it plain that social behaviour is a terrible movement away from nature:

> at the beginning it was some wild and harmful animal that was eaten, then a bird or fish that had its flesh torn. And so when our murderous instincts had tasted blood and grew practised on wild animals, they advanced to the labouring ox and the well behaved sheep and the house-warding cock; thus little by little giving a hard edge to our insatiable appetite, we have advanced to wars and the slaughter and murder of human beings. Yet if someone once demonstrates that souls in their rebirths make use of common bodies and that what is now wild becomes tame, and that Nature changes everything and assigns new dwellings . . . will not this deter the unruly element in those who have adopted the doctrine from implanting disease and indigestion in our bodies and perverting our souls to an ever more cruel lawlessness?
>
> (Plutarch 1957: 573)

Ritson replaced Plutarch's metaphysics with modern organic structure but the similarities between their stories are quite noticeable.

Plutarch was using a number of ideas which Ovid had attributed to Pythagoras, and indeed, perhaps Pythagoras should be seen as the founding voice of Neoplatonist appeals for meat avoidance and kindness to animals. Whereas Plutarch put a great deal of emphasis on the universal spirit, Pythagoras used a more metaphorical line of argument. He saw a direct analogy between the world's changing geography and the physical forms taken by the spirit. The sea had often changed the shape of the land, and, consequently, Pythagoras thought it reasonable to assume that the physical features of the human soul could change from one form to another. In particular, Pythagoras asserted that it was quite likely that animals were nothing other than the present physical form adopted by deceased loved ones. He believed that this possibility of transmigration meant that we should treat animals in much the same way as we would treat our brothers, sisters, or parents. Certainly, we should not eat them (see Pythagoras in Ovid 1986: 365). It seems that when he extended these claims into a different treatment of animals, Pythagoras was treading new ground. Ovid suggests that Pythagoras was the first thinker in the Hellenic world to advocate a ban on meat. Pythagoras had a profound effect on early nineteenth century Romanticism and people like Ritson called themselves followers of the 'Pythagorian system'.

The poet Shelley was another leading exponent of the system. He had also been influenced by Ritson (for Shelley's debt to Ritson, see Clark 1939). Shelley combined Ritson and the ancients with Romanticism. Modern classification at least in part denigrates nature; it is seen as something which has little or no place in the proper affairs of women and men, unless it is behind a cage or tamed like some Italian garden. The Romantic attitude was rather different. It saw nature as a thing of beauty and inspiration. The places where many of the poets chose to live provide clues to the Romantic response to nature. They went to the Lake District or, like Blake later on, left the city to live in a quiet village. The poets and painters believed that nature could deepen and enrich their human being, rather than undermine it. Perhaps the Rousseau we have met was a Romantic before his time, but Ritson was obviously writing in these terms, and so was Shelley.

Shelley put forward his ideas in two essays, *A Vindication of Natural Diet*, and the *Essay on the Vegetable System of Diet* (both in Shelley 1954). Now, where Ritson opposed the state of nature to civilisation through cross-cultural comparisons, and Rousseau said that the state of nature was a hypothetical historical origin, Shelley turned to mythology. His starting point was lifted from the earlier writers. In the state of nature, humans are peaceful and healthy, and only eat vegetables, fruit, and nuts. Shelley also confirmed that 'Man resembles no carnivorous animal', and went on to draw links between the structure of the human organism and orang-utans (Shelley 1954: 84). It was utterly obvious to Shelley that what is natural must be good, and that any move away from what it dictated must be bad:

> I hold that the depravity of the physical and moral nature of
> man originated in his unnatural habits of life . . . The
> language spoken . . . by the mythology of nearly all religions
> seems to prove that at some distant period man forsook the
> path of nature and sacrificed the purity and happiness of his
> being to unnatural appetites . . . The allegory of Adam and
> Eve eating of the tree of evil, and entailing upon their
> posterity the wrath of God and the loss of everlasting life,
> admits of no other explanation than the disease and crime
> that have flowed from unnatural diet.
>
> (Shelley 1954: 81–2)

The language is similar to theology, which is rather ironic since
Shelley was a professed atheist. He identified some golden age in
the past when humans were happy because they were pure. In
contrast, modern social life is typified by illness and discontent.

Had Adam and Eve not eaten the forbidden fruit, all might still
be well. 'Man' further lost touch with the benevolent dictates of
organic structure when fire was discovered and used for cooking.
Shelley found the effects of cooking in the legend of Prometheus,
who was doomed to torture and torment. The myth told Shelley
that the movement away from natural, raw food brought only
decay, because it made meat a cultural product:

> From this moment his vitals were devoured by the vulture of
> disease. It consumed his being in every shape of its loathsome
> and infinite variety, inducing the soul-quelling sinkings of
> premature and violent death. All vice arose from the ruin of
> healthful innocence.
>
> (Shelley 1954: 82–3)

Or, as Shelley might have said, but Gore Vidal actually did:
'Prometheus stole fire from Heaven so that we could not only cook
dinner but one another' (Vidal 1989: 30). Shelley's argument
followed Ritson (and John Newton's *Return to Nature, or Defence of
Vegetable Regimen*). He believed that the roots of all social problems
led back to the socialised diet of cooked meat, which contradicts
humans' natural goodness and physical constitution. After all,
meat is something that can only be gained violently. The
identification of meat as the source of evil strongly implied an
abstinence from it. The individual had a duty 'resolutely to break

this unnatural practice thus pregnant with inexhaustible calamity' (Shelley 1954: 95). Shelley made the connection between individual illness and social difficulties quite plain with his sweeping definition of 'vice' as disease, violence, death, and also 'Tyranny, superstition, commerce, and inequality' (Shelley 1954: 83).

Although Shelley was worried about the treatment of animals, the grounds of the concern were a little muddy. The protagonists of the Demand for Difference, and for that matter most of the supporters of the Demand for Similitude, broadly agreed that cruelty was wrong because it did something to humanity. The cruel person either threatened society or ignored the natural law. Animals were relevant, if only because certain things should not be done to them. Shelley did not even give animals this marginal place; he merely pointed out that if meat is unnatural and causes illness, then any treatment of animals which is not totally natural is a waste of time (Shelley 1954: 94). Throughout the essays, Shelley says next to nothing about animals. He wanted to show how much 'Man' is tied up in a natural system of similitude, only to prove that 'Man' has become horribly different, but can be different again if society and its customs are transformed. The vegetable diet, which includes teetotalism, 'strikes at the very root of evil', because 'the use of animal foods and fermented liquors directly militates with . . . equality of the rights of man. The peasant cannot gratify these fashionable cravings without leaving his family to starve' (Shelley 1954: 88). The tricolour should be the shades of the cabbage patch.

The politically revolutionary aspects of the state of nature and the Noble Savage could end up as quietude. They could easily lead to a withdrawal from social life rather than a newly moral participation in it. This is precisely what happened to Henry David Thoreau. Without doubt, ideas of a golden age and Noble Savages were high in Thoreau's mind when he built his house at Walden and started to live simply. During the attempt to make himself a living example of the pre-social innocent, Thoreau came to the conclusion that meat-eating made happiness quite impossible:

> The repugnance to animal food is not the effect of
> experience, but is an instinct. It appeared more beautiful to
> live low and fare hard in many respects . . . I believe that

every man who has ever been earnest to preserve his higher
or poetic faculties in the best condition has been particularly
inclined to abstain from animal food, and from much food of
any kind.

(Thoreau 1981: 264)

Notice how Thoreau said it is possible to get in touch with the
more creative aspects of human being. He had no faith at all in
knowledge. Instead he asserted that meat is *instinctually*
repugnant. In other words, humans know nature through
participation in it, not abstract, social observation. Also, the
Rousseauian-Romantic point that nature is morally good had been
expanded so that nature and a proper diet help develop aesthetic
abilities. A vegetable diet makes us more than just healthy; it
makes us poetic and beautiful. The full potential of the happy,
natural individual can only be realised if the intellectually
deadening effects of dead food are removed.

Richard Wagner told a similar story, although he added a nasty
anti-Semitic edge. According to the state of nature tradition as it
has been encountered so far, ill health and violence are the fault of
all civilisation. All societies everywhere are blamed for the decline
of human nobility. Wagner blamed Judaism: 'The Jewish tribal
god found Abel's fated lamb more savoury than Cain's offering of
the produce of the field'. Apparently, the Last Supper was a
vegetarian ceremony, and 'It is more than doubtful if Jesus himself
was of Jewish extraction'. Wagner did however believe that
humanity could be regenerated. Thoreau just went to Walden for
a couple of years; Wagner wanted to develop an art (his art) which
would reveal the causes of decay, and he tried to develop his own
creativity by giving up meat. He also preached extermination of
the Jews (Watson 1979: 301–2). It is more than a little ironic that
many of the people who followed the 'Master's' appeal for the
'bloodless diet' were themselves born Jews, most notably Gustav
Mahler (Lebrecht 1987: 26–9).

Something might have become obvious in the discussion of the
Demand for Similitude. None of the enthusiasts of the natural,
vegetable diet used the word 'vegetarian'. The reason is simple.
The word did not exist before 1842 and was not in wide use until
the British Vegetarian Society was formed at Northwood Villa, a
Ramsgate nursing home, in September 1847 (Twigg 1981: 66).

Vegetarianism was not only a negative refusal to eat meat. It was also a positive attempt to uphold the moral goodness of nature. Vegetarianism is about the life of all beings, as the very word indicates. Most people probably think that 'vegetarian' is derived from 'vegetable-arian'; that is, they think it means a person who eats plants. They are wrong. The word was deliberately coined from the Latin *vegetus* which means whole, sound, fresh, and lively. Vegetarianism has always involved a concern with natural well-being and health. It has never really been about carrots and turnips at all (Wynne-Tyson 1979: 10). Vegetarians only give up the flesh of animals, but vegans go a stage further and also try to do without eggs, animal milk, cheese, and butter. The word 'vegan' simply comes from the 'veg' and 'an' at the beginning and end of 'vegetarian' (Wynne-Tyson 1979: 107). Veganism believes that vegetarianism does not go far enough. If it is wrong to eat meat, if human are frugivorous organic beings, then it must also be unnatural to eat any produce which comes from animals. Both diets are codifications of points raised by Pythagoras and Plutarch, but largely reinvented by Rousseau.

The Demand for Similitude contains a fascinating semiology of food which bestrides the ambiguities of 'Man'. It is a fair assumption that the bourgeois supporters of the Demand for Difference were great meat-eaters, and as Mary Douglas points out, meat must be 'transformed from a living creature into a food item' (Douglas 1975: 271). In urban societies, the transformation of nature into culture is a relatively simple task. People like Erskine and Richard Martin, and the founders of the RSPCA, would have rarely seen the animals they were going to eat. Although there were a number of slaughterhouses in towns and cities, they tended to be in special areas. For example, the meat for London came from Smithfield Market, where animals were already reified into commodities: it was a single place which could be easily avoided. The Demand for Difference had two visions of food animals: as nature in a field or as lumps of meat. However, the meat's status as a cultural product is reinforced through cooking. The preparation of food proves that we are humans and not animals. Animals tear their meat, we cut it with a knife and fork. Animals drink blood, we drink Beaujolais. The very fact that the great culinary symbol of English national identity, roast beef, is *roast* is not coincidental. The beef is not saying, 'The English are degenerate animals who eat meat'. It is communicating the idea that 'The English are real "Men" who can tame and digest the power of an ox'. There is a social dimension to this. The bourgeoisie could eat as much meat as it wanted, but the working class would have to be watched because, as Andrew Ure put it, the workers might 'pamper themselves into nervous disorders by a diet too rich and exciting' (quoted in Twigg 1983: 25). Meat could inflame their beastly passions. The Demand for Difference suggests that flesh equals life, meat equals strength, and cooked meat equals the socialisation of nature. Consequently, the English are highly social and extremely strong because they eat so much meat (and vegetarianism is tantamount to treachery; also, remember the quotation from Orwell at the beginning of Chapter 2). It is worth considering the traditional English contempt for 'mucked-up foreign food' in this way. One of the main virtues which attaches to English cooking is its simplicity. All we do is *roast* beef and so we take in the full strength of the animal in a cultural and yet undiluted form. Meanwhile, the French are notorious for adding complicated sauces to their food. They diminish the strength of the animal and, as any good Francophobe knows, the French are absurdly effeminate.

The semiotics of the Demand for Similitude could not be more different. It is contained in Ritson, Shelley, and the concept of vegetarianism, where meat is anything but a sign of strength. They saw meat as the signification of degeneration exactly because it was social. The case for Similitude suggests that cooked meat is a uniquely social food; it is taken out of nature and can therefore only be decaying. In the Demand for Difference, humans eat meat and appropriate a new life. Those who can afford to eat most meat are the most social and therefore the most human; the meat-eater is humane. The cooked is good because it is social, the raw is bad since it remains natural. In the Demand for Similitude, if we eat meat we only take death into ourselves. Vegetables are the organically proper diet and therefore healthy. Vegetables signify a double life; the life they demonstrated as they grew (whereas meat is taken from dead animals), and the life they give humans. As such, the individuals who are most human and most in touch with humane sensibilities will be the ones who eat the most natural and least socialised diet. The raw is good because it is natural, the cooked is bad since it is social. Perhaps the way these contending meanings of food are rooted in the problem of 'Man' can explain their mutual hostility. It might explain why Joseph Ritson's madness was put down to his vegetable diet, and why the strength of so many boxers is due to their mythical fondness for steak. After attending a Vegetarian Society conference, a meat-eating reporter once made a comment which contains most of the contradictory significations:

> It is irrational and unacceptable, but most of us attribute to people the qualities of what they eat. Just as vegetarians must have thought me 'tainted' – yellow toothed and intangibly dirty, so I watched them for signs of 'zestlessness' – for sagging thighs and weak chins. In fact, for the most part they looked very healthy.
>
> (Mitchison 1987: 11)

And why shouldn't they? The passage shows the mutual incomprehension which arises across the face of 'Man'. It is impossible to answer conclusively whether our lives should be social and cooked or natural and raw.

But who were the protagonists of the Demand for Similitude? From what places in late eighteenth- and early nineteenth-century Britain did the argument appear? Some clues are provided by the Vegetarian Society. In the first years after its formation, the Society was led by members of the Bible Christian church and liberal manufacturers. Most of the members belonged to the labour aristocracy of the northern industrial cities who also had close links with the teetotal movement (Twigg 1981: 84–8). Perhaps the most significant aspect of the Vegetarian Society's membership was its overwhelmingly urban nature. Vegetarianism was a city-based attempt to turn away from the looseness of urban and social existence (Twigg 1981: 92). The workers' vegetarianism was part of a tradition of body management which tried to make them better machine operatives, and more respectable (bourgeois) members of society. Their interests should not be stressed too much, and caution should be taken over the expansion of vegetarian evidence to explain all attempts to moralise relationships between society and animals on the grounds of Similitude. Arguably, a greater clue to the social origins of the Demand is given in the biographies of Rousseau, Ritson, Shelley, and Thoreau. They were all intellectuals who had turned their backs on urban life and become social outsiders. Although they were tapping a rich vein in modern classification when they tried to prove a deep congruity between 'Man' and animals, they tended to operate at some remove from the individuals and society they were trying to change. 'It is in the country that one learns to love and serve humanity; one only learns to despise it in cities' (Rousseau 1931: 107). They were people with a highly individuated sense of self, which they felt was only constrained and destroyed by society. They were individuals with a developed sense of difference from existing 'Man'. Rousseau is the classic example; the *Confessions* only really existed in order to demonstrate that the author was a person quite unlike any other.

The Demand for Similitude was originally developed by people who who were so unwilling to live the urban, social life expected of them that they declared they would rather be like animals. They set themselves up as natural and pure taxonomic legislators, and turned society into a pollution and a taboo. The working class could play no great part in this because it had been fully socialised or demoralised; the respectable vegetarian workers were only trying to improve their lot as socially reputable workers. The bourgeoisie merely laughed at the absurdities of 'little Jean-Jacques' and his followers. The Demand for Similitude might well be a valid classification in so far as 'Man' rests on shaky foundations, but it was developed by people who wanted little to do with urban life. It was the concern of consciously interstitial individuals with a firm awareness of self. Contemporary animal rights still is.

Chapter Seven

A COMPREHENSIVE PRINCIPLE

What is it to be human? If it was possible to answer the question with some degree of certainty, it might also be possible to know what the relationships between animals and society should really be like. The many fine and fraught attempts to establish the truth of our being beyond any doubt have only caused suspicion and disbelief. They have turned out to be little more than partial resolutions of the matter. After all, the political and moral legislators encountered so far were only saying: 'Everyone should be like me. I am the paragon of virtue'. They thought that the less-than-human pariahs either had to be coerced by social discipline, or cajoled into a return to all that was meant to be natural. The paragons either ate vast amounts of meat, or they ate none at all. The two approaches to human being were utterly different, and it is no great surprise that although Granger and Rousseau, Martin and Ritson, all wanted to improve 'Man' by preaching humanity, they tended to talk past one another, and ignore any shared worries. It is highly improbable that an enthusiast for Ritson and Shelley's vegetable diet would have belonged to the Society for the Prevention of Cruelty to Animals, just as Richard Martin openly admitted that he could see no connections between working-class bull-baiting and bourgeois hunting.

The contradictory truths derived legitimacy from their social positions. The people who said that humans are similar to animals were a loose group of intellectuals who had tried to cut themselves off from the falsities and corruptions of urban life. Meanwhile, the argument that humanity must be imposed was the concern of the bourgeoisie, which established urbanised social life as the true domain of the human. The ideas were also popularised in different ways. Whereas the interstitial intellectuals relied on the impact of their writing (Shelley had announced that poets were the new legislators), the bourgeoisie created organisations which could police and condemn the behaviour of other social groups, and particularly the beastliness of the urban working class. The Demand for Similitude said that it was impossible for 'Man' to live properly in society; the Demand for Difference declared that 'Man' could not live without it. The two Demands were hostile towards each other and mutually uncomprehending. Richard Martin would have been bewildered by Shelley's eating habits in much the same way that Ritson was stunned by pheasant-shooting. Any relationships with animals which happened on the other side of the taxonomic, social, and political divide of 'Man' were repudiated as backsliding from the duties of being human.

Although the philosophers and politicians would deny it, there is not, and neither can there be, one all-inclusive relationship with animals. That is impossible whilst society is divided and 'Man' is unstable. And since society is still divided, and because we still do not really know who 'Man' is, the Demands for Difference and Similitude are of more than historical interest. Although they developed in the eighteenth and nineteenth centuries, they continue to have an absolutely fundamental influence on the treatment of animals today. Contemporary attitudes towards animals share a modernity with the two Demands. Everything that is done to animals, and everything it is said should or should not be done, is prefigured in their debates – everything, that is, except for one very important relationship with animals: the idea of animal rights, which did not appear until the late nineteenth century.

Although the protagonists of the Demands would have admitted that not everyone agreed with them, any opposition was put down to ignorance and stupidity; the ideas themselves were always assumed to be quite flawless. Rousseau and Ritson knew that they were right. They were absolutely certain that 'Man' in society was a degenerate phantom of the hardy, natural Noble Savage. They had the same confidence in the validity of their position as Erskine and Martin had that 'Man' was a beast who had to have society drummed into 'his' wild head. Indeed, they could all be certain that their definitions were right simply because no one was sure what they were trying to establish; the truth of 'Man',

yes, but what 'Man'? In Britain at least, the Demand for Difference's appeal for animal welfare and kindness has come to seem
more reasonable than the tales of Peter the Wild Boy, not because
it is more correct, but simply because 'the one class has power to
enforce its own standard, the other has not' (Freeman 1870: 677).

Both understandings of 'Man' thought – and think – that they
cut to the heart of all knowledge, when in fact they merely
revealed their own incompleteness and partiality. In this respect,
the idea of animal rights is quite special. It tries to transcend the
dualism. Animal rights deliberately tries to reconcile elements of
the case for Difference to others from the argument for Similitude.
In so doing, it tries to fuse the strengths of both and present itself
as the Whole Truth. Animal rights presents itself as the ultimate
way of knowing humanity in relation to animals. Like the Demand
for Similitude, animal rights is invariably upheld by individuals
who are highly concerned with selfhood and therefore critical of
society, and, in the specific case of understanding animals, socially
interstitial. The morality has immense strength. Because it is
upheld as an ideal independent of social relationships, it can
overcome charges of bias. It resembles the Demand for Difference
to the extent that this certainty of moral correctness is a measure
of who is or is not properly human. It allows campaigns to
discipline and police those who behave in ways which real humans
(that is, those who uphold animal rights) should not. Animal rights
does not shout across the gulf of 'Man'. It builds a bridge and
claims the legitimacy of both sides. It says that 'Man' can indeed be
made a stable figure, and therefore also says that there is only one
right attitude towards animals.

Animal rights is an alliance of themes from contradictory
traditions. Its development was not implicit to either of the two
Demands; the morality had to be made. Animal rights was
invented by people who wanted to know who 'Man' was, not
primarily because they were worried about animals. It can be
understood as a rupture, an *epistemological break*, in modern
knowledge. What do I mean? The grand phrase 'epistemological
break' is making no great claims. It does not imply that animal
rights is a scientific truth in contradistinction to all the ideological
fallacies that went before. Animal rights might see itself in that
light, but there is no reason why we should follow suit. I am only
trying to suggest that, unlike all earlier attempts to understand

relationships between animals and society, the two images of 'Man' were reconciled when animal rights appeared as a fully self-conscious concept in the 1890s. Animal rights was able to speak on behalf of a single unitary society, whereas the Demands only really spoke for parts of the social. It opened up a new set of possible truths about human being, and rewrote the past as mere prehistory.

An analogy with Western painting until the second half of the nineteenth century might help explain. Very broadly, from the Renaissance to the Impressionists, art respected the integrity of the object; the artist tried to paint the best possible representation that could be managed. However, the Impressionists tried something new. They wanted to gain a representation of the play of light on the object, which thus became less important than the impression it created to the eye. Monet's water-lilies are an obvious example. In this sense, Impressionism was an epistemological break in Western art. It took up the artistic enterprise and declared that it was a better and more truthful way of making pictures than all preceding attempts. The earlier schools and techniques were turned into the prehistory of Impressionism, and reinterpreted as that which went before Monet, Renoir, and the others. All earlier art became flawed predecessors of the new kind of painting, although they continued happily to follow their own paths of development.

Henry Salt's book *Animals' Rights* is our equivalent of Impressionism. Salt was an intriguing figure. George Bernard Shaw always said that Salt was 'the mildest-mannered man that ever defied society' (quoted in Holroyd 1988: 221). He was born in India in 1851, the son of a colonel in the Royal Bengal Artillery. Later, he went to Cambridge and became a teacher at Eton. Apart from a commitment to socialism, Salt was a rather tediously respectable Victorian, as he later realised. Then he discovered vegetarianism. Salt had happily accepted English society and manners 'as parts of the natural order' (Salt 1921: 8–9), but one day, presumably when he was eating dinner, he suddenly saw that nineteenth-century social relations might not be wholly inevitable. He began to see with the alien eye of an anthropologist:

> Why the diet of my countrymen should have been the first thing to set me pondering, I am unable to say, for as my later

discoveries convinced me, the dietetic habits of these people are not more astonishing than many kindred practices which I still regarded with mistrust. But it was so; and I then found myself realizing, with an amazement which time has not diminished, that the 'meat' which formed the staple of our diet, and which I was accustomed to regard – like bread, or fruit, or vegetables – as a mere commodity of the table, was in truth dead flesh – the actual flesh and blood – of oxen, sheep, swine, and other animals that were slaughtered in vast numbers under conditions so horrible that even to mention the subject at our dinner-tables would have been an unpardonable offence.

(Salt 1921: 9)

Although Salt could not say why he had made the connection between meat and animals, it is highly likely that his wife's influence was very important. Salt had married Kate Joynes in 1879. She was associated with Edward Carpenter's circle and its attempts to live a good life, in touch with the countryside and true human sensibilities. She also used to partner Shaw in piano duets of Beethoven and Wagner (Shaw 1970: 122–6). Although Kate Salt was a strong and determined women's liberationist, she seems to have been a rather tragic figure; she idealised Carpenter and Shaw and ended up as little more than a quiescent admirer. She exhausted her own abilities looking after Henry and massaging George's ego (Rowbotham 1977: 98). The men who preached radical social change do seem to have been especially fond of a woman's 'proper place'. Henry Salt resigned from Eton in 1884, in an act which Dr Warre, the headmaster, put down to 'the incendiary combination of socialism and *legumes*' (Holroyd 1988: 221), and went to copy Thoreau's simple life in a Surrey cottage. By 1888 he was publicly applauding Shelley's pleas for vegetable diet and contributing a steady flow of articles to socialist journals (Salt 1888: 80). He also developed a beautifully dry sense of humour; the autobiography of his life in England was to be called *Seventy Years Among Savages*. The book *Animals' Rights* managed to combine previously contradictory positions towards animals.

Salt believed that one of the biggest illusions worshipped by the not so noble savages of Britain was 'that old anthropocentric superstition which pictures Man as the centre of the universe, and

151

separated from the inferior animals . . . by a deep intervening gulf'
(Salt 1921: 13). He wanted to show that such a gulf is an arrogant
social invention, and does not really exist. Salt used evolutionary
theory to demonstrate that animals are the 'lower races' of a life
which also includes humans, and not some naturally irreconcilable
other at all. Darwin had undermined the notions that 'Man' was an
earthbound angel, but his story had a rather ambivalent impact. If
it dulled any claims for omnipotence, it could also be read as proof
that 'Man' was the high point of existence; even if 'Man' was
descended from the monkeys, 'Man' was so much better adapted
to survival that animals could be freely eaten and dissected. Salt
pushed the possibility in the opposite direction. He agreed that
humans were excellent as natural beings, and he especially
believed that 'Man' possessed far-reaching moral capacities, but
evolution told Salt that all other creatures were good in their own
way. Salt wanted an evolution of equality rather than of hierarchy,
and a recognition of 'the common bond of humanity that unites all
living beings in one universal brotherhood' (Salt 1980: 10).

Although Salt repeated the old idea that humans are naturally
and anatomically frugivorous (Salt 1980: 59), organic structure
was far less important for him than it had been for Rousseau,
Ritson, and Shelley. They saw teeth and intestines as definite signs
of the naturally right relationships between humans and animals,
but Salt turned to more metaphorical ideas of evolutionary
perfectibility. He was steeped in the ideas of late nineteenth-
century ethical socialism which often argued that each individual
should be allowed to cultivate a perfect character. Salt's point was
that if animals were simply the 'lower races' of evolution, then they
were also individuals in their own way, just as much as humans are
individuals in our own way. That common ability was the basis of
moral relevance. 'They have individuality, character, reason; and
to have those qualities is to have the right to exercise them, in so
far as surrounding circumstances permit' (Salt 1980: 16).

Now, if all living creatures are naturally similar, if we and they
are nothing more than 'races' within a wider category of
individuals, it is necessary to explain how and why that similitude
is ignored. Salt lays the blame on the names which put the
profusion of perceived things into intelligible classes. A century
earlier, Bentham had pointed out that although words refer to
humans as subjective, feeling individuals, they define animals as

mere things. According to Bentham, words degrade animals and misunderstand their true being as feeling, living creatures (Bentham 1960: 411). Salt agreed, and extended the insight to include not just the understanding, but also the physical treatment, of animals:

> It is to be feared that the ill-treatment of animals is largely due – or at any rate the difficulty of amending that treatment is largely increased – by the common use of such terms as 'brute-beast', 'live-stock', etc., which implicitly deny to the lower races that intelligent individuality which is most undoubtedly possessed by them.
>
> (Salt 1980: 17)

A deeper reality lies behind the surfaces of words. It is violated by discourse and illicitly carved up by classification. Names are fundamental to social understanding; rabbits, rats, and other small animals are treated particularly badly simply on account of their taxonomic status as 'vermin'. Salt was in no doubt that 'the application of a contemptuous name may aggravate and increase the actual tendency to barbarous ill-usage' (Salt 1980: 76). He did not confront the problem whether 'vermin' is a category of abuse because the animals it designates are revolting, or whether the animals are repulsive because 'vermin' is an unclean category, somewhere between the cuddly and domestic, and sharp-toothed and wild. The description of animals as the 'lower races' had a very important purpose; it was far more than rhetoric. Salt is telling us that we see a gulf between us and them, between the same and the other, purely because names divide the world into readily intelligible pieces. In particular, the word 'animal' places limits on the compass of humanity and sensibility. It excludes animals from moral enfranchisement. Naturally and truthfully, all creatures are equal partners in a fraternity, but the word 'animal' stops us treating other 'races' properly when they cease to be like us. Like Mary Midgley, Salt also thought that it is a mistake to forget that humans are themselves animals: 'the term "animals", as applied to the lower races, is incorrect, and not wholly unobjectionable, since it ignores the fact that *man* is an animal no less than they' (Salt 1980: 19). Animality is a difference of degree, not of kind. Salt has pulled the two faces of 'Man' together. He simultaneously upheld the position of the Demand for Similitude that 'Man' is naturally one animal amongst many, and the view of the Demand for Difference that 'Man' is separate from all other creatures. 'Man' is also different because 'he' is able to be more perfect than any other living thing.

But if 'Man' can be more perfect 'Man' might also be the most wrong. Indeed, Salt thought that the acts of difference and the category of 'animal' have had a terrible impact. It is not just that vermin are treated badly. The world as it is understood through surface perceptions and names is cruel:

> The root of all evil lies in that detestable assumption (detestable equally whether it be based on pseudo-religious or pseudo-scientific grounds) that there is a gulf, an impassable barrier, between man and the animals, and that the moral instincts of compassion, justice, and love, are to be sedulously repressed and thwarted in the one direction as they are to be fostered and extended in the other.
>
> (Salt 1980: 102)

We worry about glass in jars of baby food, but are fairly indifferent that five-day-old calves frequently have to eat chocolate-flavoured pigs' blood (*Guardian*, 17 March 1989: 28). We worry whether our leather jacket is still fashionable, and ignore the truth that we can only have trendy jackets if animals are killed. The words which shape the understanding and moral importance of things hide animals' individuality. Instead, words and names erect a high barrier which lets us do whatever we want to those on the other side.

Salt was disgusted by too much concern for some, and too little for others. He asserted that because all creatures are individuals, it is right that they are allowed to *live* as individuals. However, that normative right could not override all else; if it did, there was nothing wrong about humans living as individuals who killed animals. No, we are free to live an individual life only up to the point where we begin to impinge upon the identical individuality and freedom of others. Freedom and rights are social properties which are the defence against tyranny. The idea came from Herbert Spencer, and Salt applauded it as a way of discovering the moral truth of being. Salt writes:

> animals, as well as men, though, of course, to a far less extent than men, are possessed of a distinctive individuality, and,

therefore, are in justice entitled to live their lives with a due measure of that 'restricted freedom' to which Herbert Spencer alludes. It is of little use to claim 'rights' for animals in a vague general way, if with the same breath we explicitly show our determination to subordinate those rights to anything and everything that can be construed into a human 'want'; nor will it ever be possible to obtain full justice for the lower races so long as we continue to regard them as beings of a wholly different order, and to ignore the significance of their numberless points of kinship with mankind.

(Salt 1980: 9)

This is animal rights. The existence of the right to exercise freedom up to the point where one individual denies the freedom of another does not depend on rational validity. It is simply known to be the truth after the realisation that words and names are only inadequate handles on the world (Salt 1980: 24). Even Rousseau, Ritson, and Shelley needed some demonstration of the moral relevance of animals and their similitude to 'Man'. That is why they spent so long talking about organic structure and the illnesses of meat-eating. Salt threw the need for objective certainty into the cellar of prehistory. He does not want an abstract acknowledgement of animal rights; he wants individuals to know it as the truth which escapes all words. Animal rights almost becomes the truth which can only be felt. After all, how could it be spoken if words are questionable? Salt's animal rights is a truth which is so obvious to all humane beings that any demands for proof merely show a lack of humanity. It is rather difficult to know how Henry Salt could have reached any conclusion other than that animals are morally and taxonomically congruous with humans since he explicitly bracketed off anything outside the 'numberless points of kinship'. It is rather like saying that the score of a football match will be nil–nil if all the goals are disallowed.

Salt believed that all individuals should ungrudgingly respect the individuality of others. The assertion had a profound impact on what a person could or could not do to an animal. If humans and animals are individuals, and if, therefore, we should acknowledge the restricted freedom of each other, we are so similar that we must remain apart. The paradox has appeared on a number of occasions already, and Salt expresses it very clearly. He creates a featureless physical taxonomy and then says that humans can only show what it is to be human by doing nothing to animals. Humanity is increased as relationships with animals decrease. Any touching of animals which restricts their freedom too much, or any treatment of them as things, is cruel and immoral – an infringement of their rights.

> Yet no human being is justified in regarding any animal whatsoever as a meaningless automaton, to be worked, or tortured, or eaten, as the case may be, for the mere object of satisfying the wants or whims of mankind. Together with the destinies and duties that are laid on them and fulfilled by them, animals have also the right to be treated with gentleness and consideration, and the man who does not so treat them, however great his learning or influence may be, is, in that respect, an ignorant and foolish man, devoid of the highest and noblest culture of which the human mind is capable.
>
> (Salt 1980: 16–17)

The Demand for Difference never doubted that the moral legislators were morally and socially correct, but Salt did. Moreover, where the Demand for Similitude condemned culture, Salt believed that it could educate and reveal the truth of being. Salt was not saying that only other people should change their relationships with animals; rather, he was proposing that as individuals everyone should change, and thereby begin to change society. He did not think he was intrinsically better than anyone else; it was just that he had come to realise the truth and was obliged to put it into action.

Salt reconciled 'Man' with animals, culture with nature, and the individual with society. None of those alliances had been formed in the prehistory of animal rights. The ambiguities of 'Man' had led to deep dualisms in the treatment of animals as well as radically different ideas about the best and right path of reform. Henry Salt had managed to accept both the privileged 'Man' who is a subject as well as the unprivileged one who was a natural object. This is the core of the epistemological break in *Animals' Rights*. It explains why Salt was so certain about what the single, true relationship between animals and society should be. He knew who 'Man' was, and therefore knew how animals should be treated. The fact that

156

the truth was invented in a social context which obviously contradicted it, as British society still does, was quickly brushed to one side. Salt was confident enough to believe that few people agreed with him simply because they were unable to see the validity of the argument; their mockery just made the moral case more obvious and unquestionable.

From this perspective, nearly every existing treatment of animals is fundamentally bad. All social behaviour was covered by the absolute principle of the right of all individuals to a life of restricted freedom. The principle had no place for special pleading like that of Martin for fox-hunting. But if individuality is the basis of rights, it is also the basis of duties. *Animals' Rights* contains a survey of the main areas where the rights of animals are infringed and criticises the life of domestic and wild animals, food animals, field sports, science, and fashion. For the first time, it is possible to see links between animal welfare laws and vegetarianism, the attack on field sports and an attack on science. Cruelty is cruelty because it infringes the right of restricted freedom. Every act which ignores animals' individuality is equally disgraceful: 'each of these hydra-heads, the off-spring of one potent stem, has its own proper characteristic, and is different, not worse or better than the rest' (Salt 1980: 88–9). The basic assertion is that animals have a right to individual restricted freedom, and any treatment which transgresses that core of individuality is immoral. The principle makes great demands on the way individuals and society treat animals. It certainly means that vegetarianism is absolutely essential: 'Now it must be admitted, I think, that it is a difficult thing consistently to recognize or assert the rights of an animal on whom you purpose to make a meal' (Salt 1980: 55). Similarly: 'It is idle to spend a single moment in advocating the rights of the lower animals, if such rights do not include a total and unqualified exemption from the awful tortures of vivisection' (Salt 1980: 94).

By the time Henry Salt started to think about animal rights, vivisection had been in the public mind for many years. The RSPCA had always taken a soft line on the medical use of animals; of course, it was worried about the pain which the animals felt, but the perpetrators were highly educated professionals working in the privacy of their own laboratories. Had they been working class the problem would have been easier, but was it possible that doctors and professors could be cruel? The antivivisectionists argued that it was indeed possible. (A comprehensive history of the debates surrounding vivisection in nineteenth-century Britain is given in French 1975.) The London-based Society for the Protection of Animals Liable to Vivisection was formed in March 1876, followed two months later by the London Anti-Vivisection Society and the International Association for the Total Suppression of Vivisection. The societies agreed that vivisection was disgraceful because it was cruel (French 1975: 308) and, perhaps more fundamentally, a waste of time. As Anna Kingsford once said 'how is it possible to suppose that the study of biological function in the beast is capable of explaining satisfactorily the mysteries of human life?' (quoted in French 1975: 316). Although Salt was undoubtedly familiar with the antivivisection struggle, he did not want to criticise animal experimentation on the grounds that it was bad medicine. Rather, vivisection fell foul of the moral principle and it therefore needed to be abolished. As in all else, Salt accepted no back-pedalling. Perhaps the first sentence of the following passage is Salt's guiding light for how humans should treat animals:

Nothing is necessary which is abhorrent, revolting, intolerable, to the general instincts of humanity. Better a thousand times that science should forego or postpone the questionable advantage of certain problematical discoveries, than that the moral conscience of the community should be unmistakably outraged by the confusion of right and wrong. The short cut is not always the right path; and to perpetrate a cruel injustice on the lower animals, and then attempt to excuse it on the grounds that it will benefit posterity, is an argument which is as irrelevant as it is immoral. Ingenious it may be (in the way of hoodwinking the unwary) but it is certainly in no true sense scientific.

(Salt 1980: 98)

Bloodsports were opposed on an identical basis. Salt followed Edward Freeman in calling the sports 'amateur butchery' (Freeman 1869: 373; Salt 1980: 67). He also copied Freeman's tendency to pour vitriol on the hunters. Freeman doubted whether they were capable of thought (Freeman 1869: 381), whilst Salt dismissed the hunter: 'a man of slow perception, he naturally finds it much easier to follow the hounds than to follow an argument' (Salt 1980: 68). Both also agreed that fox-hunting continues, whilst bear-baiting is forgotten, only because it is a pastime of the bourgeoisie. It was impossible to make any moral distinctions between the sports, 'except that the one form of brutality is cherished by those who make the laws, the other only by those who break them' (Freeman 1869: 677; it must be said that the nineteenth-century opponents of hunting did have a nice way with epigrams). However, the links between Edward Freeman and Henry Salt should not be pushed too far. The latter believed that any moral defence of animals was impossible without vegetarianism, whereas the former happily ate steaks (Freeman 1869: 354).

It might seem that Salt's principle of animal rights put iron in the moral soul. It was the truth and had to be accepted because, once it is possible to see behind words and classification, it is simply known as the truth. That is certainly how Salt presented the argument and, undoubtedly, how he thought it should be taken up. However, it is interesting to note that Salt was reticent to apply the principle equally to all animals. In particular, he seems to have thought that domestic and wild animals could be treated differently without undermining the integrity of animal rights. Peter Singer, Tom Regan, and Stephen Clark were earlier accused of a little dishonesty. They said that their moralities covered all animals, but it was discovered that really they only fully spoke about mammals. Something comparable had also happened with Salt. He was in no doubt that all the animals which are already involved in social relationships (as meat, potential coats, research tools) should be accorded full rights, but the same case was not made for the wild animals who remain outside of social domination.

Salt established the right of domestic animals to be treated with courtesy and fairness. They are fellow creatures 'and in many cases the familiar associates and trusted dependants' of our homes (Salt 1980: 44). They share our lives to such an extent that under the pretence of kindness, compassion, and rights, we create a physical distance and call it morality. But all the certainty evaporates when the discussion turns to wild animals who live in a separate geographical environment and therefore potentially escape rigid classification. Admittedly, Salt says that wild animals have a right to their freedom just as much as any other creature, but he edges back from an absolutist imposition of the principle:

We are justified by the strongest of all instincts, that of

159

self-defence, in safe-guarding ourselves against such a
multiplication of any species of animal as might imperil the
established supremacy of man; but we are *not* justified in
unnecessarily killing – still less in torturing – any harmless
beings whatsoever. In this respect the position of wild
animals, in their relation to man, is somewhat analogous to
that of the uncivilised towards the civilised nations. Nothing is
more difficult than to determine precisely to what extent it is
morally permissible to interfere with the autonomy of savage
tribes – an interference which seems in some cases to conduce
to the general progress of the race, in others to fasten the
worst forms of cruelty and injustice; but it is beyond question
that savages, like other people, have the right to be exempt
from all wanton insult and degradation.

(Salt 1980: 47)

And when he is talking about the treatment of wild animals a little
later: 'We may kill, if necessary, but never torture or degrade' (Salt
1980: 47). That is a qualification of what Salt tells us should really
be an inviolable principle.

Why the ambivalence? Why are the animals which live in a
laboratory treated differently from the ones which live in a forest?
Perhaps because the wild animals are so obviously distinct from
urbanised society that they can be handled and made metonyms,
whereas domesticated animals are so close, already so metonymical, that careful steps must be taken to protect humanity
against consubstantiality. Certainly, Salt's discrimination against
wild animals is relatively mild, but the moralists of animal rights
should try to confront such curiosities honestly. They should try to
explain their uncertainties rather than erect *post hoc* justifications.

So much, then, for Henry Salt's theory of animal rights. Now it
is useful to turn to his accounts of how the principle of animal
rights should be enforced, and why. Obviously, much of the answer
to the questions revolves around the need to recognise that the
right to restricted freedom is inalienable, and a product of
individuality. The individuals who knew the truth would reshape
their lives in its terms; like Salt they would become vegetarians,
denounce hunting and medical research, and, quite possibly, stop
wearing leather (Salt 1980: 81). These are the ends of a fairly
orthodox Demand for Similitude, but Salt also took up the method

of the Demand for Difference where the morally right and good should legislate and educate for social change. He was able to beat the heirs of Erskine and Martin at their own game. Although they were only exploiting one side of 'Man' and aiming it at the not-quite humans, Salt spoke on behalf of a unified figure. He looked at the activities of 'Man' from the outside; Salt had no real class axes to grind and tried to take a total view.

Shelley had said that many of the ills of modern society were due to commerce. For him, as for Rousseau, 'Man' was naturally good but had been corrupted by society. Salt agreed, but where 'society' was a vague concept in the Demand for Similitude, Salt managed to make it more subtle by following the aim of the Demand for Difference. People like Erskine blamed working-class cruelty on the insufficient hold of social allegiances; Salt blamed it on people like Lord Erskine. The parliamentarians and preachers were not slow to condemn groups like butchers or slaughterhouse workers; they were said to be cruel, and, indeed, Kant applauded the English legal system because it was thought to exclude butchers from jury service (Kant 1930). The butchers were not properly human, and, therefore, the bourgeoisie prevented them from playing a full part in society. Henry Salt was outraged:

> This . . . is a libel on the working men who have to earn a livelihood by the disgusting occupation of butchering. The ignorance, carelessness, and brutality are not only in the rough-handed slaughterman, but in the polite ladies and gentlemen whose dietetic habits render the slaughterman necessary. The real responsibility rests not on the wage slave, but on the employer. 'I'm only doing your dirty work', was the reply of a Whitechapel butcher to a gentleman . . . 'It's such as *you* makes such as *us*.'
>
> (Salt 1976: 143–4)

Salt never forgot that he was a socialist. Certainly, butchers are cruel and rather dubious characters, but Salt wants to see their inhumanity in social and economic terms. Although modern social life is rotten to the core, the decay is due to capitalism and class-divided society as opposed to social existence as such. Salt hints that the bourgeois condemnation of working-class cruelty was basically a case of the pot calling the kettle black. He does not want the bourgeoisie to change everyone after its own image, as

161

happened with the Demand for Difference. Henry Salt wants the morally good, whoever they might be, to help transform all social relationships and halt the infringement of human and animal freedom alike. He did not want to demolish society, instead he wanted to make it better. It is no coincidence that the full title of Salt's book was *Animals' Rights Considered in Relation to Social Progress*.

Progress involved two simple tasks: education and legislation. When Baroness Burdett-Coutts set up the Bands of Mercy in the 1870s, she thought that only working-class children needed to be instructed in the ways of kindness and compassion. She was merely projecting her attitudes on to others; the problem was somewhere else. Salt totally rejected the identification of others as bad in opposition to one's own innate or social goodness: 'It is society as a whole, and not one class in particular, that needs enlightenment and remonstrance' (Salt 1980: 120). Consequently, education is far more than what happens to children at school; all social groups need to learn the proper treatment of animals, and especially scientists, preachers, and the intelligentsia (Salt 1980: 121). It needed immense effort which would establish animal rights as a moral law, rather than a mere sentiment. Salt wanted an education which would transcend the special concerns of the vegetarians, antivivisectionists, anti-hunters, and defenders of animal welfare. He wanted a new moral instruction which would link all the separate concerns in a truth to destroy 'the disregard of the natural kinship between man and the animals, and the consequent denial of their rights' (Salt 1980: 122). He was more than a little bit vague how this ambitious project should be carried out and, unfortunately, he believed 'that education must always precede the law, and that we can only make penal those offences which are already condemned by the better feeling of the nation' (Salt 1980: 127). But if he was uncertain how to develop the feelings of the nation, which is rather harder than the more straightforward task of enlightening individuals, it is difficult to know how legislation could be validated.

Salt managed to get around the dilemma by reintroducing an idea of evolution – not the evolution of species, but, this time, the evolutionary progression of humanity to a state of perfection. He believed that the moral social outsiders were the vanguard of a change which would eventually affect all society and make everyone more humane and more human. It was only possible if the mistaken pictures painted by words and false taxonomies were taken down and, instead, humans discovered the fraternity linking them with animals. The Demand for Difference would have been horrified by such a destruction of an urbanised understanding of the universe, and even the Demand for Similitude never wanted to question the primacy of human understanding, but Salt did:

It is not human life only that is lovable and sacred, but *all* innocent and beautiful life: the great republic of the future will not confine its beneficence to man. The isolation of man from Nature, by our persistent culture of the ratiocinative faculty, and our persistent neglect of the instinctive, has hitherto been the penalty we have had to pay for our incomplete and partial 'civilization' . . . . But let it not for a moment be supposed that an acceptance of the gospel of Nature implies an abandonment or depreciation of intellect – on the contrary, it is the assertion that reason itself can never be at its best, can never be truly rational, except when it is in perfect harmony with the deep-seated emotional instincts and sympathies which underlie all thought.

(Salt 1980: 114)

The right-thinking person does not need to be told about animals' rights; she or he simply *knows* them.

The argument is clear. If humans look behind the rational world of society, they will grasp the interconnections between all life. In so doing, the idea of humanity will be extended beyond surface appearances, which are now seen as crumbling façades, and individuals and society will become more humane. Humanity and humanitarianism can only approach its destiny of perfection through a reassertion of the place of instincts in understanding. And so, although animal rights certainly involves less cruelty towards animals, 'it is not only, and not primarily, for the sake of the victims that we plead, but for the sake of mankind itself' (Salt 1980: 111). Salt tells us that it is the destiny of 'Man' to be ever more perfect and the summit of the world, through an increasing acknowledgement of the congruities of the universe which classification hides. The humane humans have the job of pulling the rest of society along.

Salt manages to make a historical adventure out of the story of moral progress. 'It is for each age to initiate its own ethical reforms, according to the light and sensibility of its own instincts' (Salt 1980: 110). The point was, of course, that by the late nineteenth century, the time had come when society had to accept that animals possessed unequivocal rights; the light illuminated previously dark wastes. Indeed, Henry Salt might well have suggested that one day in the future, when the light was still brighter, humane people would be worrying about rainforests. This chronicle had the great advantage that it allowed a total rewriting of the history of animal rights. It is fairly obvious to anyone who looks at the parliamentary debates that the early nineteenth-century anti-cruelty acts were about the unruliness of the urban working class, and that the Noble Savage rested on rather flimsy evidence. The only real link between the legislators and the Savages was the joint interest to say something definite about 'Man' in so far as 'Man' had problematic relationships with animals. But Salt pulled the stories together in a wonderful pageant of the evolutionary decline, fall, and recovery of the conclusively true morality and a final encounter with the question 'What is "Man"?' Richard Martin's Act of 1822 was reinterpreted as 'a memorable date in the history of humane legislation' (Salt 1980: 7). This ability to rewrite the recent past gave the notion of animal rights a degree of inevitability, and made the rather contradictory aims of the Demands for Difference and Similitude prehistorical ancestors of a morality which saw itself as an absolute necessity. And so Britain becomes the home of animal lovers and the kindest nation in the world; and so the glorious history of humanitarianism can be told to people whose great-great-grandparents laid bets on cock-fights or murdered cats for a joke. Some people continue to believe the tale of humanitarianism.

Although Salt's *Animals' Rights* was making new and radical statements, the book's career was far from brilliant. Gandhi said that Salt's *A Plea for Vegetarianism* of 1886 made him a vegetarian by conviction rather than habit (quoted in Salt 1980: 227), whilst George Bernard Shaw once declared that his plays had been 'sermons preaching what Salt practised' (quoted in Holroyd 1988: 221). Shaw contributed an essay to a collection Salt edited on hunting. It added little to Salt's own arguments except abuse: coursing 'reduced them all, men and terriers alike, to a common denominator of bestiality', whilst hunters enjoyed 'the sports in which men revert to the excitements of beasts of prey' (Shaw 1915:

xxi). Shaw also wrote a preface to *The Doctor's Dilemma* which contained a spirited attack on vivisection (Shaw 1971: 259–85). However, Peter Singer gets close to the mark when he comments that Salt's book changed nothing (Singer 1980b: ix).

Indeed, Salt's book was forgotten until Peter Singer reinvigorated the question of the morally right attitudes which humans ought to adopt towards animals. Of course, throughout the century, people had continued to criticise various treatments of animals, but the idea of rights was not very important. The antivivisectionists attacked animal experiments because they were bad medicine as much as anything else, whilst the RSPCA rarely criticised any treatment of animals which was not obviously cruel. Despite the continuing protests, which also continued in the hunting fields and in vegetarianism, animal rights was stagnant before Singer. But Singer has doubted whether he could have written *Animal Liberation* without the help of Henry Salt. According to Singer, *Animals' Rights* is the best nineteenth-century contribution to the issue and anticipates much of the contemporary debate. Singer felt unable to add very much: '*Animals' Rights* is of more than merely historical interest: it remains a living contribution to a continuing debate' (Singer 1980b: ix). He put himself in a tradition largely invented by Salt, but gave it a new twist when he called his book *Animal Liberation*.

With the word 'liberation' Singer created the possibility that animal rights would become an item on the political agenda. Henry Salt had proved that animals possess rights, and he was happy to try to undermine the classification which meant that rights were forgotten. Singer went further. He added the new element that animals have to be liberated. Singer gives accounts of experiments and factory farming before announcing that we should all be vegetarians; Singer's utilitarian critique is a practical affair, whereas Salt had largely operated at the level of a true moral principle. Moreover, Singer attacked a society which was defined in the global, monolithic terms of a Rousseau rather than the social and economic categories of a Salt. For Singer, the social treatment of animals is wholly speciesist; he makes no allowances for social class, as Salt did, or the countryside as Rousseau did, or for the cynical origins of morality as an Edward Freeman might. Instead, Singer condemns humans simply because they are humans:

> Most human beings are speciesists . . . ordinary human beings
> – not a few exceptionally cruel or heartless humans, but the
> overwhelming majority of humans – take an active part in,
> acquiesce in, and allow their taxes to pay for practices that
> require the sacrifice of the most important interests of
> members of other species in order to promote the most trivial
> interests of our own species.
>
> (Singer 1976: 9–10)

Singer is arguing that we should change our behaviour so that animals are liberated from our speciesism. We have a moral duty to make animals free. Now, this is rather different from Salt's position that animals already possess a free individuality which humans restrict too much; Singer is saying that animals have an interest in the avoidance of our speciesism. In Singer's analysis, humans should only do those things which are compatible with the interest of the animal to avoid pain; we should only do those things which – or should not do that which does not – liberate them from suffering. Perhaps this is one reason why he liberally condemns each person, as both an individual and a member of society, rather than concentrate on some groups more than others.

It is fair to say, however, that although Salt's and Singer's arguments are different, they fundamentally support each other. Why, then, did Singer talk of 'liberation'? Why did he adopt this particular political vocabulary? Some of the explanation is due to Singer's commitment to a utilitarian denial of rights, but the phrase 'animal liberation' does not lack a political resonance. The book could have been called *Be Kind to Animals* or *The Errors of Speciesism* just as easily, but it was not. Why did Singer choose 'liberation'? Some clues are given by Henry Salt and the reasons he gave for 'animal rights'.

Salt saw the case for animals' rights as the latest development in a process which began in 1789, and had resulted in a recognition of the 'world-wide spirit of humanitarianism' (Salt 1980: 4). The idea is comparable to the expanding circle thesis which identifies a historical process of the moral enfranchisement of classes and categories of life which are decreasingly similar to the Same of the white male bourgeoisie. Humanity 'is beginning to extend itself to the lower animals, as in the past it has been gradually extended to savages and slaves' (Salt 1980: 112). Women should be added to the list, because Salt expressly located his book in the rights tradition of Tom Paine and Mary Wollstonecraft. Salt's is the final volume in that radical trilogy.

Salt rewrote the history of human rights to make it part of the prehistory of animal rights. In so doing, he put his argument in a specific context. Similarly, it might be possible to see why Singer suddenly brought together the vocabularies of animal rights and human liberation, by looking at the context in which he was working. Singer wrote *Animal Liberation* in the early 1970s; anti-imperialist struggles had been rumbling on for decades, black liberation and civil rights were powerful issues in the United States, 1968 was fresh in the mind, and the first wave of the women's liberation movement was in full flow. Singer took the idea of animal liberation from the political discourse of these other movements. He borrowed their radical clothing and gave the moral case for animals an immediacy which it had always lacked before (Salt's book sounds like a philosophical treatise; Singer's does not). As Singer said:

> The title of this book has a serious point behind it. A liberation movement is a demand for an end to prejudice and discrimination based on an arbitrary characteristic like race or sex. The classic instance is the Black liberation movement. The immediate appeal of this movement, and its initial, if limited, success, made it a model for other oppressed groups. We soon became familiar with Gay liberation and movements on behalf of American Indians and Spanish-speaking Americans. When a majority group – women – began their campaign some thought we had come to the end of the road.
> (Singer 1976: x)

But we had not. Singer made the issue of animals another last piece in the jigsaw of freedom. Salt made animal rights seem inevitable by talking about evolutionary progress; Singer made it inevitable through revolutionary slogans. The first chapter of *Animal Liberation* has the tub-thumping title: 'All Animals Are Equal . . . or why supporters of liberation for Blacks and Women should support Animal liberation too' (Singer 1976: 11). They must support it if the ideas of black and women's liberation are worth the paper they are printed on; to deny their extension to the relationships between animals and society is to fall into the trap of speciesism. And if one is being speciesist, why cannot one be racist and sexist as well?

All these struggles are preoccupied by selfhood. They are all attempts to establish what it means to be a member of society, and how society should relate to the individual. They all uphold, and try to develop, a space in which the individual can live her or his life with a suitable degree of freedom and self-responsibility. Henry Salt saw animal rights as a way of life as much as a moral principle, and Peter Singer tied it in with most of the other concerns about lifestyle and selfhood which appeared in the 1960s. Whether Singer was being entirely honest when he did this is another question again.

Singer's attempt to connect the moral status of animals to a political agenda had undoubtedly been made rather easier by the activities of the Hunt Saboteurs' Association in Britain, a group which tried to stop any possibility that hunters might inflict pain or suffering on animals. The Saboteurs were practical proof that individuals could become morally good subjects and then play a part in the liberation of animals. They linked selfhood to moral conviction. This had happened out of frustration with the conventional struggle against hunting which had not really changed since Henry Salt inspired a campaign of public opinion against the Royal Buckhounds at the beginning of the twentieth century. For the most part, hunting was opposed by individuals who thought it was cruel or an example of the genetic stupidity of the aristocracy. There were few attempts to link the moral conviction that it was wrong to kill for sport with the idea that, consequently, the individual should personally do something about it; something more than just writing letters to *The Times*. The League Against Cruel Sports took the first steps towards a linkage in the late 1950s. It also went some way towards ideas of liberation when it started to lay false trails to take hounds off the scent of foxes. The Hunt Saboteurs' Association was formed in 1964 with the stated aim of saving animals by actually getting in the way of the hunt 'until such time as these practices [namely, hunting] are banned by law' (R. Thomas 1983: 104). The saboteurs were using themselves, and not just abstract discussions, to impose the moral law. Peter Singer came up with a similar argument.

The idea of animal rights has only existed since the 1890s.

Certainly, precursors can be found, but they are rather different from the new field which Henry Salt opened up. Indeed, the precursors continue to exist, and it is important to stress that animal rights is very different from the separate strands that can be seen within it. For example, animal rights would agree with Edward Freeman that it is silly to draw a distinction where 'To chase a calf or a donkey either till it is torn to pieces or till it sinks from weariness, would be scouted as a cruel act. Do the same to a deer and it is a noble and royal sport' (Freeman 1869: 356). But Freeman felt no qualms about eating meat, whereas Henry Salt of course did. Similarly, although the antivivisectionists said that animal experimentation was useless and cruel, they were never especially close to vegetarianism, and Frances Power Cobbe, who was a leading antivivisectionist, was renowned for her fondness for meat (French 1975: 230). As Henry Salt said:

> The terrible sufferings that are quite needlessly inflicted on the lower animals under the plea of domestic usage, food-demands, sport, fashion, and science, are patent to all who have the seeing eye and the feeling heart to apprehend them; those sufferings will not be lessened, nor will man's responsibility be diminished by any such irrelevant assertions as that vivisection is less cruel than sport, or sport less cruel than butchering, – nor yet by the contrary contention that vivisection, or sport, or flesh-eating, as the case may be, is the one prime origin of all human inhumanity. We want a comprehensive principle which will cover all these varying instances, and determine the true lines of reform.
>
> (Salt 1980: 106)

The true lines of reform. By the mid 1970s, they had come to involve a concentration on what the individual did in her or his daily life, and a belief that animals should be released from speciesism.

Chapter Eight

ANIMAL MAGIC

Henry Salt wrote with considerable certainty. He knew that although humans are animals, they are also responsible for the moral progress of the world. He knew that the words and categories which make the universe intelligible also create a terrible misunderstanding of the real order of things. Salt was sure that society could only edge closer to its evolutionary destiny of perfection if it was made to explore an almost Magrittian world where objects and relationships only seem odd because they are said to be incongruous; and of course such a saying has no great depth or validity. Salt asserts that if it feels acceptable to bring together a glass of water and an umbrella, if their meeting seems right in some unspeakable way, then it must also be good. The fact that the meeting would be repudiated 'by our persistent culture of the ratiocinative faculty' only shows how much work remains to be done. Salt saw moral rights in these terms; rights can only be felt, like hunger or like pain. And because it is felt by all individuals who do not want to suffer, and who want to be free, there can be no reason why the 'lower animals' could not feel the moral good as well. Animals have rights. The sphere of moral enfranchisement was consequently widened. Salt mentioned the structural identity of humans and animals as living organisms, and more importantly denied human difference by denigrating the language which was identified as the medium of the illicit claims for uniqueness. Yet he could not deny that humans retained a place of universal significance. We might well only be animals, but precisely the recognition of similitude consolidates and advances social progress. Animal rights pushes humans into the order of the beasts, whilst simultaneously pulling us into the starry heaven of perfection and virtuous civilisation.

The ability to give a reasonable answer to the problem of being human in relation to animals was the stuff and the signal of the epistemological break contained in *Animals' Rights*. The book offered a comprehensive principle which had never been imagined before. It looked forward to the day when the right of animals to a life of restricted freedom would be widely upheld, and resisted the temptation to peer back at some dim anthropological past, or to the uncultivated and masterless wastes outside the city boundary. Salt stared into the future – and drew a curtain across the past. The epistemological break had the effect of creating a new and apparently inevitable moral orbit around animals, whilst making it possible to forget that there was nothing inevitable about the extension of morality at all. Henry Salt was able to ignore the uncomfortable fact that he was writing little more than a century after the first hesitant, now prehistorical, stirring of claims on behalf of animals; stirrings which were in any case trying to tackle rather different problems. Salt was so wrapped up in the new-found necessity of animal rights that he could not see that it was really a thing of his own invention. None of the subsequent protagonists have seen what Salt was blind to either. Indeed, by the time Peter Singer reinvigorated the tradition in the 1970s, animal rights was a quite unassailable natural right. Since the 1890s, there has been a systematic denial of something which is perfectly plain to anybody who has read to this page: animal rights is not natural; it is a social and a historical invention. Society is worshipping a thing of its own creation when it falls down before this truth.

When he used the concept of the fetish, Marx was trying to explain the grip and fascination of commodities in capitalist social and economic relations. Obviously, commodities meet needs, but why is a very complicated car, for example, said to be intrinsically better than a simple one? And why do we worry about it? Marx thought that commodities like cars have such value because in the capitalist system they confront individuals as ready-made objects. They are things which are already waiting to be bought and used. They take on almost metaphysical qualities. Marx gives a useful example. He points out that although a table is just made up of a few bits of wood, 'so soon as it steps forth as a commodity, it is changed into something transcendent' (Marx 1938: 42). The table has mystical properties because, as a commodity, it is something rather more than the sum of its parts. The conditions of the transformation of wood into furniture are hidden by the almost miraculous table. Moreover, the table is itself important because it goes with other commodities like chairs; its production is fairly irrelevant. The social origin of the commodity in capitalist relations of production is pushed aside and replaced with the objective, natural relations between things. Marx could only compare the transformation of the produced thing into the commodity to religion: 'In that world the productions of the human brain appear as independent beings endowed with life, and entering into relation both with one another and the human race' (Marx 1938: 43). This is fetishism: commodities and religious ideas are social productions, but they are worshipped as immutable things in their own right. The social relationships surrounding the product divorce it from its social origins. It is forgotten that the idols of the market or the church are made in the image of 'Man'.

Animal rights is a fetish. It is prey to exactly the same illusions of grandeur as the commodity. Now, a vital dimension of fetishes is their worship; and to be worshipped they must have some influence over the behaviour of the individuals who are initiates of the truth. The followers of the Sect of the Table would kneel before a Chippendale, whilst the Disciples of Porsche take their moral code from a maintenance manual. Similarly, if animals are interpreted as fetish objects – that is, as things surrounded by social and historical meanings – the invention of which is forgotten, then it is to be expected that the individuals who uphold the truth of those meanings will participate in very distinctive practices. Mary Douglas provides a helpful illustration with the Lele treatment of the pangolin. Let us recall her analysis. The pangolin is a scaly creature which lives in trees. It contradicts the rigid taxonomy of animals developed by the Lele; the pangolin can be put into more than one category at a time. The Lele respond to the pangolin's anomalous status by investing it with magical properties which particularly surround human fertility (Douglas 1966: 168). Douglas's analysis explores the social rites which surround the pangolin. The animal is only eaten on certain occasions in a highly ritualised way, and can only be touched and consumed by the initiates of the cult. Douglas argues that in their pangolin cult, the Lele symbolically confront the reality that the categories which make the world intelligible are just social fictions (Douglas 1966:

170). The Lele are, so to speak, practising an honest fetishism.

But the pangolin cult can be interpreted rather differently. Although the Lele might well eat the pangolin to show how arbitrary their classification of the world and the human place in it really is, perhaps they are more fundamentally taking part in a reinvention of that knowledge. On the bottom line, there is one less pangolin to escape classification, but more broadly, the Lele are demonstrating how special the pangolin must be since its death is wrapped up in very specific social practices. Although they might well know that their definitions of reality are fictive, the Lele also know that they work. The pangolin is both a taxonomic and a practical fetish. The rituals which surround it reaffirm the place of society and humanity in the wider plenitude of things. Moreover, the Lele confront the truths of their fetish in cyclical time. Presumably the rites always happen on certain feast days; this is a recreation of order and humanity, not a confrontation with its limits as Douglas suggests. Every year they do exactly the same things. They have done them since time immemorial, and will continue to do so for as long as they can imagine, and consequently the categories which the Lele reinvent are made ahistorical. There has never been a time when the pangolin has not been a symbolic animal; there has never been a treatment of the animal unlike this. They never have to come to terms with the now long-forgotten day when a group of their ancestors invented the pangolin cult for the first time. The Lele forget the social and historical conditions of the cult's existence. Their relationships with the pangolin are made as natural as nature itself. Perhaps the Lele are not quite so honest after all; perhaps they worship a fetish every bit as much as the protagonists of animal rights.

The clearest indication of the contemporary status of animal rights as a fetish of the animal is provided by its establishment as the ineffable truth. The speakers for the Demand for Difference and the Demand for Similitude were quite aware that they were treading new ground. They knew that the moral claims of animals still had to be demonstrated and proved to a sceptical public. However, since Henry Salt it has been a more or less obvious truth that animals possess individuality and therefore rights. Salt was trying to understand why the rights of animals were not respected, whereas Erskine and Ritson were still attempting to get an accurate picture of something that was disguised. The doubts of the late eighteenth and early nineteenth centuries were rewritten in terms of an utter certainty that animals made definite, unchanging, ahistorical claims. The debate triggered by Singer operates in the confident epistemological field opened by Salt, and by the 1970s it was impossible to imagine a time when animal rights did not exist. Today, there is little doubt that a deeper, more truthful reality lurks behind the constructions of social life. But, sociologically speaking, the impassioned condemnations of the treatment of animals which have been voiced since the 1890s could be called the rage of Caliban seeing his face reflected in a mirror (with apologies to Oscar Wilde!). The problem is that Caliban has forgotten that he made the mirror himself, and holds it in his own hand.

Consider the following story. It shows how deep a hold the fetish has taken, and how the entire world is reconstructed as some magical commonwealth. In 1970, a 28-year-old man went to the Annual General Meeting of a major animal welfare society in London. He had been raised in rural Somerset, and this was his first visit to the city. At the meeting, he became friendly with a couple with whom he went to eat a sandwich in St James's Park. Apparently, the scene was quite astonishing and a complete contrast with the city, which was in full flow a couple of streets away. St James's Park was a dream world,

> where smiling, relaxed human beings strolled leisurely in the sun, sat alone or in groups on the grass near shimmering lakes and where, in the shade of huge and beautiful trees, birds of many species cavorted, fluttered and chirped happily amongst the very feet of human beings.
>
> (Bryant n.d.: 3)

The author calls it a Utopian vision: 'Millions of other people have also had a "peep" of "what could be" but, sadly, most would not have recognised it' (Bryant n.d.: 3). St James's Park was a vision which shimmered like the lakes. It was a little world where humans and animals were all able to enjoy themselves freely, and where there was no trespass of the boundaries of restricted freedom. The author comments that it might seem odd that the moment of awareness came in a London park. After all, he had lived all his life in Somerset. He explains. Humans still harm animals in the countryside, but in the park they do not (Bryant n.d.: 3). This is a significant point. It has been encountered already. If society uses animals to establish the truth of human being and the acts of being human, then rural relations are likely to be based on coercion; humans and animals share the same world and distanciation can only be created through the barrel of a rifle. However, the urban world is already detached from animals – women and men already know themselves to be city-dwellers – and so animals can be let into daily relationships without transgressing or diluting 'Man'. The inhabitants of London only have to turn a corner, and the beast is left behind. They do not need to harm.

The story is saying that London all the more clearly shows the peaceful and relaxed relationships of nature exactly because it is a noisy and teeming metropolis. The park is a glimpse of how the world could and should be: a place where humans and animals leave each other alone, and flourish in each other's company. The trees, lakes, and birds are a more truthful reality than the traffic, lights, and bargains of Oxford Street. But not everyone knows this. The author could only *feel* the full significance of the fleeting glimpse of a more than real world. It was not something that could be taught or put into words, and when it is, the writing is more than a little banal. The truth could only be felt in a flash of insight, in a moment that was outside social mediation. It is an inviolable and yet unspeakable fact that all life is equal and perfectible in its own way. The few individuals who have managed to recognise the proper meaning of the park have the responsibility to prepare everyone else for it.

The incident smacks of a conversion scene. The author had a brief, yet profound, contact with the greater truth and reality of nature, and conveniently forgets that St James's Park is not wild nature at all. It is just a green patch in the middle of a big city, looked after by gardeners and permanently recreated so that it *seems* like a place which has no social or historical conditions of existence. The park was turned into a transcendent reality when, in fact, it is nothing of the sort. It is just a human artifice. Unsurprisingly, the magic of the fetish had a spellbinding effect on the man's personal life. He adopted a vegetarian diet and, like Henry Salt, became increasingly convinced that the relationships between animals and society are intrinsically cruel if they take no heed of the suffering of the animals. Animals had been imprisoned by society, and only an animal rights which released them was compatible with the vision of the park. Only a recognition of the right of animals to their individual freedom from suffering can 'stimulate a desire amongst others to work for the Golden Day when Man can tread the earth lightly – without causing fear amongst a world of "unfettered kingdoms"' (Bryant n.d.: 84). Humans should live a life which does not touch animals in any way except as equals, and if they are our equals, we should not touch them anyway.

The practical implications of the need to 'unfetter' animals were inevitably anticipated by Salt. The twentieth century has added little to his statements of how animals should be treated by the proper humans who know the truth of 'Man'. However, there have been interesting developments around the question of pets. Henry Salt thought that pet-keeping was fairly acceptable so long as it was based on fairness and equality (Salt 1980: 44). The situation was radically different by the 1980s. Now, pet-keeping can be denounced as a treatment of animals which is, morally speaking, unacceptable, like putting them into zoos. The moral principle is absolute; it is an invariant norm which cannot be qualified in any way:

> Once we have accepted that we may utilize animals for so trivial a reason as our enjoyment of the taste of their flesh, it is easy to use them for any purpose which is equally frivolous, such as domesticating them as pets or confining them in zoos to amuse us, or for those which are more serious, such as using them in medical experiments that we believe will save human lives.
>
> (Schleifer 1985: 70)

Humane humans know that animals are free individuals. Therefore any treatment which restricts their freedom too much must be cruel. The people who uphold animal rights should have nothing whatsoever to do with animals. It might seem curious that the individual who lavishes affection on a poodle is condemned in the same breath as a zoo-owner or medical experimenter, but there is a simple explanation. The status of animals as creatures which make claims cannot be violated; their claims are quite real, and therefore any behaviour which infringes their rights is equally disgraceful. The compassion for animals which the rights argument emphasises does not demand that we love them; it just asks that we leave them to themselves.

There is a world of difference between animal love and animal rights. As a leading antivivisectionist once said of herself and her animal rights colleagues: 'We strongly dislike the term "animal lover" . . . It is a derogatory term like nigger lover' (quoted in Harris 1985: 170). The horror of being called an animal lover represents the fear of a position which defines itself as a moral fact, being reduced into an irrelevant emotion which provides easy comfort for 'the old lady with twenty cats and two fur coats' (see Harris 1985: 170). Animal love, indeed even liking animals, is repudiated as an inclination and a sentiment. It is quite possible actually to dislike animals but still believe that they possess inalienable rights. To repeat: animal rights is not about animals, and as a fetish it is arguing that if we construct a selfhood which is divorced from animals, we will become better humans.

Obviously, it is forcefully argued that the individuals who practise animal rights will improve themselves either because they are the vanguard of progress and perfection (Salt), or on the grounds that they will be living the morally good life (Singer, Regan, Clark). Certainly, animal rights is preoccupied with the actual being of 'Man', but it also offers important rewards. For the most part, the rewards are simply derived from the knowledge of doing what is right, but there are also benefits in our daily lives. If we practise animal rights with diligence and vigour, we will become physical temples and symbols of our initiation into the truth. In particular, animal rights sees itself as a path towards bodily health. The idea was originally put forward in the Demand for Similitude, and the equation of the 'natural diet' with health remains influential (if it did not, it is unlikely that there would be so many health food shops). Animal rights rewrites the dietary statements of Rousseau, Ritson, and Shelley so that the natural diet is seen as a key to a healthy physique which is itself a symbolic testimony of moral goodness. I eat well, therefore I am well. In particular, the individual who only eats vegetarian food will lose weight and gain a socially prestigious body (Wynne-Tyson 1979: 103) which is slim and highly desirable to the opposite sex (for the prestige of slimness, see Featherstone 1982). Perfection increases in proportion as the reliance on animals decreases. Indeed, the person who has no dietary relationships with animals – and of course diet is just one part of a greater principle – will be a beacon who stands out from the dullness of society:

It would be overstatement, or at least an oversimplification, to suggest that all the blood that bespatters the pages of our history books can be traced to the meat that has irritated and inflamed the human bloodstream. But there is little doubt that it has played a significant part. The decomposition of animal proteins in the unsuitably long gut of our species creates poisons that affect both mind and body. All other factors being equal, vegetarians are second to no meat-eater in strength, stamina, good health and longevity.

(Wynne-Tyson 1979: 71)

Vegetarians eat natural food. They also know that animals have rights, and their moral goodness sets them apart from the violence and illnesses of society. It would be wrong to underestimate the association of moral and physical goodness. The prizes of attractiveness and health that are held out by the hand of moral truth are comforting and seductive in Western urban cultures, which have very strict standards of the beautiful body, and where deviant physiques stick out all the more easily. Where the bourgeoisie of the Demand for Difference wanted to police the urban working class, the preoccupation with selfhood of modern animal rights might lead to the slim and moral watching over the flabby and violent.

The moral principle is detached from the social and historical conditions of its existence. It is far removed from the cynicism of Richard Martin or the legends of Peter the Wild Boy, and since Henry Salt and the debate which Peter Singer inspired, it has been invested with quite miraculous properties. The pangolin fetish is nothing compared with animal rights. Today, and in the name of a natural, ahistorical truth, some individuals radically change their lives. They certainly distance themselves from any relationship with animals and thereby begin to know themselves all the better. They also move out of kilter with relationships which the rest of society has with animals and, in this respect at least, can be defined as interstitial; they are the individuals who treat animals perfectly in an imperfect society.

It is quite impossible to know how many people practically respect the rights of animals. The membership numbers of the different societies can provide no clue. None of the societies, whether they exist to stop hunting, look after welfare, oppose vivisection, or promote vegetarianism, is fully included within the orbit of animal rights. Certainly, a significant proportion of their members probably share Salt's assumptions or Singer's attack on speciesism, and the proportion is likely to increase, but it will never include each member. The magazine published by the Vegetarian Society provides a good illustration of why not. Although it occasionally talks about animal rights, it more closely resembles a food and lifestyle journal. Like all the other separate concerns, vegetarianism appeals to a wider audience than just animal rights enthusiasts. Moreover, even if 'animal rightists' did all join societies, it is likely that they would join more than one since any single group could not cover all their worries. A considerable amount of double counting would take place. All this is notwithstanding the point that, given the distance which the individuals who uphold animal rights take from society, it is possible that they would be averse to joining any organisations in the first place. Animal rights can easily lead to a modern Thoreauian self-righteous withdrawal from a society which is condemned as corrupt and cruel. But it can, on the contrary, possibly lead to a hyperactive encounter with society; to an attack on cruelty rather than a resigned turning away from it. It is possible that the initiates who worship the fetish could begin to knock over what they see as the speciesist heresies.

In Britain, one group in particular has been trying to lay siege to speciesism: the Animal Liberation Front (ALF). The ALF originally came from the world of hunt sabotage. The Hunt Saboteurs' Association brought together morally right individuals with the need to change the behaviour of others which transgressed the bounds of humans' restricted freedom. It criticises hunting because it is unnecessary and involves coercion of the animal. But the moral principle which establishes the rightness of its cause also means that the Hunt Saboteurs' Association recognises definite limits on quite how far its opposition can go. If the infliction of pain on an animal reflects an action which has gone beyond the right to restricted freedom, it is also wrong to inflict any sort of pain on a human (R. Thomas 1983: 104). In practice, this means that the humane people who sabotage hunts restrict themselves to attempts at distracting the hunt's hounds with noise or false trails. Officially at least, the Saboteurs condemn anything which might harm a sentient individual, even if they were only hurt whilst being prevented from killing a fox. This has always been the guiding principle of the Hunt Saboteurs. It is a comprehensive and equal application of a moral norm. However, it has not met with universal acceptance. In the early 1970s a small group called the Band of Mercy was set up by Ronnie Lee, a disenchanted saboteur, and a few associates (Windeatt 1985: 190).

The Band of Mercy believed in the pressing necessity of animal rights, and thought that it allowed a vast expansion beyond the limits set by the Hunt Saboteurs. The Band of Mercy contained the stirrings of a rather fundamentalist, fetishistic participation in the social world. Its members were inevitably trying to have no part in the relationships which violated animal rights and, instead, felt that they had an absolute responsibility to do something about animal suffering. Moreover, the suffering was not confined to the hunting field; it could be found in all the existing relationships between animals and society. The Band of Mercy began by damaging hunt vehicles (the Hunt Saboteurs would never have carried out such acts), but became rather more flamboyant in November 1973 when it burned down a building in Milton Keynes which was going to be used for experimentation on animals. A note was subsequently sent to the press. It was written in square block capitals and claimed responsibility for the arson. It also showed the amazing properties which animal rights had come to possess. The note said:

> The building was set fire to in an effort to prevent the torture and murder of our animal brothers and sisters by evil experiments.
> We are a nonviolent guerilla organisation dedicated to the liberation of animals from all forms of cruelty and persecution at the hands of mankind.
> Our actions will continue until our aims are achieved.
>
> (Reproduced in the
> *Animal Liberation Front Supporters Group Newsletter*,
> no. 17, 1985).

Animal rights is a compelling natural fact which the self-styled guerrillas know to be true in their full humanity. It has no social and historical conditions of existence at all.

Let us look at the note in a little more detail. Certainly, it shows how far the worry about the treatment of animals had moved in barely two hundred years. Erskine and Rousseau were trying to change the world, but accepted that some of their ideas were rather speculative. Even Henry Salt still spent a little time establishing the basis of animal rights. The Band of Mercy did not; it relied on assertion rather than debate. It knew that animals and humans are individuals but, more importantly, also brothers and sisters. Consequently, the experiments which a vivisectionist performs on a laboratory monkey or rat are as moral as the experiments which Mengele performed in the death camps. There is no difference. All living creatures share a bond of oppression and suffering. All the brothers and sisters need to be freed from persecution. To this extent, the Band of Mercy was saying that 'Man' should renounce any claims to being unique and, instead, return to the fraternity of equal life. The flames which engulfed the laboratory also destroyed the false social order of things. But 'Man' is also something more: 'Man' is able to liberate animals. The similitude is one of organic structure, but the Band of Mercy was prepared to concede that 'Man' is different; so different that 'he' is able to release animals from their oppression. Humans are – or at least under the right moral guidance can be – suffering individuals with freewill and intentionality. The traces of Similitude played on an anthropology which was identified as the basis of true reality, whereas the strands of Difference emphasised the extent to which real and proper humans were animals quite unlike any other. To remember a thesis which has been used before: humans are so similar to animals that they need to be made radically different. By the 1970s, the moral principle had become defined as so much of an approximation to the natural state of things that it was a fundamental(ist) measure of how relationships between animals and society could, and should, be changed.

The Band of Mercy was probably only a small group of friends, yet it continued to destroy property associated with 'cruelty and persecution' until August 1974, when the police finally caught up with the militants. Whilst the leading members were serving prison sentences for a number of offences related to their activities, Peter Singer published *Animal Liberation*. The book had an immense impact. The title was a slogan as much as a name, and the book cross-cut with ideas which were already circulating in the

Band of Mercy (Windeatt 1985). The note which the Band left after the Milton Keynes fire referred to the 'liberation of animals', a phrase which would have gained Singer's philosophical, although probably not political, support. The coincidence led to the formation of the ALF. The similarity between the title of Singer's book and the Front was not itself an accident, even though it was probably a great surprise to Singer. Arguably, it was a deliberate attempt to imply that a considered philosophical discussion of the question of animals had directly led to the formation of a new political movement. Singer lent moral inevitability and legitimacy to practices which were being carried out anyway. The ALF was formed in June 1976 by Ronnie Lee and about thirty others (Windeatt 1985: 191). Lee started to call himself Captain Kirk – another bold traveller into the unknown. The ALF has always aimed to copy the Band of Mercy, but on a far larger scale. It tries to destroy and economically undermine any activity which is involved in the cruel treatment of animals. The ALF wants to liberate animals from pain, by breaking windows, burning buildings, burgling laboratories, or issuing hoaxes that food has been poisoned. The Front will do many things which other people would frown on, in the name of its moral conviction.

Although the ALF did have some coherent organisation before it was rather successfully infiltrated by a special police unit in the mid-1980s (Henshaw 1989), it could not be called an organisation as such. Ronnie Lee was fond of saying that 'the ALF is not an organization; it's a state of mind' (quoted in North 1985: 24). A person does not join the ALF by paying membership fees; she or he becomes a member by doing something. The Front is concerned with the morally perfect individual who tries to change the world singlehandedly. However, the sophistication and planning which the ALF could achieve if it wanted to was underlined in December 1988, when three letter bombs were posted and incendiary devices were planted in five department stores in the South and Midlands of Britain. The targets were all involved in the fur trade. A store in Plymouth was gutted in what was said to be the city's biggest fire since the Blitz, and stock worth £180,000 was damaged in Cardiff. Fire-bombing became more popular within the ALF through the 1980s. Part of the reason was pragmatic; the bombs caused immense harm to those who harmed animals, but they also had a great tactical advantage. As police interest grew, people were scared off from carrying out ALF action simply on account of their 'state of mind'. The remaining activists drew more on organisational structures. The bombs could be planted by very small cells of militants who could be more confident about secrecy, and who could develop support networks. According to the Front's own estimate, the fire bombs caused at least £9 million of damage in Britain between 1986 and 1988 (*Guardian*, 20 December 1988). The power of the fetish has increased. It has taken an increasingly firm hold on its militants and has led to an aggressive assault on the false idols of anthropocentrism and human apartness. Animals themselves have no place in this conflict; it may be waged in their name, but it rages over their heads.

The ALF fundamentally believes that modern society is based on lies and a misplaced arrogance. Its politicised version of animal rights – which, it must be stressed, is not supported by everyone, and was by no means inevitable – takes aim at a society which is identified as a web of corruption. Anyone who participates in society is equally blameworthy. However, special blame is directed at capitalism and its stooges, the political parties and the state. Acts like bombing department stores are acceptable to the extent that they attack animal abuse. But they are part of the only kind of action that has any chance of success. The Front must assault the hearts of capitalism from without; within is a cosy conspiracy. In 1986, the Leeds cell of the ALF produced a pamphlet which, amongst other things, reasserted the natural similitude of life. Now where Salt thought that similitude was masked by words, or Singer that it was oppressed by speciesism, the Leeds militants blamed exploitative social relationships, and drew a direct link between human and animal liberation: 'Only when all the crimes and evils caused by the governments are attacked, is there hope for us all'. It also declared that the struggle for animal rights needs much activity. It is

a war built out of compassion and respect for our fellow living-beings. They cannot wait hundreds of years for the next reform. . . . Our inaction is their condemnation. The whole political system is interwoven with, and propped up by big business. Political parties are funded by big companies and multinationals, and in return, you can bet that politicians look after the interests of these companies. In fact, many MPs and politicians have shares in these companies or the prospect of a good job after leaving the political arena.

(From *Snarl! Handbook of the Leeds Animal Liberation Front*, 1986)

There is no point in appealing to politicians since they are at the heart of the problem, and it is useless asking the companies because they profit from the use of animals. The only answer is to go on to a war footing and ignore social conventions. The breaking of laws is only incidentally interesting since they only exist to protect the animal-exploiting capitalists. The initiates of the truth – the militants who have glimpsed the timeless similitude behind the modern order of things – have the duty and the justification to override anything which society holds dear. The militants might like to travel the parliamentary road to animal rights (although that is probably doubtful), but they are confident that the road would prove to be a dead end. Although the militants might accept that their actions contradict the rules of democratic politics, their entire argument is that Britain is speciesist and, therefore, cannot possibly *be* democratic. According to them, democracy is quite impossible if no heed is paid to the preferences or nature of animals. The militants argue that they are practising the true democracy – they are the only ones who are aware of the real extent of the *demos* – and that, therefore, what is socially condemned as mindless violence is, when properly understood, a defence of the truth. The interstitiality of the militants in relation to society is quite total.

However, the fact the the ALF recognises no social restraints on what it can do does not mean that it can do anything. That is not surprising. After all, animal rights wants to promote the restricted freedom of all individuals, or, in Singer's terms, the interest of all sentient creatures in a life free from suffering. The militants also use these principles as the measure of their own actions. The activists will do nothing at all which is violent on the grounds that violence is oppressive and causes pain. But precisely what 'violence' means is open to question. The ALF carries out a strategy of economic sabotage and damage, but, by its own terms, shies away from violence. This might sound like an odd thing to say. Surely, it is a trifle aggressive to burn down a department store?

Not necessarily. The ALF equates violence with an act which a sentient other would rather not have done to it. Violence is associated with the suffering which arises from the infringement of individuality. The point is that a department store cannot suffer pain; therefore it has no rights, and it is impossible to behave violently towards it. On these grounds, it is perfectly reasonable to destroy a shop if one is certain that no living creature will be harmed. 'While we may not give a toss about a butcher's right to have his shop window left intact, we must allow that *rights* are important' ('Rose' 1985: 16). So the militant activist can smash a window with a clear conscience, but she or he must remember that the moral constituency also includes butchers. In so far as animal rights is indeed a comprehensive principle, and humans are really animals, butchers share the inalienable and intrinsic right not to be harmed.

> Despite differences . . . all sentient beings have the right not to be killed, physically harmed, tortured, degraded by being involuntarily used as a resource by others If this is accepted, then it strikes at much which most humans take for granted. At a stroke it implies the end to using nonhuman animals as mere resources for human animals. It demands the end of the meat and dairy industry, blood and other animal 'sport', animal experimentation, the keeping of pets, etc., and it imposes a duty, on those of us who can, to try to put an end to them – by direct action because this is the only effective way.
>
> ('Rose' 1985: 16)

Given the conspiratorial network of society, direct action is pragmatically valuable. But, the passage is saying, pragmatism should never get the upper hand over the philosophical argument. The position owes rather more to Salt and Tom Regan than Peter Singer, and it has tended to be a guiding thread for the ALF. However, as the 1980s progressed, there were frequent denials that the norm should be extended to include farm-owners, fur-traders, and vivisectionists. The ALF felt able to send a few letter bombs. Indeed, by the middle of 1990, a smaller number of potentially lethal car bombs had been planted under vehicles belonging to scientists involved in animal experimentation. The bombs caused a great deal of outrage, and they managed to shatter the common front which the speakers of the ALF had previously presented to the press and public.

How could the ALF send bombs which were intended to hurt people? Surely a letter bomb is violent? Again, not necessarily. The ALF generally accepted what may be called an 'absolutist' definition of violence: the right of all creatures not to experience cruelty is an unchanging imperative which places invariant limits on action. It is rooted in the rights tradition. But ever since Jeremy Bentham, and, of course, especially Peter Singer, the attempts to decide the correct relationships between society and animals have also drawn upon utilitarianism. And utilitarianism denies intrinsic rights to moral subjects. The way was paved for the ALF to start sending bombs through the post by a shadowy group called the Animal Rights Militia (ARM), which realised the tactical implications of a simple reading of utilitarian theory. The ARM held to a relative definition of violence. The ARM is formally separate from the ALF, but its grandly named 'Communiqués' have been published by the ALF, and it is highly likely that the Militia is made up by people who also wear the Front's hat.

The ARM came to public attention in 1982 when a letter bomb was sent to Margaret Thatcher. In early 1985, it claimed to have injected eggs with rat poison. It soon moved to even more extravagant measures. Towards the end of 1985, the cars of scientists who worked at a laboratory in Surrey were destroyed, and in January 1986, the ARM managed simultaneously to plant bombs under cars belonging to people associated with animal experiments in Sussex, London, Harrogate, and Staffordshire. As the ARM declared:

> we do not shy away from violence against individual animal abusers for, even if a vivisector were to die, it would be just a tiny fraction of the blood and terror on which animal abuse industries are based. . . . What we plan to do is attack the real abusers, the vivisectors, huntsmen and slaughterhouse owners. . . . [E]veryday our comrades and fellow animals stay behind bars their torment will be avenged, even if this means that some of the filth will lose their lives.
> (Animal Rights Militia 'Communiqué 2' in the *Animal Liberation Front Supporters Group Newsletter*, no. 17, 1985)

Notice the rather Mary Douglasian association of improper

humanity and pollution taboos in the final sentence. Compared to the filthy scientists, the bombers of the Militia, who have nothing to do with animals, are quite pure. The ARM argument is very simple. One scientist causes pain in, say, one hundred animals. Therefore, in a crude utilitarian analysis, if that one scientist (or hunter, or farmer) is killed, the unhappiness caused by his or her death would be wholly outweighed by the liberation of animals from suffering. Violence is redefined as a relative quantity. It was undoubtedly this line of reasoning, mixed with a measure of blatant coercion, which led to the car bombs of 1990.

Peter Singer has been outraged by such views. Although the ARM drew on a thread which is not wholly absent from *Animal Liberation*, the Militia did rather contradict the more liberal drift of Singer's work. Singer replied to the bombs with the argument that it is imperative that the struggle on behalf of animals avoids the trap and error of utilitarian violence. Singer at least has always been aware that the militants still need to convince rather than just coerce people who are at present happy to be speciesists. He wanted to rock the statues on their foundations, not plant a stick of dynamite under them. He says that animal liberation must always guard its place on the high moral ground:

> Animal liberation activists must set themselves irrevocably
> against the use of violence, even when their opponents use
> violence against them. By violence I mean any action which
> causes direct physical harm to any human or animal; and I
> would go beyond physical harm to acts which cause
> psychological harm like fear or terror.
>
> (Singer 1985: 13)

This is not just the repentance of some latter-day Pandora, trying to slam down the lid on a box of woe. It is intended to be a strict application of Singer's philosophical argument, and it reveals the conservative bias which Tom Regan detected. Singer is saying that it is wrong to use violence because it causes an increase of unhappiness compared to the here and now. The ends do not justify the means.

The Animal Rights Militia would argue that the torching of a store is a fairly mild action. The ALF would be inclined to accept such an action to the extent that it infringed no rights. Meanwhile, Peter Singer is obviously rather disturbed that his utilitarian assumptions have been taken up and moulded into terrible new forms. It must be said that Singer did rather create the problem for himself. He linked the moral status of animals to calculations of happiness over suffering, and said that all sentient creatures within the calculation should be counted equally. That straightforward position was unable to avoid the possibility that people like those in the ARM would read the case for animal liberation as a licence for any acts which would bring about a net decrease of suffering. Certainly, it would be wrong to suggest that the ARM was implicitly prefigured in Singer's book, but he in no way closed down the possibility that such a group might appear. Indeed, given his earlier aversion to any trace of metaphysics, it is rather hard to know what the plea for the defence of the high moral ground can possibly mean. Where is the ground? How can it be approached? Either the moral ground is somewhere outside the utilitarian concentration on immediate relationships, in which case careful calculations of the greater good seem to be a little pointless; why not go to the heart of the matter? Alternatively, Singer could reassert that utilitarianism is the way to morality, but that would just restate the difficulty of whether or not it is justifiable to kill a scientist.

All the moralists and practitioners who believe that animals make claims on humans accept that violence is reprehensible. They look at the usual relationships between animals and society and see only cruelty: an illicit touching which corrupts humanity; an aggression which does violence to our human being. The political difficulty is that there is a lack of agreement about what violence actually is. None of the animal rights militants believe they fall into it, and they can provide more or less coherent explanations of why not. The situation is reminiscent of the speeches which Richard Martin and his supporters made in the House of Commons to defend hunting and shooting. They were also unable to admit that they were behaving violently. They too were truly human; they too were the exemplars of all virtue and could, therefore, do almost anything they wanted. Meanwhile they remorselessly tracked down any evidence that the urban working class was slipping from the standards of being human. Richard Martin saw the violence of others from his prestigious social situation. Today's militants see the violence of others from the vantage point of their prestigious moral situation. Violence is little more than an epithet which is used by the right and good guardians of the truth of being to launch an attack on the behaviour and beliefs of other social groups.

Violence is wrong, the world should be made without it. Essentially, groups like the ALF see themselves as the heralds of the new world. They are the people to live in it. They are trying to bring society closer to the moment of ultimate goodness. Henry Salt saw the moment of goodness as a kind of unity between the rights of all individuals and the structures of social classification. He glimpsed perfection in the unification of the two into one and the transcendence of falsity. The stroller in St James's Park perceived something similar: a world where all arrogant distinctions were pushed aside to uncover a fraternity of complete joy. Both were yearning for a future which recreated an ideal of what life was like before the towns and cities were built. Their visions are a nostalgia for *Gemeinschaft*.

The contemporary militants also have dreams of nostalgia; they too want to return to the future. But they also have clear practical ideas on what the future society will be like. Obviously, in the specific case of relationships with animals, the aim is to create a world which is non-oppressive for 'Man' and beast alike. Human and animal rights and freedoms are sides of the same coin because the very division between humans and animals is illegitimate. But the militants want rather more. Writing under his code-name, Captain Kirk, Ronnie Lee said that 'True freedom for all the Earth's creatures demands a decentralized non-hierarchical society with much lower levels of technology and a massive cut in the human population' (Lee 1985a: 10). In the future, society will fly a green and black flag.

Lee wants a world which has reconciled culture and technology with nature, and 'Man' with animals. All life, and the conditions which sustain it, provides a non-oppressive model for the correct relationships between society and animals. Another leading militant has explained Lee's vision and suggested that the reduction of human numbers could be achieved by compulsory sterilisation (see Harris 1985: 169). They do not seem to have noticed a problem. Who chooses which members of the global population should be sterilised, and what criteria would they use? It is a reasonable bet that the morally good militants would give to themselves the ability to choose and would want to begin with the forcible sterilisation of the inhumane, polluted individuals who paid no heed to the rights of animals: the vivisectionists, factory farmers, and hunters. Presumably, however, they would eventually turn to meat-eaters and people who wear leather shoes. An interesting dilemma which the militants never seem to have confronted is whether abortion is an acceptable way of reducing human numbers. How could the pure and humane, the true humans, be stopped from carrying out their *obligation* to purify the planet? They could not. They would never doubt the immutable rightness of their cause. Because they have the faith, they can change the world. The future belongs to them: 'If we can create within ourselves the prophecy of victory, there is little doubt that we will see that prophecy fulfilled'. Yet caution is needed; victory 'will not be achieved unless activists have a fervent faith in its ultimate achievement' (Lee 1985b: 14).

Peter Singer, Tom Regan, Stephen Clark, and all the other moralists of animal rights are in no way responsible for Ronnie Lee's eco-fascist future. It would be a libellous misinterpretation to say that they are. Lee is combining animal rights with Kropotkinesque and propaganda-by-deed anarchism, and a large dose of millenarian fervour. This is a fetishism of a most unshakeable kind. Lee and groups like the ALF and the ARM are a vivid example of what can happen when ideas are fetishised, and their social and historical conditions of existence ignored. I am not saying that everyone who believes that animals possess rights will turn into a militant activist. But a significant and noisy minority have done, and some people will do so in the future, despite the opposition or wariness of most of their colleagues. It is quite impossible to suggest what the social background and number of the militants will be; just as impossible as it is to predict the constituency of any other cult which appeals to individuals *as* individuals, rather than any definite social groups. Animal rights is not important on the grounds of who upholds it, but because of the very fact that it is upheld at all.

Is it upheld as a peculiar strand of a wider environmental concern? Is Ronnie Lee just an odd sort of ecologist? Although there might well seem to be some coincidence, and although it can be assumed that many ecologists think that animals have rights, and many 'rightists' agree that society should be more environmentally aware, there is a great gulf which separates the ideas from each other. Indeed, there are serious tensions between them. The ecological approach accepts that humans should look after questions of animal welfare, and also that animal species should be conserved. However, at least in Jonathon Porritt's presentation of green politics, animals are simply one part of a global nature. He presents ecology as a systems approach to the world in which human activity in relation to nature should be regulated if human well-being is to be possible. As Porritt writes:

> It is calculated there are between 3 million and 10 million
> species of plants and animals, of which only 1½ million are
> recorded, and very little is known even about these. The fact
> that thousands of species will disappear by the turn of the
> century is not just an academic irritation: our own survival
> depends on our understanding of the intricate webs of life in
> which we're involved. Nor is it just a question of the 1,000 or
> so familiar and appealing mammals which are now
> threatened; our concern must be based on something more
> than the instinct to cuddle warm, furry creatures.
>
> (Porritt 1984: 98–9)

Porritt wants an awareness of supposedly 'intricate webs of life'. It is ironic then that he seems seems slow to draw any real distinctions between plant and animal species. All non-human life is put into an analytic bucket which muddies as much as it clarifies. Certainly, Porritt is saying laudable things, but the passage locates the importance of animals at the level of species. The 'webs of life' require the continued existence of the up to 10 million species of life, and so they should be conserved. The well-being or suffering of any individual animal is a distant second to global worries.

Animal rights holds the conservation of ecology in complete anathema. As Ronnie Lee commented with characteristic assurance: 'An individual animal doesn't care if its species is facing extinction – it cares if it is feeling pain' (quoted in Wynne-Tyson 1985: 174). A considerably less militant, indeed a distinctly moderate, worker for animal rights has expanded the assumption behind Lee's assertion:

> While the value of the work of organisations in the field of
> conservation cannot be overstated, it can be argued, as far as
> suffering is concerned, that when the last great whale is killed

to feed man's greed for its oil, blubber and meat, never again will one of the most intelligent non-human animals in the world be subjected to such an obscene and lingering death. The death of the last whale will be man's loss, not the whales'.

(Hollands 1985: 170)

The problem with Porritt is that he forgets the rights and claims of the individual in his emphasis on the well-being of the planet. Ecology preserves whales for the benefit of the earth's biological systems, whereas animal rights argues with a bleak logic that the death of the last whale will be the end of the suffering of whales.

Politically, animal rights exists in something of a fund-amentalist ghetto. Other groups and organisations steer clear of the issue because they do not want to get their fingers meta-phorically blown off by a bomb. The militants themselves criticise nearly everyone else for a lack of faith and woolly thinking. The militants can also end up in some curious political alliances. Hans Ruesch, who is a leading Swiss antivivisectionist, has given interviews to British Nazi journals on the grounds that any chance of talking about animal rights is better than none (Henshaw 1989: 192–3). Ronnie Lee wrote that Nazis who joined animal rights groups should not necessarily be expelled: 'To advocate that we have nothing to do with such people, in my view, is a serious mistake because it . . . deprives the animals of some of their defenders' (Lee 1985a: 10). It must be said that the groups which have a higher public profile than the ALF, such as the Hunt Saboteurs and the British Union for the Abolition of Vivisection, have a far more honourable record in their dealings with Nazis. For Ronnie Lee at least, it is impossible to taint the magical purity of animal rights.

The militant activists who appeared in Britain in the 1970s and 1980s were the product of a long process of historical creation which was stimulated during the eighteenth century and firmly in train by the final decades of the nineteenth century. The main questions in the invention of animal rights have been: what is it to be a human who lives an urban life? What should we do, how ought we behave? What is expected of us? All the answers involved an attempt to determine the basis of human being in contra-distinction to the animal. That is why *all* the relationships between society and animals are at arm's length. In the countryside, humans and animals are metonymical; the distinction of being human is established by the hunters and the landworkers who prove their supremacy over animals by killing them. Meanwhile in the city humans and animals are metaphorical. We are already firmly separated from them. Consequently, animals can be let into our houses as objects of affection and we can start worrying about them. Our human being is already certain; to be human is to be humane, it is to not touch animals. We feel happy to enfranchise them morally. Now, animals are the same as us; all life is identical, and we are keen to say so because all our knowledge, everything which creates truth, confirms that real humans are not animals at all.

Animal rights is one strand of a wider urban-centred order of things. It firmly slams the door between proper humans and animals by saying and practising the assertion that humans should have no relationships with animals. Animal rights also creates the space in which the real 'Man' can glory in certainty by locking another door to protect moral purity and goodness from social corruption and filth. It locks 'Man' into a classificatory prison where 'he' can finally say what 'he' is without fear of mockery or contradiction – a prison in which idols are worshipped and an amnesia swamps the lingering memories of how those idols came to be fashioned in the first place. The activities of the militants are just one especially fundamentalist way of living the truth of the fetish of animal rights. The ALF is only trying to do the same modest things as its predecessors in the history of the claims for animals. The ALF is simply saying that it is absolutely right, it really does know best, and it is merely trying to make sure that everyone else agrees. The animals only wander into the picture when they are dying or dead. The humans are too busy painting their own image throughout the world to take any notice of them.

Chapter Nine

IF A LION COULD TALK

By the middle of the 1970s, animal rights had been firmly fetishised. This book has explained much of the history and sociology which made possible the claims which are currently made on behalf of animals' moral status. Since Henry Salt more or less invented animal rights in the nineteenth century, and thus turned the earlier Demands for Difference and Similitude into prehistory, the conditions of existence of the narrative have been systematically repressed. Now, for the twentieth-century protagonists like Peter Singer, Tom Regan, and Stephen Clark, the moral claims which animals make are a quite immutable natural truth. According to those writers, it is upheld today, when it would have been mocked two centuries ago, simply because we have progressed to a higher level of moral goodness. I have argued that it is misplaced and not very useful to think that the truth of animals exists 'out there', waiting to be directly and unproblematically appropriated within knowledge. The analysis has insisted on precisely the thing that Salt and all the others have tried to forget: animal rights is a social construction and exclusively a social practice. All else, all statements that the morality is a true reflection of the natural being of animals, is fictional. However, the statement that animal rights is a fiction does not imply that it is a delusion or wanton artifice. On the contrary, people like the militants of the ALF mould large parts of their personal, subjective lives around it. For them, it is an absolutely certain reality, and they should not just be ridiculed.

I am not condemning animal rights because it is untrue, but I do think it is reasonable to criticise the enthusiasm to tell the world that the narrative is naturally given. If this book has any polemical intent, it is to ask the militants and the philosophers to realise that they are fetishistically upholding obligations which are made and not found. I have endeavoured to tell the story of the making. The fetishisation of the treatment of animals is no more inevitable than Marx thought it was inevitable that all commodities in all societies would be invested with magical properties. It is not the thing itself (the morality, the animal, the product) which is the cause of fetishism; rather, it is the social relationships within which the thing is located. The point is that the social relationships practised by the militants are irrevocably attempting to elevate to a position of overwhelming obviousness and domination a moral principle which is not obvious at all.

Animal rights is only obvious, and only seen as a natural truth, to the extent that within the epistemological field which Salt opened up there is a degree of confidence over who or what 'Man' is. Within that field 'Man' is defined as the potentially perfect animal; so Different that 'he' is the beacon of progress and well-being, but so much the Same that 'Man' and animal are linked by strong moral bonds. The fascinating anthropological and taxonomic dimension of animal rights is how it revolves around the seeming contradiction that as 'Man' increasingly recognises similitude with animals, 'Man' restates difference through practical actions. The modern individual who acknowledges the identity of humans and animals refuses to eat, wear, use, or touch them. In other words, the distinctive place of humans in the order of the things of the world, which is potentially qualified by the ambiguous faces of 'Man', is reconfirmed through pragmatic behaviour. Animals are only made the site of moral worries to the extent that they are useful in establishing social definitions of the properly human. Does that mean that this analysis is idealist? In particular, if the question of the relationships between animals and society is crucially taxonomic, what status can be given to the social processes and relationships which, it was argued, had to be a key to any explanation?

The relationships retain an absolutely fundamental importance. Certainly, the analysis provided in this book has obviously been somewhat influenced by Michel Foucault's work on the historical discontinuity of Western knowledge, and it is fair to say that he does tend to place too heavy an emphasis on purely ideational events. However, knowledge does not change for simply internal reasons. If knowledge involves a project of classifying and ordering social reality, then it will be transformed as and when there is a change in the material circumstances it is trying to apprehend. Despite possible first impressions, the moralisation of the way society deals with animals is not only rooted in ideas and taxonomy. More fundamentally, the emphasis on morality is the product of the eighteenth- and nineteenth-century process of urbanisation and the conflictual relationships between different urban groups. Both these events were in addition to the tensions between the invariably contradictory urban and rural definitions of the practices of being human. Animal rights is inextricably part of the same social processes which allowed Marx to vilify the idiocy of rural life, and others to bewail the dirty sloth of the urban working class. I have explained the form and content of those processes. Perhaps more importantly, I have endeavoured to provide an account of animal rights which lapses into neither a social history ('what happened'), nor a history of ideas ('what was believed'). Instead, I have identified animal rights as a moral system which integrates ideas and practices into coherent forms of social subjectivity. Such an approach is a significant advance on the naturalist assumptions of the protagonists.

However, one of the relationships between animals and society has not yet been made wholly explicit. Although it has been implicit throughout the book, it has not been spelt out. Yet it is probably the most obvious and influential of all. It is the *freedom* of individuals and society to do what they want with animals, and the freedom we presently enjoy to make of animals what we will. Animal rights might restrain the social treatment of animals, but that restraint is only possible and necessary because we are otherwise free in relation to them. Singer, Regan, and Clark offer clear meditations on the problems and opportunities of human freedom in Western, urbanised societies. Their moral theories pretend to say something conclusive about animals, but they are perhaps more fundamentally indicating what actions individuals can and should rightly take. The animals are nothing more than objects to which something is done. Indeed, when something substantive is said about animals it tends to be fairly banal. Let us be honest; it is not actually too profound to say that certain things hurt other species. The mere fact of animals' pain is exactly the blank page which Mary Midgley argued would, on the contrary, be revealed to be sublimely written upon, if only we learnt how to decipher the marks. But Midgley forgot that it takes skill, know-how, and subjectivity to write anything on the pages, abilities which only fully social human individuals are said to possess. Only society invests animals and the natural world with moral meaning, because only society is sufficiently free to be able to carry out that investment.

Indeed, perhaps all the moral codes can be usefully understood as attempts to make the relationships between animals and society more aesthetic. If that is the case, it is the finest illustration of social freedom. Animals are turned into poor, suffering, cuddly creatures precisely because they constitute no threat at all, precisely to the extent that we are free from any compulsion in the treatment of them. The only compulsion is that which we ourselves make. After all, endangered species are only a problem since, firstly, we are able to kill them very easily, and, secondly, we do not need to. If animals like tigers still represented a very real threat, as presumably they do for a number of people elsewhere in the world, they would quite probably be shot without hesitation. If animals were in themselves a direct and demanding dimension of British social life, if they came before us in a natural way, and not through the social mediations of the factory farm, television screen, or philosophy book, our treatment of them would be very different, as indeed it frequently is. It is no coincidence that aesthetic and moral sensibilities towards animals have almost exclusively emerged in the highly urbanised societies which practise a far-reaching freedom from, and over, the natural world. The urban way of life sees animals as experiential and geo-graphical outsiders or, at least, subordinates who need to be looked after. Relationships with animals would have other characteristics if the urban had not been quickly and firmly established as the home and garrison of the fully social in eighteenth- and nineteenth-century Britain.

The composer Harrison Birtwistle has interestingly stated that 'we look at Nature externally with mystic feelings . . . [But] when you get close you see that it's incredibly violent. Everything's eating everything else. Nature is hell on earth' (quoted in Lebrecht 1987: 85). Angela Carter in some ways reiterated Birtwistle's point that it is impossible to aestheticise or moralise a

197

natural world which is still compelling. In the story 'The Company of Wolves', Carter wrote:

> You are always in danger in the forest, where no people are. Step between the portals of the great pines where the shaggy branches tangle about you, trapping the unwary traveller in nets as if the vegetation itself were in a plot with the wolves who live there, as though the wicked trees go fishing on behalf of their friends – step between the gateposts of the forest with the greatest trepidation and infinite precautions, for if you stray from the path for one instant, the wolves will eat you. They are grey as famine, they are as unkind as plague.
>
> (Carter 1981: 111)

Of course, in modern Britain, in Britain as it has developed since the eighteenth century at least, the natural world *is* viewed externally. We *are* divorced from it both by the urbanisation of social life and through the taxonomy which orders the things of the world. Woods and wolves are not an oppressive danger. The nearest most of us get to a forest is a day trip to a park or wildlife sanctuary where, if we wander off the path, we meet not wolves but the urban terror of a party of schoolchildren. It is not especially important whether Harrison Birtwistle's and Angela Carter's image of nature as red in tooth and claw is historically accurate. The picture is important because it offers an insight into what they think the world *might* be like if it was experienced as an overpowering reality. The statements are also important precisely because they have been made by people who will not be eaten by wolves, and who are detached from the wild and the natural. Like the rest of us, Birtwistle and Carter are free to turn forests and wolves to any ends they want. When the social directly experienced animals, they were treated either as a danger symbol, a stupid plaything, or so much meat. Birtwistle and Carter are voicing a late twentieth-century horror of the loss of freedom, and a fear of the collapse of the Nietzschean pathos of distance. Without distance and freedom, animal rights would be impossible.

That is to offer a very flat and easy interpretation which is similar to the one offered by Harriet Ritvo and criticised earlier. It asserts the freedom of *all* society over *all* animals. But, as we have seen, society is not an internally homogeneous whole. Quite the opposite; it is riven with conflict and only takes on the appearance of a solid totality, a society as opposed to the looser ensemble of the social, through the political resolution of those conflicts, and strategies of domination. For that matter, the 'we' I keep appealing to is a rhetorical figure, and the creation of social processes and relationships rather than the simple product of any prior biology or common essence. Freedom, too, is a social relationship, and not some bright, immutable reality which is the same for all people at all times. The discussion of the Demand for Difference and the Demand for Similitude showed that the meaning and practice of freedom is a pressing site of social dispute. Is 'Man' free when the beast has been extirpated, or when the suffocations of social convention have been thrown aside? Later, towards the end of the nineteenth century, Henry Salt thought that we could be free only if we accepted the intrinsic restricted sovereignty of the individual. Each of the definitions had its own social base; it was part of the world view of the bourgeoisie, free-floating intellectuals, or self-appointed defenders of the truth. Also, each has established some validity solely because of its success and practical usefulness, not because any one definition was 'better' or 'more true' than any other.

Freedom is not 'a property, a possession of the individual . . . it is a quality pertaining to a difference between individuals; . . . it makes sense only as an opposition to some other condition, past or present' (Bauman 1988: 7). The bourgeois legislators like Lord Erskine or Richard Martin were only free to the extent that they were the defenders of the special 'Man' in contrast to the human beasts, typified by Tom Nero, who rotted in city slums. Meanwhile, Rousseau and Ritson were free since they had torn apart social bonds, unlike the people they condemned as the pampered windbags of parliament. More recently, Salt and his heirs have been free to the extent that they have managed to ignore species and have instead realised the inalienable moral equality of all individuals. The freedom of each group is a social relation. It is something it uniquely possesses in contradistinction to what is thus defined as the constraint of others. Each group struggles to establish its definition as *the* definition of freedom. The analysis of the Demands for Difference and Similitude, and the discussion of the 'comprehensive principle' of animal rights told the story of many of the features of the conflict between them. However, it has not been fully resolved today, and indeed probably never will be played out to a consensual solution. Had the disputes over freedom been worked through, if the freedom of humans and society in relation to animals had been decided beyond all doubt, groups like the ALF would not need to be active. Either that, or they would not generate such hostility.

The social definitions of the right and proper treatment of animals operate on two levels: firstly, the freedom of urban society from the compulsions of nature; and secondly, the intra-social struggle of certain social groups to impose their own standards and perspectives on all other groups. Both levels of historical definition have particularly involved the ability of the social to understand animals as things which are bereft of all intrinsic symbolic meaning, and only mean whatever society projects upon them. Animal rights is one aspect of a whole set of social relationships which confirm and consolidate the place of 'Man' in contradistinction to the profusion of other things. Animal rights is one way 'Man' can be free, and so 'Freedom is power, in so far as there are others who are bound' (Bauman 1988: 23). We could not be free to give animals rights if they were not bound to our ability to give them rights. Just as animals are subordinately tied to social relations, certain social groups are bound by the freedom of other groups. That is why the working class has had no more of a constructive role in this analysis than the animals themselves. It is also why the only forms of opposition to the enforced curtailment of the historical pleasures of the working class tend to be just a little unpleasant.

Now, if freedom is a relation which exists only in distinction to some past or present state of compulsion, then it should be possible to date the moment when society became free to give animals rights. It should also be possible to discuss the strategies by which the historical situation of freedom has been protected from the backsliding of the human beasts and the dilution of humanity which would be the consequence of any illicit touching of animals. If the freedom which is the heart of modernity is all these things, it should display a degree of social and historical coherence. Indeed it does. The freedom which permits the moral treatment of animals can be understood in terms of *gardening* relationships. When society, and social groups, felt nature and animals as an oppressive reality, in the days before modern freedom, the relations and practices were similar to those of *gamekeeping*.

The words 'gamekeeping' and 'gardening' are a metaphor for two different historical strategies of social relations. Each has implications for the relationships between animals and society. The metaphor is taken from the work of Ernest Gellner (1983) and Zygmunt Bauman (1987). Ernest Gellner begins to explain:

> Cultures, like plants, can be divided into savage and cultivated varieties. The savage kinds are produced and reproduce themselves spontaneously, as parts of the life of men . . . [They] reproduce themselves from generation to generation, without conscious design, supervision, surveillance or special nutrition.
>
> Cultivated or garden cultures are different, though they have developed from the wild varieties. They possess a complexity and richness, most usually sustained by literacy and by specialised personnel, and would perish if deprived of their distinctive nourishment in the form of specialised institutions of learning with reasonably numerous, full-time and dedicated personnel.
>
> (Gellner 1983: 50)

It might seem that Gellner's use of the metaphor says little about freedom. Certainly, his use of the word 'savage' is quite unacceptable. Gellner tends to talk as if the processes and relationships of wild and garden cultures are largely inevitable and present society with a set of necessary requirements. To an extent, such an objection is valid, but Bauman has taken the image a stage further. For him, wild and garden cultures do not just exist; on the contrary, they are themselves ways of understanding specific social relationships, and therefore imply definite practices. If the metaphor is used in that way, in a fully *sociological* sense, the issue of freedom becomes very important.

Consider the place of individuals in each of the different cultures. The wild culture is held to be something which reproduces itself without human intervention. Culture and society are simply found. They are in no way made. The world is apprehended as something quite beyond the human and the social. All society can do, or all the most powerful social groups at least can usefully do, is behave like a collective gamekeeper, and simply try to preserve its place in a world which is potentially as dark and threatening as Angela Carter's wolf-infested forest.

201

Social knowledge and practices will bear the definite stamp of the gamekeeper's fear and modesty:

> Gamekeepers are not great believers in the human (or their own) capacity to administer their own life. They are naturally, so to speak, religious people. Having practised no 'patterning', 'moulding' or 'shaping' of the wild culture they supervise, they lack the experience from which one can fashion the idea of the human origin of the human world, the self-sufficiency of man, the malleability of the human condition, etc. Their own lack of interference with the spontaneous working of the wild culture, which has constituted the virtual 'untouchability' of the latter, is reflected in their philosophy . . . of the superhuman character of the world order.
>
> (Bauman 1987: 52–3)

The story has been encountered twice before. Keith Thomas implied it in his analysis of pre-modern definitions of nature as resolutely anthropocentric, and Michel Foucault also came near to it when he painted the picture of the Renaissance *episteme*.

Thomas's account of the decline of anthropocentrism is rather curious. Although anthropocentrism perceived humanity as the centre of the universe, all its legitimacy was derived from a simple assertion of the God-ordained status of the human. It seems to have had no reliance on any discussion of society as such, as one might reasonably expect that anthropocentrism would. Anthropo-centrism rested all its strength and validity on the word of God. God had made humans the high point of His creation, and so humans had to behave according to His compelling and intransigent word. Consequently, Thomas is able to link the story of the disenchantment of the world to the decline of anthro-pocentrism, and suggest that knowledge was shaped by a newly detached scientificity by the beginning of the nineteenth century. Meanwhile, Foucault's Renaissance *episteme* necessarily had to see the universe as something pre-ordained, since it was founded on the assumption of a magical connection between the word and the thing. Only a figure with the abilities of God could have forged the bonds of resemblance.

In both contexts, the social could only behave like a gamekeeper. The philosophers of the Renaissance thought that the world, and existence within it, was an immutable reality which merely turned back on itself in repetitious cycles and mirror images of resemblance. All the old philosophers could do was scan the true texts and endeavour to spell out the proper place of humans in the impassive system. The anthropocentric-theological thinkers discussed by Thomas were in much the same situation. They thought that they should only seek to tell of the indivisible human place in the world. The universe itself was something which God had created in His wisdom, and was therefore quite beyond their interference. The resulting social practices, which both Thomas and Foucault for very different reasons are inclined to push out of the main frame of analysis, would be of the most trivial freedoms. Since the world existed independently of society itself, the place of humans could only be very small. To be sure, within that place they could do much as they pleased; the women and men of the Renaissance could kill animals, but only so long as they continually looked over their shoulder to see if their behaviour was compatible with the truth. They were not really free at all. They were prisoners of God and resemblance, and only free to hit out wildly against the walls of their safe and secure little cell.

Everything changed with the development of the new strategy of gardening, and with the redefinition of truth as the preserve of socially generated and protected knowledge. Everything changed when God died and the bonds of Renaissance order were torn apart. Now, for the purposes of the study of animal rights, the transition from a wild to a garden culture in Britain, and the transition from gamekeeping to gardening social practices, can be dated to the eighteenth century. However, the transformation was not easy and neither was it achieved all at once. Certainly, Bauman is a little too prone to overdraw the distinction. He almost seems to imply that, one night in the eighteenth century, society went to bed wearing its gamekeeper clothes and, although it had many disturbing nightmares, awoke wearing the clean boots of the gardener. The transition was not so quick, nor so simple. Foucault provides some indication of the transformation with the identification of a Classical *episteme* which is dated to exactly the same period. The Classical *episteme* was fundamentally unsound. The problem was that humans and society had no place in the Classical tables of knowledge and the classification which was founded upon the principle of representation. The human was the Same *par excellence*, and thus turned into that which could not be known because there was nothing it could represent.

'Man' emerged as an epistemological figure from the ruins of the Classical system. Arguably, Foucault's modern *episteme* indicates the moment and form of the implementation of gardening social relations. Gardeners are people who have a great deal of faith and trust in their own abilities. They do not think that culture can be left to itself. Instead they tear up weeds, plant beautiful flowers, and make sure that the environment fits their designs. The order and truth of the world is something they create, and they tend to think it is a nonsense to say that any truths are simply 'there', waiting to be found. Gardeners do not rely on God and supernatural sanctions; they only depend on knowledge and themselves:

> Intellectually, the redefinition of social power as a product of human convention, as something not 'absolute' and beyond human control, was by far the most important milestone on the road to modernity. But for such a redefinition to happen, a revolution in the way social order was reproduced must have taken place.
>
> (Bauman 1987: 53)

The crucibles of that revolution were the geographical and cultural growth of the town and the city, and the political linkage of the urban with the properly human and fully social. Gardeners are people who think that the order of things needs surveillance and protection, lest it be undermined by transgression. In this light, the early nineteenth-century legislators such as Lord Erskine and Richard Martin were making typical gardening demands. They were indeed trying to establish knowledge as the ruling force in the world, and attempting to confirm a definition of the urban as the place where 'Man' behaves in peculiarly human ways. The gardener's political point was that, unfortunately 'Man' was also little more than an animal. As such, people like Bentham, Erskine, and Fowell Buxton condemned what they thought to be passionate and emotional behaviour on the grounds that it revealed the beast beating in the human breast. Instead, they applauded their own refined and affected, *cultivated* practices, and struggled to make such behaviour the only truly human mode of life. The Nietzschean insight that the good and moral is simply that which is carried out by the bourgeoisie, in contradistinction to the beastly and base actions of the working class, can be seen as the historical ideational basis for the crushing of popular pastimes, the formation of the RSPCA, and the enactment of anti-cruelty laws. Indeed, even the Rousseau–Ritson line, which attacked the Demand for Difference, was fully a gardening social relationship since it was self-consciously created by more or less deliberately interstitial individuals who voluntarily, or at least knowingly, defined the world as an immutable reality. The real historical gamekeepers could never choose; they were never free enough.

Although gardening relationships are predominantly concerned with intra-social disputes and struggles, they also have a profound impact on the social treatment of nature and, of course, animals. If God had not created the universe, or if it did not reveal some superhuman design, then the truth could not possibly be revealed from 'out there'. It could only be made and rationally known. And, socially, only the privileged 'Man' was capable of gaining knowledge and knowing how to use it properly. Consequently, the truth of animals, their status as the makers (or not) of moral claims, could only be a social product. Gardening relationships entirely subordinate animals to social knowledge. In themselves, animals only provide ambivalent meanings; they are simultaneously weak and strong, docile and frightening, suffering or useful. Their moral status is simply a result of the historical freedom of society to invest animals with any symbolic or philosophical meaning it pleases. If it is society, and the conflicts within it, which makes and practises the truth, then it is society, and the conflicts within it, which makes and practises the truth of animals. Since the eighteenth century, animals have been made meaningless without social and historical intervention. With the collapse of anthropocentrism, the introduction of the modern *episteme*, the deployment of gardening social relations and, underlying all this, the consolidation of the urbanisation of social life, 'Man' has become free to use animals as nothing more than a measure of the nature of human being and the practices of being human. Hamlet anticipated matters somewhat when he announced that 'Man' is 'in action, how like an angel! in apprehension, how like a god! the beauty of the world! the paragon of animals!' Hamlet was aware that we are able simultaneously to define ourselves as linked to all other animals, but also as beings approaching metaphysical perfection. He did not realise, however, that the angels and the animals would be different social groups.

In modern Britain, animals cannot escape social definition. They can never be things in and for themselves. They are only given rights, and seen to make moral claims, because individuals and society are able to give them rights. All the lofty talk of animal liberation or rights is more than a trifle mischievous. The prospect of liberation and sovereignty which the narrative contains is just one more entrapment of animals. The morality is rather clever at hiding the utter meaninglessness of animals, but, at heart, it emphasises the meaningfulness only of the social. With the moral offer, society is very skilfully and surreptitiously reinforcing the already virtually total grip it enjoys over animals. In modern Britain, animals cannot escape being bound by our freedom. Society can only demonstrate and enhance freedom over them. It is delighted to do so. In behaving morally in relation to animals, individuals and society are simply proving how much better than animals they have become; just showing how privileged 'Man' really can be. Real 'Man' can do all this for animals; after all, they cannot do it for themselves.

Richard Rorty might offer a way out of this rather melancholy, now seemingly eternal, return of domination over other species. He asks whether the losses and constraints which modernity involves might not be compensated for by the decrease of pain. Indeed, Rorty does not doubt 'that this decrease does, in fact, compensate for those constraints' (Rorty 1989: 63). The assertion could be useful. Certainly, animals might at present be totally trapped within the social and historical situation of human freedom when they were not before, but Rorty could have a point when he suggests that entrapment might be a small price to pay if it means that animals do not have to suffer as much pain as they once did, when humans were less free. Unfortunately, there are few reasons to agree with him. Quite simply, it is impossible to know how Rorty's question might be given a valuable answer. If social and historical relationships and processes are given analytic primacy, and I have suggested throughout this book that they must, then it must also be accepted that those relationships are the context for the formation of individual social subjectivity. Rorty himself admits that subjectivity is a contingent state and in no way the product of any intrinsic qualities or essence (Rorty 1989: 23–43). Now, simply, if the problem of animals' moral status, the question of their pain, and the answer that compensation is worthwhile are all socially and historically dependent, as is the individual who considers the problem, then the answer itself will always be dependent as well. It will rely upon, and be shaped by, precisely the sociological context which created the initial difficulty. In other words, the answer to the question will always be 'Yes, the loss of freedom is more than compensated for by the loss of pain'. It could not be anything else. A non-relative and fully independent answer could only be given by an individual who has somehow remained outside of social and historical relationships; and such an individual is an impossibility. We cannot know whether the present treatment of animals is preferable to the treatment of two or three centuries ago. There is no supra-historical basis upon which it is viable to ask the question, nor indeed answer it, in anything other than the most trite fashion.

Neither, of course, can we ask the animals themselves. If the problem of the treatment of animals is a social problem, then it can only be given a social resolution. Yet the resolution again only increases the power of society over animals. That is something which we can only accept with a resigned shrug. It is most seriously irresponsible to pretend that the morality has been developed exclusively for the good of animals, or to suggest that they naturally demand a certain treatment, or, indeed, to maintain that they are being released from social power. Animals have been made moral subjects because society demands that they be made moral subjects for *purely social reasons*.

Wittgenstein once remarked 'If a lion could talk, we could not understand him' (Wittgenstein 1953: 223e). He was making the largely philosophical point that the world of the lion and the world of the social are totally unconnected and, therefore, communication between them is impossible. But the rupture between the two worlds is not only philosophical; it is also historical and sociological. Animal rights is one way in which the rupture is emphasised and made quite unbridgeable. The struggles over the status and meaning of 'Man' the city dweller have helped guarantee that the lion can never be known in itself. Indeed, outside of our investment of it, there is nothing about the lion for us to know. The lion is only given meaning to the extent that the values which are projected on to it help say something about what it is to be human.

All of us would rather a lion did not suddenly start up an intelligible conversation because we have taken it upon ourselves, as a mark and a vindication of our difficult, double-faced, and yet privileged status within the world, to speak on the lion's behalf. The lion has been given the right to hold a conversation only because we know that talking is a uniquely human and social activity. If, one day, a lion were to stroll up to one of the protagonists of its rights and say, in perfect grammar, 'Hello, thank you for helping me', the reaction would probably be one of utter horror. It is easier, more comforting, and far more superior, to talk about the rights or liberation of things that cannot answer back.

BIBLIOGRAPHY

Archer, John E. (1985) '"A Fiendish Outrage"? A Study of Animal
  Maiming in East Anglia: 1830–1870', *Agricultural History Review*,
  vol. 33: 147–57.
'B' (1791) 'Humanity to Brute Creation Strongly Recommended',
  Gentleman's Magazine, vol. 61: 334–6.
Bataille, Georges (1986) 'Metamorphosis', *October*, 36.
Bauman, Zygmunt (1987) *Legislators and Interprotors. On Modernity,
  Post-modernity and Intellectuals*, Oxford: Polity.
—— (1988) *Freedom*, Milton Keynes: Open University Press.
Baumgardt, David (1952) *Bentham and the Ethics of Today*, Princeton,
  NJ: Princeton University Press.
Bentham, Jeremy (1960) *An Introduction to the Principles of Morals and
  Legislation*, Oxford: Basil Blackwell.
Bryant, John (n.d.) *Fettered Kingdoms. An Examination of a Changing
  Ethic*, Chard: J.M. Bryant.
Carter, Angela (1981) *The Bloody Chamber and Other Stories*,
  Harmondsworth: Penguin.
Censorinus (1803) Letter to the *Gentleman's Magazine*, vol. 73: 915.
Charbonnier, Georges (1969) *Conversations with Claude Lévi-Strauss*,
  London: Jonathan Cape.
Chatwin, Bruce (1987) *The Songlines*, London: Jonathan Cape.
Clark, David Lee (1939) 'The Date and Source of Shelley's *A
  Vindication of Natural Diet*', *Studies in Philology*, vol. 36: 70–6.
Clark, Stephen R.L. (1977) *The Moral Status of Animals*, Oxford:
  Clarendon Press.
Clerus (1821) Letter to the *Gentleman's Magazine*, vol. 91: 386.
Cohen, Esther (1986) 'Law, Folklore and Animal Lore', *Past and
  Present*, 110: 6–37.
Darnton, Robert (1985) *The Great Cat Massacre and Other Episodes in
  French Cultural History*, Harmondsworth: Penguin.
Douglas, Mary (1966) *Purity and Danger, An Analysis of the Concepts of
  Pollution and Taboo*, London: Routledge & Kegan Paul.

—— (1975) *Implicit Meanings. Essays in Anthropology*, London: Routledge & Kegan Paul.

Duffy, Maureen (1984) *Men and Beasts. An Animal Rights Handbook*, London: Paladin.

Durkheim, Emile (1915) *The Elementary Forms of the Religious Life*, London: George Allen & Unwin.

Elias, Norbert (1956) 'Problems of Involvement and Detachment', *British Journal of Sociology*, vol. 7: 226–52.

—— (1978a) *The History of Manners. The Civilizing Process, vol. 1*, Oxford: Basil Blackwell.

—— (1978b) *What is Sociology?*, London: Hutchinson.

—— (1982) *State Formation and Civilization. The Civilizing Process*, vol. 2, Oxford: Basil Blackwell.

Elias, Norbert and Dunning, Eric (1986) *Quest for Excitement. Sport and Leisure in the Civilizing Process*, Oxford: Basil Blackwell.

Erskine, Lord (1809) Speech to the House of Lords, *Parliamentary Debates*, 15 May 1809: columns 553–71.

Evans, Edward P. (1906) *The Criminal Prosecution and Capital Punishment of Animals. The Lost History of Europe's Animal Trials*, London: William Heinemann.

Fairholme, E.G. and Pain, W. (1924) *A Century of Work for Animals. The History of the RSPCA 1824–1924*, London: John Murray.

Featherstone, Mike (1982) 'The Body in Consumer Culture', *Theory, Culture & Society*, vol. 1 (2): 18–23.

Foucault, Michel (1970) *The Order of Things. An Archaeology of the Human Sciences*, London: Tavistock.

—— (1977) *Discipline and Punish. The Birth of the Prison*, London: Allen Lane.

—— (1978) 'About the Concept of "The Dangerous Individual" in Nineteenth-Century Legal Psychiatry', *International Journal of Law and Psychiatry*, vol. 1: 1–18.

—— (1983) *This is not a Pipe*, Berkeley: University of California Press.

—— (1986) *The Use of Pleasure. vol. 2 of The History of Sexuality*, Harmondsworth: Viking.

Fowell Buxton, Thomas (1823) Speech to the House of Commons, *Parliamentary Debates*, 21 May 1823: columns 434–5.

Freeman, Edward A. (1869) 'The Morality of Field Sports', *The Fortnightly Review*, no. XXIV new series. 1 October: 353–85.

—— (1870) 'The Controversy on Field Sports', *The Fortnightly Review*, vol. IV. 1 December: 674–91.

French, Richard D. (1975) *Antivivisection and Medical Science in Victorian Society*, Princeton, NJ: Princeton University Press.

Gablik, Suzi (1985) *Magritte*, London: Thames & Hudson.

Gellner, Ernest (1983) *Nations and Nationalism*, Oxford: Basil Blackwell.

Giddens, Anthony (1971) *Capitalism and Modern Social Theory. An Analysis of the Writings of Marx, Durkheim, and Max Weber*, Cambridge: Cambridge University Press.

Goudsblom, Johan (1977) 'Responses to Norbert Elias's work in England, Germany, the Netherlands and France', in P.R. Gleichmann, J. Goudsblom and H. Korte (eds), *Human Figurations: Essays for Norbert Elias*, Amsterdam: Amsterdams Sociologische Tijdschrift.

Grass, Gunter (1973) *Local Anaesthetic*, Harmondsworth: Penguin.

Hall, Catherine (1979) 'The Early formation of Victorian Domestic Ideology', in S. Burman (ed.), *Fit Work for Women*, London: Croom Helm.

Harris, Martyn (1985) 'The Animal Rights Brigade', *New Society*, 31 January: 168–71.

Harrison, Brian (1967) 'Religion and Recreation in Nineteenth-Century England', *Past and Present*, 38: 98–125.

—— (1973) 'Animals and the State in Nineteenth-Century England', *English Historical Review*, vol. 88: 786–820.

Henshaw, David (1989) *Animal Warfare. The Story of the Animal Liberation Front*, London: Fontana.

Hollands, Clive (1985) 'Animal Rights in the Political Arena', in P. Singer (ed.), *In Defence of Animals*, Oxford: Basil Blackwell.

Holroyd, Michael (1988) *Bernard Shaw. 1856–1898: The Search for Love*, London: Chatto & Windus.

Humanus (1789) 'Love of Mischief Early Imbibed', *Gentleman's Magazine*, vol. 59: 15–17.

Ignatieff, Michael (1978) *A Just Measure of Pain. The Penitentiary in the Industrial Revolution 1750–1850*, New York: Columbia University Press.

—— (1984) *The Needs of Strangers*, London: Chatto & Windus.

Kant, Immanuel (1930) *Lectures on Ethics*, London: Methuen.

—— (1988) 'Critique of the Faculty of Judgment', in *Kant. Selections*, L.W. Beck (ed.), New York/London: Scribner/Macmillan.

Lansbury, Coral (1985) *The Old Brown Dog. Women, Workers and Vivisection in Edwardian England*, Madison: University of Wisconsin Press.

Leach, Edmund (1964) 'Anthropological Aspects of Language: Animal Categories and Verbal Abuse', in E.H. Lenneberg (ed.), *New Directions in the Study of Language*, Cambridge, MA: MIT Press.

—— (1982) *Social Anthropology*, London: Fontana.

Lebrecht, Norman (1987) *Mahler Remembered*, London: Faber & Faber.

Lee, Ronnie (1985a) 'Let the Same Flame . . . ', *Animal Liberation Front Supporters Group Newsletter*, no. 17: 10.

—— (1985b) 'The Bad Old Days Will End', *Animal Liberation Front Supporters Group Newsletter*, no. 17: 14.

Lee, Sidney (1896) 'Ritson, Joseph', *Dictionary of National Biography*, vol. LVIII. London: Smith, Elder.

Lévi-Strauss, Claude (1966) *The Savage Mind*, London: Weidenfeld & Nicolson.

—— (1987) *The View from Afar*, London: Peregrine.

211

Lorenz, Konrad (1952) *King Solomon's Ring. New Light on Animal Ways*, London: Methuen.
—— (1977) *Behind the Mirror. A Search for a Natural History of Human Knowledge*, London: Methuen.
Lyotard, Jean-François (1989) 'Complexity and the Sublime', in L. Appignanesi (ed.), *Postmodernism, ICA Documents*, London: Free Association Books.
Macfarlane, Alan (1987) *The Culture of Capitalism*, Oxford: Basil Blackwell.
Malcolmson, Robert (1982) 'Popular Recreations under Attack', in B. Waites, T. Bennett and G. Martin (eds), *Popular Culture: Past and Present*, London: Croom Helm.
Martin, Richard (1824) Speech to the House of Commons, *Parliamentary Debates*, 26 February 1824: columns 486–9.
Marx, Karl (1938) *Capital. A Critical Analysis of Capitalist Production*, vol. 1, London: George Allen & Unwin.
Mennell, Stephen (1985) *All Manners of Food. Eating and Taste in England and France from the Middle Ages to the Present*, Oxford: Basil Blackwell.
Menninger, Karl A. (1951) 'Totemic Aspects of Contemporary Attitudes Toward Animals', in G.B. Wilbur and W. Muensterberger (eds), *Psychoanalysis and Culture. Essays in Honor of Géza Rohéim*, New York: International Universities Press.
Midgley, Mary (1976) 'The Concept of Beastliness', in T. Regan and P. Singer (eds), *Animal Rights and Human Obligations*, Englewood Cliffs, NJ: Prentice-Hall.
—— (1979) *Beast and Man. The Roots of Human Nature*, Hassocks: Harvester.
—— (1983) *Animals and Why They Matter*, Harmondsworth: Penguin.
Mill, John Stuart (1910) *Utilitarianism*, London: J.M. Dent.
Mitchison, Amanda (1987) 'Vegetating in Loughborough', *New Society*, 25 September: 10–11.
Monboddo, Lord (1785) 'Account of Peter the Wild Boy, Formerly Brought from the Woods of Germany', *Gentleman's Magazine*, vol. 55: 113–14.
Moss, Arthur W. (1961) *Valiant Crusade. The History of the RSPCA*, London: Cassell.
Nietzsche, Friedrich (1956) *The Genealogy of Morals*, New York: Doubleday.
North, Richard (1985) 'Night Raid on Animal Farm', *The Sunday Express Magazine*, 8 September: 22–4.
Orwell, George (1959) *The Road to Wigan Pier*, London: Secker & Warburg.
Ovid (1986) *Metamorphoses*, Oxford: Oxford University Press.
Papayanis, Nicholas (1985) 'The Coachmen of Paris: A Statistical Profile', *Journal of Contemporary History*, vol. 20 (2): 305–21.
Paulson, Ronald (1975) *The Art of Hogarth*, London: Phaidon.

Plutarch (1957) *Moralia*, vol. 12, London: William Heinemann.

Porritt, Jonathon (1984) *Seeing Green. The Politics of Ecology Explained*, Oxford: Basil Blackwell.

Pratt, S.I. (1803) Letter to the *Gentleman's Magazine*, vol. 73: 1030–1.

Prochaska, Frank (1974) 'Women in English Philanthropy 1790–1830', *International Review of Social History*, vol. 19 (3): 426–45.

R——Y (1800) 'Humanity to Beasts', *Gentleman's Magazine*, vol. 70: 848.

R.E.R. (1804) Letter to the *Gentleman's Magazine*, vol. 74: 297–8.

Regan, Tom (1983) 'Animal Rights and Human Wrongs', in H.B. Miller and W. Williams (eds), *Ethics and Animals*, Clifton, NJ: Humana Press.

—— (1984) *The Case for Animal Rights*, London: Routledge & Kegan Paul.

—— (1985) 'The Case for Animal Rights', in P. Singer (ed.), *In Defence of Animals*, Oxford: Basil Blackwell.

Regan, Tom and Singer, Peter (1976) (eds), *Animal Rights and Human Obligations*, Englewood Cliffs, NJ: Prentice-Hall.

Ritson, Joseph (1802) *An Essay on Abstinence from Animal Food, as a Moral Duty*, London: Richard Phillips.

Ritvo, Harriet (1987) *The Animal Estate. The English and Other Creatures in the Victorian Age*, Cambridge, MA: Harvard University Press.

Rorty, Richard (1989) *Contingency, Irony, and Solidarity*, Cambridge: Cambridge University Press.

'Rose, Martial' (1985) 'Utilitarianism and Rights Theory', *Animal Liberation Front Supporters Group Newsletter*, no. 17: 15–16.

Rousseau, Jean-Jacques (1931) *The Confessions of Jean-Jacques Rousseau*, vol. 2, London: J.M. Dent.

—— (1984) *Discourse on the Origins and Foundations of Inequality among Men*, Harmondsworth: Penguin. Originally published in 1755.

Rowbotham, Sheila (1977) 'Edward Carpenter: Prophet of the New Life', in S. Rowbotham and J. Weeks, *Socialism and the New Life. The Personal and Sexual Politics of Edward Carpenter and Havelock Ellis*, London: Pluto.

Ryder, Richard D. (1975) *Victims of Science. The Use of Animals in Research*, London: Davis-Poynter.

Salt, Henry S. (1888) *Percy Bysshe Shelley. A Monograph*, London: Swann, Sonnenschein, Lowrey.

—— (1921) *Seventy Years Among Savages*, London: George Allen & Unwin.

—— (1976) 'The Humanities of Diet', in T. Regan and P. Singer (eds), *Animal Rights and Human Obligations*, Englewood Cliffs, NJ: Prentice-Hall.

—— (1980) *Animals' Rights Considered in Relation to Social Progress*, London: Centaur. Originally published in 1892; London: George Bell & Son.

Schleifer, Harriet (1985) 'Images of Death and Life: Food Animal

Production and the Vegetarian Option', in P. Singer (ed.), *In Defence of Animals*, Oxford: Basil Blackwell.

Serpell, James (1986) *In the Company of Animals. A Study of Human–Animal Relationships*, Oxford: Basil Blackwell.

Shaw, George Bernard (1915) 'Preface', in H.S. Salt (ed.), *Killing for Sport. Essays by Various Writers*, London: George Bell & Sons.

—— (1970) *An Autobiography 1856–1898*, London: Max Reinhardt.

—— (1971) 'The Doctor's Dilemma: A Tragedy', in *The Bodley Head Bernard Shaw Collected Plays with their Prefaces*, London: Max Reinhardt/The Bodley Head.

Shelley, Percy Bysshe (1905) *The Poetical Works of Percy Bysshe Shelley*, Oxford: Oxford University Press.

—— (1954) *Shelley's Prose*, D.L. Clark (ed.), Albuquerque: University of New Mexico Press.

Sheppard, Julie (1986) *Food Facts. A Statistical Guide to the UK Food System*, London: The London Food Commission.

Singer, Peter (1976) *Animal Liberation. Towards an End to Man's Inhumanity to Animals*, London: Jonathan Cape.

—— (1980a) 'Utilitarianism and Vegetarianism', *Philosophy and Public Affairs*, vol. 9 (4): 325–37.

—— (1980b) 'Preface', to H.S. Salt *Animals' Rights Considered in Relation to Social Progress*, London: Centaur.

—— (1981) *The Expanding Circle. Ethics and Sociobiology*, Oxford: Clarendon Press.

—— (1982) 'Ethics and Sociobiology', *Philosophy and Public Affairs*, vol. 11 (1): 40–64.

—— (1985) 'Animal Rights and Wrongs', *The Times Higher Education Supplement*, 29 March: 13.

Smith, J (1824) Speech to the House of Commons, *Parliamentary Debates*, 26 February 1824: columns 490–1.

Soler, Jean (1979) 'The Semiotics of Food in the Bible', in R. Forster and O. Ranum (eds), *Food and Drink in History*, Baltimore, MD: Johns Hopkins University Press.

Sykes, John (1973) *Local Records or Historical Records of Northumberland and Durham, Newcastle-Upon-Tyne, and Berwick-Upon-Tweed*, Stockton: Patrick & Shotton. Originally published in 1866.

Tambiah, Stanley J. (1973) 'Classification of Animals in Thailand', in M. Douglas (ed.), *Rules and Meanings. The Anthropology of Everyday Knowledge*, Harmondsworth: Penguin.

Tester, Keith (1989) 'The Pleasure of the Rich is the Labour of the Poor: Some Comments on Norbert Elias's "An Essay on Sport and Violence"', *Journal of Historical Sociology*, vol. 2 (2): 161–72.

Thomas, Keith (1977) 'The Place of Laughter in Tudor and Stuart England', *The Times Literary Supplement*, 21 January: 77–81.

—— (1978) 'The Rise of the Fork', *The New York Review of Books*, vol. XV (3): 28–31.

—— (1983) *Man and the Natural World. Changing Attitudes in England 1500–1800*, Harmondsworth: Allen Lane.
Thomas, Richard H. (1983) *The Politics of Hunting*, Aldershot: Gower.
Thompson, Edward P. (1980) *The Making of the English Working Class*, Harmondsworth: Penguin.
Thoreau, Henry David (1981) *Walden and Other Writings*, New York: Bantam.
Turner, Bryan S. (1984) *The Body and Society. Explorations in Social Theory*, Oxford: Basil Blackwell.
Turner, James (1980) *Reckoning with the Beast: Animals, Pain, and Humanity in the Victorian Mind*, Baltimore, MD: Johns Hopkins University Press.
Twigg, Julia (1981) 'The Vegetarian Movement in England 1847–1981: With Particular Reference to its Ideology', Unpublished Ph.D. thesis: London School of Economics.
—— (1983) 'Vegetarianism and the Meanings of Meat', in A. Murcott (ed.), *The Sociology of Food and Eating*, Aldershot: Gower.
Vidal, Gore (1989) 'Gods and Greens', *The Observer*, 27 August: 29–30.
Voltaire (1947) *Candide or Optimism*, West Drayton: Penguin. Originally published in 1759.
Wallis, R.,T. (1972) *Neoplatonism*, London: Duckworth.
Watson, Derek (1979) *Richard Wagner. A Biography*, New York: McGraw-Hill.
Wilson, Edward O. (1975) *Sociobiology. The New Synthesis*, Cambridge, MA: Harvard University Press.
—— (1978) *On Human Nature*, Cambridge, MA: Harvard University Press.
Windeatt, Philip (1985) '"They Clearly Now See the Link": Militant Voices', in P. Singer (ed.), *In Defence of Animals*, Oxford: Basil Blackwell.
Windham, William (1809) Speech to the House of Commons, *Parliamentary Debates*, 13 June 1809: columns 1029–40 and 1025*–28*.
Wittgenstein, Ludwig (1953) *Philosophical Investigations*, Oxford: Basil Blackwell.
Wokler, Robert (1978) 'Perfectible Apes in Decadent Cultures: Rousseau's Anthropology Revisited', *Daedalus*, Summer, vol. 107 (3): 107–34.
Wynne-Tyson, Jon (1979) *Food for a Future. The Complete Case for Vegetarianism*, London: Centaur Press.
—— (1985) *The Extended Circle. A Dictionary of Humane Thought*, Fontwell: Centaur Press.

NAME INDEX

Bataille, G. 87
Bauman, Z. 90, 199, 200, 201–2, 203, 204
Bentham, J. 96–8, 99, 100, 152–3, 186
Birtwhistle, H. 197, 198
Borges, J.L. 77
Bryant, J. 174–5, 176

Carpenter, E.151
Carter, A. 197–8, 201
Chassenée, B. 19
Chatwin, B. 74, 77
Clark, S.R.L. 2, 10–12, 13, 14, 15–16, 85, 159, 177, 190, 194, 196
Clerus 111

Darnton, R. 68–70, 72–3, 107
Darwin, C. 152
Douglas, M. 37–9, 40, 43, 46, 49, 64–5, 78, 91, 143, 172–3
Duffy, M. 18
Durkheim, E. 45–6, 49, 59, 60

Elias, N. 56, 58, 68, 69, 70–1, 73
Erskine, Lord 104–7, 108, 118, 148, 161, 173
Evans, E.P. 72, 73–5, 79

Foucault, M. 71, 77–87, 89, 121, 195, 202, 203, 204
Fowell Buxton, T. 109–10, 113
Freeman, E.A. 158–9, 169
French, R.D. 188

Gellner, E. 201
Granger, J. 112–13
Grass, G. 119

Harrison. B. 115
Hogarth, W. 64–5, 75, 90, 99, 109, 136
Hollands, C. 192
Humanus 117

Ignatieff, M. 95, 98

Kant, I. 7, 29–30, 64–5, 99–100, 105, 161
Kingsford, A. 158

Leach, E. 40–1, 43, 46, 49, 64–5, 76, 78
Lee, R. 180, 182, 189–90, 191, 192
Lévi-Strauss, C. 32–6, 38, 39–40, 46, 49, 53, 62–5, 78, 130
Lorenz, K. 19–24, 31, 59
Lyotard, J-F. 30

Macfarlane, A. 52
Margritte, R. 77
Mahler, G. 142
Malcolmson, R. 101
Martin, R. 104, 108–10, 114, 148, 178, 188
Marx, K. 171–2, 194
Mennell, S. 67
Menninger, K.A. 17–19, 20
Midgley, M. 14, 27–31, 153, 197
Mill, J.S. 3
Mitchison, A. 145
Monboddo, Lord 128–9

Nietzsche, F. 101, 113, 118–19

Orwell, G. 17, 144
Ovid 138–9

216

Plutarch 137–8
Porritt, J. 191–2
Primatt, H. 113
Pulteney, Sir W. 107
Pythagoras 137–9

Regan, T. 2, 5–7, 9–10, 12–13, 14, 15, 16, 85, 159, 177, 185, 187, 190, 194, 196
Ritson, J. 132–7, 139, 145, 148, 173, 177
Ritvo, H. 92, 118, 198
Rorty, R. 206–7
'Rose, M.' 185
Rousseau, J.J. 122–8, 129–32, 133, 139, 145, 146, 148, 161, 177
Ryder, R. 4

Salt, H.S. 75, 150–65, 166–7, 168, 169, 170–1, 173, 174, 175, 176, 178, 183, 185, 189, 194, 195, 199
Salt, K. 151
Schliefer, H. 176
Shaw, G.B. 8, 150, 151, 164–5

Shelley, P.B. 2, 139–41, 145, 161, 177
Singer, P. 2, 3–5, 6, 7, 8–9, 10, 12–15, 16, 24, 27, 85, 97, 159, 165–8, 174, 177, 178, 181–2, 183, 185, 187–8, 190, 194, 196
Smith, J. 109
Soler, J. 36–7
Spencer, H. 154, 155

Thomas, K. 50–6, 57, 70–1, 75, 79, 80–1, 83, 84, 92, 102, 202, 203
Thompson, E.P. 49
Thoreau, H.D. 141, 145
Turner, J. 76

Vidal, G. 140
Voltaire 94–5

Wagner, R. 142
Wilson, E.O. 24–7, 31, 32
Windham, W. 107
Wittgenstein, L. 207
Wynne-Tyson, J. 178

SUBJECT INDEX

altruism 24–6
Animal Liberation Front 179, 182–6,
    187, 190, 192, 193, 194, 200
Animal Rights Militia 186, 187, 190
animal trials 72–5, 91–2
anthropocentricism 50, 52, 54, 74, 76,
    80, 92, 102, 151, 183, 202, 203
anti-Semitism 142

Band of Mercy 180–2
bear baiting 68, 104, 108
bull baiting 90, 121–2

cats 70; burning of 67–8, 71, 73;
    massacre of 69, 83
civilising process 58–63, 64–5, 67, 73
cruelty 101, 109, 114, 117, 157;
    legislation 103–10, 164

ecology 190–2
episteme 78–87
ethology 19
evangelism 111–12, 114

fetishism 171–3, 174, 175, 179, 183,
    190, 193, 195
freedom 196–7, 198, 199–201, 203–4,
    205, 206

health 134–5, 140, 177–8
humanitarianism 75–6, 77, 93, 100,
    116, 163, 164, 166
hunting 13, 68, 90, 109–10, 136, 157,
    158–9, 164, 168, 169
Hunt Saboteurs' Association 168,
    179–80, 192

Impressionism 150

'ladies' 116
League Against Cruel Sports 168

meat, eating 65–6, 140, 141, 143,
    150–1; restrictions 36–8
middle class 54–5, 57, 100
moral education 162

nation 118, 120, 133
natural diet 132–3, 135–6
Neoplatonism 137–8
Noble Savage 125–9, 130–1, 133, 134,
    141, 142, 164

pets 52–3, 176
pigs, execution of 72–3

Romanticism 139
RSPCA 55, 89, 111, 113–15, 116, 157

sociobiology 24, 27
speciesism 4–5, 8, 14, 85, 165, 166,
    168, 169, 169, 179, 184
sport 101–2, 108–9

urbanisation 52, 56, 57, 71, 75–6, 81,
    90, 102, 196, 198, 205
utilitarianism 3, 96–7, 166, 186–7, 188

vegetarianism 8, 10, 12, 13, 17, 67, 84,
    142–4, 145, 157, 169, 178
violence 184–9
vivisection 13, 99, 157, 158, 169

welfare, animal 13, 89, 90, 149, 157, 191
working class 90, 99, 102–3, 106, 107,
    109, 110, 111, 112–13, 117, 118,
    119, 121, 123, 144, 146, 161, 164,
    200